Business Process Oriented Implementation of Standard Software

How to Achieve Competitive Advantage
Efficiently and Effectively

2nd Edition

Springer
Berlin
Heidelberg
New York
Barcelona
Hongkong
London
Milan
Paris
Singapore
Tokyo

Mathias Kirchmer

Business Process Oriented Implementation of Standard Software

How to Achieve Competitive Advantage
Efficiently and Effectively

Second Edition

With 107 Figures

 Springer

Dr. Mathias Kirchmer
President & CEO
IDS Scheer, Inc.
Chadds Ford Business Campus
Brandywine 2 Bldg., Suite 307
Chadds Ford, PA 19317
USA

"Originally published in German with the title:
Mathias Kirchmer, „Geschäftsprozeßorientierte Einführung von Standardsoftware.
Vorgehen zur Realisierung strategischer Ziele"
© Betriebswirtschaftlicher Verlag Dr. Th. Gabler GmbH, Wiesbaden 1996"

ISBN 3-540-65575-1 Springer-Verlag Berlin Heidelberg New York
ISBN 3-540-63472-x 1st. ed. Springer-Verlag Berlin Heidelberg New York

Cataloging-in-Publication Data applied for
Die Deutsche Bibliothek - CIP-Einheitsaufnahme
Kirchmer, Mathias:
Business process oriented implementation of standard software : how
to achieve competitive advantage efficiently and effectively /
Mathias Kirchmer. - 2. ed. -
Berlin; Heidelberg; New York; Barcelona; Hong Kong; London; Milan; Paris; Singapore;
Tokyo : Springer, 1999
Einheitssacht.: Geschäftsprozeßorientierte Einführung von
Standortsoftware <engl.>
ISBN 3-540-65575-1

© Springer-Verlag Berlin · Heidelberg 1999
Printed in Germany

The use of general descriptive names, registered names, trademarks, etc. in this publica-
tion does not imply, even in the absence of a specific statement, that such names are
exempt from the relevant protective laws and regulations and therefore free for general use.

Hardcover-Design: Erich Kirchner, Heidelberg

SPIN 10713663   42/2202-5 4 3 2 1 0 - Printed on acid-free paper

Preface

Facing increasingly tough competition, enterprises must address the business issues at hand with lean, flexible and nimble structures. A key solution is business process oriented engineering of organizational structures. Business processes are generally supported by information technology – and deploying standard software is increasingly the method of choice. Today, the implementation of standard software is a key element of information system planning and execution, enabling enterprises to reach their corporate goals by systematically supporting business processes.

The procedure shown in this real-world oriented work illustrates how enterprises are capable of reaching strategic goals by business process oriented implementation of standard software. The methods and tools commonly used to successfully implement standard software are discussed – yet always keeping in step with the respective applications.

The procedure described here has been proven time and time again. Here it is also illustrated by practical examples of implementation projects in various vertical markets. This work demonstrates how scientifically sound solutions are the cornerstone for efficiently and effectively addressing business administration issues.

August-Wilhelm Scheer

Foreword to the Second Edition

The market for standard business application software continues to grow rapidly worldwide, where there is still a major focus on ERP systems. However, more and more companies are considering the use of so-called "Post ERP" applications, especially for Supply Chain Management. Therefore, the importance of a business process oriented implementation approach, based on the goals of a company, has continued to grow since the release of the first edition of this book.

The described implementation approach in this book is also used as a framework and extension for standard software vendor specific approaches, such as SAP's AcceleratedSAP (ASAP). In this context, there is high practical relevance of the business process definition based on company goals and best practices (chapter 3), and of the post implementation activities leading into a continuous process improvement (chapter 5).

The process oriented implementation is suited to both the use of ERP and more importantly to the use of Supply Chain Management systems. Therefore, specific hints have been included (especially in chapter 1, 3 and 4). In addition, some stylistic improvements have been made and some new references added.

I would like to give special thanks to Prof. Dr. Dr. August-Wilhelm Scheer for his continued encouragement, support, and for numerous interesting and enlightening discussions.
Thanks also to my co-workers at IDS Scheer, Inc. for their support, especially to Jeff Graber for his editing and to Susan Griffith for updating the manuscript.

Mathias Kirchmer

Foreword to the First Edition

The deployment of standard software is becoming an increasingly important factor in business process optimization. At the same time, standard software implementation is shifting its focus from purely technical tasks to business administration issues. Installation of software systems has evolved to strategy driven engineering of business processes.

This book discusses a procedure, proven time and again in the real world, for business process oriented implementation of standard software to achieve competitive advantage. It demonstrates how strategic goals can be reached by implementing software. We have made a point to emphasize efficiency in the implementation process, enabling enterprises to react to changing business environments -- quickly and cost-effectively. Essential implementation activities are covered in their chronological sequence and explained by means of examples, especially in SAP R/3 software implementations.

I authored this book while a project manager and director at IDS Prof. Scheer GmbH and President and CEO at IDS Scheer, Inc. I would like to thank Prof. Dr. August-Wilhelm Scheer for his personal and scientific support. His advice and his encouragement have been of greatest value. I also wish to thank Prof. Dr. Karlheinz Küting for his co-sponsorship. Special thanks also go to Dr. Alexander Pocsay, President and CEO of IDS Prof. Scheer GmbH, who gave me the opportunity to combine this work with my professional work at IDS.

I am endebted to Kaeser Kompressoren GmbH for the extraordinary cooperation in their world-wide implementation of SAP R/3, providing real-world results with which to verify the theoretical procedures: special credit is due Mssrs. Thomas Kaeser and Falko Lameter.

I also wish to express gratitude to my co-workers at IDS Prof. Scheer GmbH for always being available for discussions and for their moral support. Special acknowledgments go to Christian Aichele, Katja Boßlet, Dr. Reinhard Brombacher, Thomas Joachim, Claudia Klingshirn, Dieter Leinen, Katharina Rock, and Andreas Waldow.

The excellent illustrations were prepared by Mr. Matthias Büttner and Mr. Johannes Schymura. Ms. Sabine Hofmann and Ms. Rita Landry-Schimmelpfennig deserve special recognition for their stylistic corrections.

Special thanks to all my co-workers at IDS Scheer, Inc. for their support while preparing this English edition. I would like to mention especially Carmen Kaechler for her great support as well as John Prendergast and David Shaw.

I also wish to thank Mr. Christian C. Tiews of The Localizer for the meticulous translation of the text into English.

Finally, I am especially grateful and appreciative for the understanding and motivation of my parents, who helped to make this work a success.

Mathias Kirchmer

Table of Contents

1 Business Process Oriented Organizational Structures and Function Oriented Standard Software -- Implications for the Implementation

In order to deal with increasing competition effectively, both nationally and globally, companies must implement lean, flexible and market oriented structures. Work processes should be reviewed and reengineered, in order to meet various goals, such as trimming throughput time, reducing costs, increasing flexibility and improving the quality of products (services and goods).

This reengineering is extremely complex. In order to plan or execute corporate activities, countless functions and objects must be carried out or processed (see SCHEER 1993b, p. 85). This complexity can be lessened by designing appropriate organizational structures to define and coordinate sub-tasks. These structures focus either on individual functions, such as Sales or Production of all of a company's products or they can focus on "objects", such as a certain product and every function relating to it. The operations of process oriented organizations are based on object oriented views. These views do not recognize individual functions, but rather a *series* of functions that carry out an overriding task by providing the customer with a meaningful result. An example would be order processing, starting from the entry of the customer order, right up to the delivery of the appropriate item. In reengineering organizational structures, there is a growing consensus that process orientation is beginning to take the place of the hitherto prevailing function orientation concept (see HAMMER, CHAMPY 1994, pp. 52-53; SCHEER 1994c, p. 4). Complete business processes, rather than individual functions, are now the center of discussion.

Business processes are usually optimized by leveraging information technology (IT), which is frequently responsible for more efficient and effective work processes (see HAMMER, CHAMPY 1994, p. 67, 112, 113; PORTER 1989a, p. 223; SCHEER 1993b, 85, 86; WOMACK et al.. 1992, pp. 199-201). Specifically, the **use of standard application software** (such as **ERP** (Enterprise Resource Planning) and **Supply Chain Management** (SCM) systems) offers many advantages over the use of individual software programs. This is the reason for the increasing popularity of standard application software (see AMR 1998, BECKER et al. 1991, p. 153; HANSEN et al. 1983, pp. 3-4; KEEN 1991, pp. 157, 158; MORVAN 1988, p. 264; OCDE 1989, p. 28; SCHEER 1990c, pp. 140, 141; SCHEER 1994a, p. 398; STEINKE 1979, pp. 105-110). Implementing standard applications in enterprises is often the key component of business process optimization.

In the following chapter we will show why, in planning organizational structures, **process** orientation is being preferred as a design paradigm, whereas today's standard applications are predominately **function** oriented. We will then show the implications for implementing standard applications. The objective and structure of this work will be explained based on this.

The structure of this chapter is depicted in Fig. 1.1.

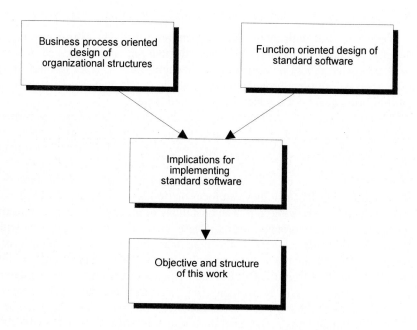

Fig. 1.1: Structure of Chapter 1

1.1 Business Process Oriented Design of Organizational Structures

After characterizing and defining the term "organizational structure", the reasons for the predominance of process orientation in designing organizational structures will be explained. Subsequently, the key characteristics of process oriented organizational structures will be presented.

1.1.1 Characterizing and Defining the Term "Organizational Structure"

In organizational theory, there are many approaches, leading to different aspects of the organization and various definitions of the terms in question. This is due to the fact that the „big picture" can only be observed and displayed in "snapshots", in a subjective manner (see GAITANIDES 1983, p. 1; KIESER, KUBICEK 1992, p. 33). As a rule,

❑ The activity of "organizing" (instrumental / functional organizational term) as well as
❑ The outcome of this "organizing" (instrumental / institutional organizational term)

is defined as "the organization" (see HOFFMANN 1980, pp.1425-1431). We will subsequently discuss the instrumental / institutional organizational term, in order to deduct the key characteristics of the term "organizational structure".

Basically, another description of a "resource pool" would be "organization". Resource pools are created when individuals place some of their resources (e.g., capital, labor or skills, knowledge, certain rights) at the disposal of a central entity not identical to themselves (see KIESER, KUBICEK 1992, p. 1; PROBST 1992, p. 25). Organizations are social structures that

❑ Have a consistent goal and
❑ Have formal structures, within which organization members execute functions, in order to meet these goals.

(see FRESE 1993, p. 6; KIESER, KUBICEK 1992, p. 4).
These organizations can be regarded as systems, in which

❑ Organizational elements (tasks, responsible persons or entities, tangible items and information) are
❑ Interrelated (in hierarchical and process organizations, respectively) and which
❑ Regulate time, space and quantity dimensions

(see SCHMIDT 1991, pp. 17-21). The key element is the task carried out by people (such as responsible persons) by means of tangible items and information. This regulates aspects regarding time, space and quantities, i.e., organizational dimensions.

We will subsequently discuss the "relationships" between organizational elements, i.e., hierarchical and process organizations, respectively.
Process and hierarchical organizations represent a **dynamic** and a **static view** of the organization:

- ❑ **Process organizations** describe *how* organization members execute the functions (work processes).
- ❑ **Hierarchical organizations** describe *what* is to be executed. They lay down a system of rules (such as decision making authorization) for focused execution of the work processes.

Hierarchical organizations break up the corporate mission of an organization into any number of sub-tasks. On the one hand, this means that hierarchical organizations enable individual members to specialize (in certain functions necessary to carry out sub-tasks). On the other hand, it assures coordination of these activities. The **smallest sub-task unit** that can be carried out by one person, is known as a "**position**". A "**management system**" defines the **parent / child relationships of positions** for coordinating sub-tasks. Consequently, process organizations and hierarchical organizations necessitate each other. Positions are their mutual reference points. **Process organizations and hierarchical organizations** are only theoretically differentiated. De facto, they both deal with the same entity (see FRESE 1993, p. 6; GAITANIDES 1983, pp. 1, 2; KIESER, KUBICEK 1992, pp. 16-18; PROBST 1992, pp. 44, 45, 108-110). Therefore, the term **organizational structure** should include both hierarchical and the process organizations.

Organizations should not be regarded as isolated structures because they are **closely interrelated with their environment**. They take in certain external elements (e.g., raw materials, energy, labor or capital) and subsequently emit other elements into their environment (e.g., tangible items, services, salaries, profits, etc). The actual structure of organizations is greatly influenced by existing environmental factors (see FRESE 1993, p. 5; KIESER, KUBICEK 1992, pp. 45-47; PROBST 1992, pp. 26-28; SCHEER 1993b, p. 97).

The statements made hitherto are applicable to **many types of organizations**, such as associations, governmental agencies, political parties or companies (see KIESER, KUBICEK 1992, pp. 27, 28). The following discussion will refer to **companies** only. In hierarchical organizations, for the corporate mission to be processed in work processes (i.e., in process organizations), it is broken up into sub-tasks. There is a strong correlation between the business environment and market transactions, mainly consisting of the purchasing and selling of goods and services.

The **hierarchical organization** in a company is usually depicted in organigrams or organizational charts. These break up the company into several **levels**, reflecting management relationships. A parent level "manages" its child levels (by means of decision making authorizations or directives). Every level is **subdivided into areas**, according to the structure of the corporate mission. Typical definitions of these various areas are divisions, departments or groups (see SCHEER 1990b, p. 90). These structures make up the framework for **process organizations**. On the other hand, work processes (in hierarchical organizations) also necessitate these structures (see PROBST 1992, p. 45).

Organizational units, for example departments, can be

❑   Uniquely subordinate (**mono-linear system**) or can be
❑   Allocated to several senior units (**multi-linear system**).

A good example of a multi-linear system is a matrix organization. Here, each employee reports to a responsible person, such as a product manager, but also to a person responsible for an organizational function (such as Sales), (see FRESE 1993, pp. 166-168).

Each **individual structural level** (e.g., a division level or department level) can be **classified according to various criteria** (see FRESE 1993, pp. 168-174; KIESER, KUBICEK 1992, pp. 86-89; PROBST 1992, pp. 60-69). This structuring can be

❑ Function oriented or
❑ Object oriented

(see GRÖGER 1992, p. 126). The classification can be according to

❑   A criterion (mono-linear structures), (e.g., only according to certain functions or only according to an object, e.g., products) -- or according to
❑   Several criteria (multi-dimensional structures), (e.g., according to one or several objects and/or functions).

This classification is a key characteristic of organizational structures because it defines the work processes of each employee (process organization) and also defines the structure of the hierarchical organization.

Fig. 1.2: Function oriented hierarchical organization

In **functionally oriented organizational structures**, the corporate mission of an enterprise is broken up into the functions to be carried out (see FRESE 1993, pp. 171, 172; KIESER, KUBICEK 1992, pp. 86, 87; PROBST 1992, pp. 61-63). Thus, individual areas of the company contain identical single functions that they execute for the whole enterprise (the Sales function working for all the products of the organization). An organization could thus be broken up into Sales, Production, Accounting and Human Resources Management (see Fig. 1.2). The work processes are characterized by the execution of one function or several functions for many objects.

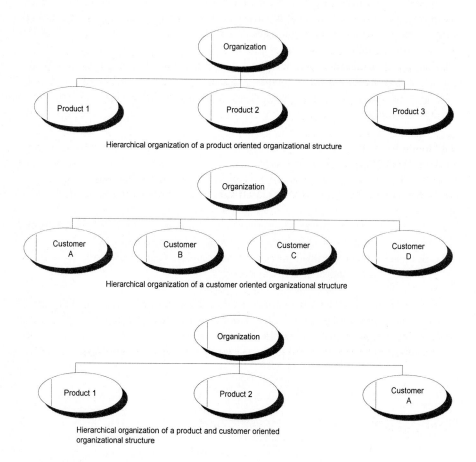

Hierarchical organization of a product oriented organizational structure

Hierarchical organization of a customer oriented organizational structure

Hierarchical organization of a product and customer oriented
organizational structure

Fig. 1.3: Object oriented hierarchical organizations

Object oriented organizational structures group the enterprise by objects, according to which various functions (by different product groups) are executed.

For example, a corporate division and the corresponding process organization would include every function of a certain product group. Key **classification objects** are as follows:

❑ Products (division organization)
❑ Markets and
❑ Customers or Customer Groups

(see FRESE 1993, pp. 169-171, 173-174; KIESER, KUBICEK 1992, pp. 87-89; PROBST 1992, pp. 63-69).

Examples of a hierarchical organization containing object oriented organizational structures are given in Fig. 1.3.

Multidimensional organizational structures can be designed according to **object and function oriented** criteria. For example, in a product oriented structure, in order to achieve a synergistic effect in every department, functions that are identical for every product area can be grouped (see FRESE 1993, pp. 174-187; SCHEER 1993b, pp. 96-100). Fig. 1.4 illustrates an example of a hierarchical organization within a multi-dimensional, multi-linear organization, in which the first hierarchical level was designed with a product *and* a function orientation. An organization focuses its activities on product areas A and B, but creates an overlapping function area, "Research and Development (R&D)", in order to achieve a synergistic effect. "Region 1" and "Region 2" sales departments (and their respective customers) are subordinate to both product areas.

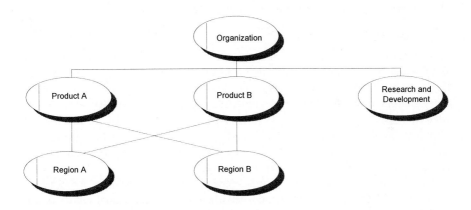

Fig. 1.4: A multi-dimensional, multi-linear hierarchical organization

1.1.2 Business Process Orientation in the Development of Organizational Structures

Today, **organizational structures** are **usually still function oriented** (see FRESE 1993, p. 171; SCHEER 1993b, p. 85). They are based on the basic principles of Taylor (see TAYLOR 1913) and are characterized by

❑ A rigid demarcation of function blocks / areas of responsibility,
❑ Extreme work-sharing,
❑ Numerous hierarchical levels and
❑ Separation of administrative or decision support activities and operational processes.

These structures have certain **advantages**, such as

❑ A simple definition of individual processes,
❑ Systematic utilization of tools and persons,
❑ A precise definition of responsibility and
❑ A lower degree of investment.

However, organizations structured according to Taylor also have **considerable disadvantages**, such as

❑ Complex coordination of processes,
❑ Poor flexibility,
❑ Little experience from administrative areas flowing back to the operational areas and
❑ Too many interfaces within the information flow.

(see AWK 1987, p. 88).

The disadvantages of pure, function oriented organizational structures stem from an isolated view of the individual business functions. This is despite the fact that they are closely entwined regarding logic and content. For example, order entry can begin in Sales, and then trigger planning and procurement functions in Materials Management. This in turn triggers manufacturing and assembly functions in Production, the process ends in Shipping. This whole process is accompanied by appropriate activities in Accounting (e.g., Accounts Receivable, Accounts Payable or in a product costing analysis).

Optimizing individual function areas generally does not result in optimization of the whole process because, within departments, only individual activities are "goal oriented". The demands of preceding or succeeding areas are not considered at all or, at best, insufficiently. When a task (for example, in Order Processing) needs to be processed across several areas, this leads to adjustment periods. This is generally true, in every department. Then everyone processes only the information that they need themselves. Consequently, if activities in individual areas need coordinating, in order to achieve the corporate mission, information between areas must be swapped and adjusted. Sometimes it must even be stored and maintained redundantly. Information delivery and adjustment periods frequently take up to 70-90% of the total processing time of an order (see SCHEER 1990a, p. 4). Inconsistent and non up-to-date information can lead to errors and an increase in expenditure. Function oriented procedures can also lead to secondary conditions in other functional areas or external companies that are accepted as a given and, consequently, are not optimized. This, in turn, impedes flexible reaction to customer demands or changes in the market place (see BECKER 1991a, pp. 136-141; BULLINGER et al. 1993a, pp. 122, 133; EVERSHEIM et al. 1994, pp. 57, 58; FRESE 1993, pp. 318, 319; SCHEER 1990a, pp. 3-5; SCHEER 1993b, pp. 85-87; WARNECKE 1993, pp. 65, 66).

These **disadvantages** should be **avoided** by introducing "**business process orientation**" as a design paradigm when developing organizational structures (see AMPONSEM, MARKHOFF 1994, pp. 137-146; BECKER 1994, pp. 43-45; FRESE 1994, p. 130; URBAN 1991, pp. 78-82; WILDEMANN 1992, pp. 19). Structuring activities focus on "**business processes**" rather than on individual, isolated functions. Business processes are defined as

❑ A series of functions that are executed
❑ By organizational units,
❑ According to an appropriate process logic, using
❑ The necessary data. This ensures that
❑ An overriding task (relating to **certain objects**)
❑ Is completely carried out.

One example is order processing, starting from the entry of the customer order, to the delivery of the appropriate products (see HAMMER, CHAMPY 1994, pp. 52, 53; KLEIN 1990, pp. 11-14; SCHEER 1992a, pp. 144-145). Thus, a business process has a **clearly defined beginning** and a **clearly defined end.** The beginning of the process is triggered by a -- usually external -- event. The end of the process is determined by the result, i.e., carrying out of the task (see JOST 1993b, pp. 10-12; ELGASS, KRCMAR 1993, p. 43).

For the following reasons, optimizing processes is greatly simplified when individual **departments** are responsible for **entire business processes**:

❑ The number of interfaces between organizational departments is reduced. This is due to a grouping of every function, making it possible to carry out complete tasks in one department.
❑ Structuring the necessary interfaces (e.g., coordinating departments), some of which are still necessary, is simplified. This is possible because only certain objects in an area are processed. Thus, only the data required for this area need to be swapped.

(see KELLER 1993, pp. 171-176; SCHEER 1993b, pp. 85-87).

Therefore, in business process oriented organizational structures, optimizing activities in individual departments leads to the optimization of entire business processes. When a single entity is in charge of the entire scope of tasks, this simplifies and accelerates a comprehensive reaction of individual organizational units (e.g., every department in a company) to the requirements of the procurement market (see WOMACK et al. 1992, pp. 153-155, 188-195).

The transition from a functionally oriented to a process oriented development of organizational structures is illustrated in Fig. 1.5.

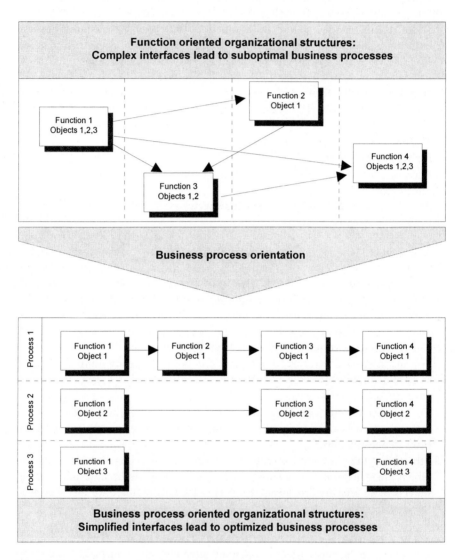

Fig.1.5: From function oriented to process oriented organizational structures

1.1.3 Characteristics of Business Process Oriented Organizational Structures

Organizational structures grouped by objects are a key result of business process orientation. This is due to the fact that business processes, allocated to individual departments, are characterized by a task referring to objects (e.g., products) (see BECKER 1991a, pp. 136-142; KELLER 1993, pp. 168-171; SCHEER 1993b, pp. 96-100). This not only results in optimized coordination of the various functions, but also in **less complexity** of the individual functions within a process (see SCHEER 1992a, p. 145). In a mechanical engineering company, for example, a simple order entry for the business process "order processing for standard products" would be sufficient. Employees in the field would be able to use it, without having to interact with internal order entry departments. Grouping by objects requires a "natural sequence" of functions and ensures **simplification** of entire work processes. Process logic is then no longer based on rigid work-sharing aimed at multiple products or markets (see HAMMER, CHAMPY 1994, pp. 75-77).

Organizational structures grouped by products (in the most general sense, i.e., also including services) or by product groups are preferred (see FRESE 1994, p. 130; PETERS, WATERMAN 1984, p. 360; WARNECKE 1993, pp. 73-75). In this case, organizations focus on objects that are the focal point of the business activity.

Product orientation also requires **market orientation** of business process oriented organizational structures. The manufactured products must be marketed against the current competition. Competition is primarily characterized by

❑ Potential new competitors,
❑ The danger posed by alternative products,
❑ Negotiating skills of buyers and suppliers and
❑ The rivalry between existing competitors.

(see PORTER 1989a, pp. 22-27). If products are tendered in various types of markets, different competitive situations can lead to different business processes. In developed countries, products could be more complex and labor costs higher. Thus, the requirements of services offered by companies in these countries could be greater than in developing countries. Constant change in the marketplace also requires continuous adaptation or reengineering of business processes (see AMPONSEM, MARKHOFF 1994, pp. 129-131; HAMMER, CHAMPY 1994, pp. 77-78; KEEN 1991, p. 96).

Product and market orientation of organizational structures focused on business processes leads to the

❑ Integration of functions and data,
❑ Decentralization and

❑ Dynamic,
❑ Employee oriented, lean hierarchies.

Integration of functions and data is a direct result of the elimination of the function oriented classification of organizational structures. In organizational units, previously separated tasks regarding the same objects are grouped, in order to complete business processes. Consequently, functions are grouped (**function integration**) and executed based on integrated data (**data integration**). **External partners** (customers and/or suppliers) can also be affected by this integration, for example, when quality control activities are transferred from the customer to the supplier. Integrating external partners enables companies to outsource certain activities, making these companies more capable of focusing on their key business (see FRESE 1994, pp. 130-131; HAMMER, CHAMPY 1994, pp. 72-74, 83-87; SCHEER 1990a, pp. 3-5; SCHEER 1993b, pp. 85-87).

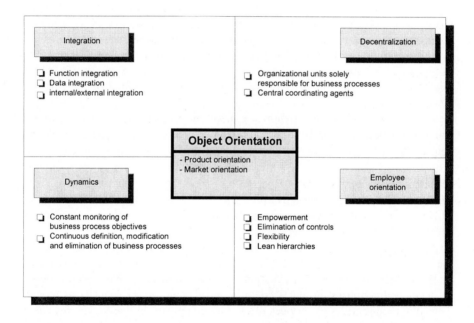

Fig. 1.6: Central characteristics of organizational structures focused on business processes

Product and market orientation also lead to **decentralization** of tasks. **Organizational units,** executing business processes completely, can be grouped into decentralized units. This is because they operate by themselves and are **solely responsible** for positioning themselves in the marketplace. This is done by means of profit centers, i.e., organizational units solely accountable for their own success. On the other hand, mutual resources (manufacturing plants or suppliers) must be centrally planned, in order to ensure a coordinated procedure and to avoid "friction loss". Synergies must be utilized to a maximum extent. Therefore, creating **central coordinating agents** often goes hand in hand with decentralizing individual tasks.

Tasks should be carried out where it is most feasible, leading to decentralized organizational units and central coordinating agents (see FRESE 1994, p. 130; HAMMER, CHAMPY 1994, pp. 78-80, 87-89; SCHEER 1993b, pp. 96-100; WARNECKE 1993, pp. 101-104, 154-157).

Constantly **changing environments** (changing markets) lead to **dynamic** organizational structures in companies. Business processes change, end or are redefined. These changes must be reflected in organizational structures. Individual organizational units must **constantly monitor their objectives** and redefine them if necessary (see HAMMER, CHAMPY 1994, pp. 77-78; WARNECKE 1993, pp. 160-169).

Dynamics, integration characteristics and the tendency of organizational structures focused on business processes to decentralize, these all call for strong employee orientation. Function integration rewards individual employees with greater responsibility. However, they are forced to **make more decisions themselves**, thus optimizing "their" processes. This, in turn, leads to **greater flexibility** and to a **decreasing need for monitoring and control** within the organization. Each employee bears the responsibility for his/her decisions. Monitoring and controls are only necessary if this is economically justified. This leads to **leaner hierarchies** because monitoring by superiors is no longer necessary (see HAMMER, CHAMPY 1994, pp. 74-75, 80-83; WARNECKE 1993, pp. 157-160).

The central characteristics of organizational structures focused on business processes are illustrated in Fig. 1.6.

1.2 Function Oriented Design of Standard Software

After characterizing and defining the term "standard software", the reasons of the predominance of function orientation in designing standard software will be given. Thus, the main characteristics of today's standard software will be illustrated.

1.2.1 Characterizing and Defining the Term "Standard Software"

In professional publications, the term "software" is defined in various ways. The most common definition describes **software** as **the sum of all computer programs** available for data processing systems. A **computer program** is the complete set of commands necessary to carry out a task on a data processing (DP)

machine. The only exceptions are micro-programmed hardware elements (see FRANK 1980, p. 13; HANSEN et al. 1983, p. 7; MORVAN 1988, p. 184).
Software can basically be divided into

❑ System software and
❑ Application software.

Together with the appropriate hardware, **system software** provides the foundation for operating a data processing system. It comprises the operating system, configured on the existing hardware. It controls the DP system, executes help functions and monitors the hardware. Furthermore, system software comprises database management systems, telecommunication systems and program development systems. **Application software** comprises all programs that process and carry out business related user tasks (see FRANK 1980, p. 14; HANSEN 1986, p. 323; KLOTZ 1993, p. 19; SCHEER 1990c, pp. 10-11). The following discussion will refer to application software.
Application software can be divided into

❑ Individually developed applications and
❑ Standard software (standard application software).

Individually developed applications are programs developed by companies or by third parties on their behalf. They are customized to carry out the specific tasks of these companies. **Standard software** comprises programs that have been developed by software companies or hardware manufacturers for an anonymous market. Besides the actual programs, standard software also includes **additional goods and services**, such as

❑ Documentation,
❑ Training,
❑ Installation support and
❑ Maintenance.

It is characterized by

❑ The ability to deliver certain functions or solutions,
❑ General usability (running on various DP systems in different companies), a
❑ Clear definition and reduced dp-technical system adaptation within a certain limited time-frame, e.g., by setting parameters. There is a

❑ Fixed price for these programs and for the additional services mentioned above.

(see BALANTZIAN 1992, p. 149; FRANK 1980, pp. 14-15; MORVAN 1988, p. 264; SCHEER 1990c, p. 139; STAHLKNECHT 1990, pp. 400, 401). In order to amortize development costs, individually developed software is also frequently available in the marketplace. However, this can not be considered to be standard software, as described above because it is usually not widely usable. This becomes apparent in light of their limited installation base (see SCHEER 1990c, p. 139). In order to solve specific problems (specific evaluations), standard software can be complemented by individually developed applications (see SCHEER 1990c, 147). The use of standard software has the following **advantages** over individually developed software:

❏ Lower cost of procurement because development costs can be spread out among many users
❏ Migration to standard software is smoother because any migration and adjustment issues are a known entity and can therefore be avoided or planned
❏ Lower maintenance costs because program maintenance can be outsourced to the software manufacturer
❏ Timesaving in the procurement process
❏ Less strain on DP departments, leaving them more time to solve non-standard problems; avoids " application backlog"
❏ Investment protection by being adaptable to business requirements
❏ Implementation of standard software suites enables data and function integration
❏ Takes advantage of the business skills of the standard software vendor and of the methods provided (e.g., for corporate management).
❏ Generally, more modern software technology is used, leading to superior software
❏ Consistent user interface and, on the whole, a higher ergonomic standard
❏ Usually also includes personal productivity software (electronic mail, word processing or on-line documentation, etc.) for each module

(see BECKER 1994, p. 154; BECKER et al. 1991, p. 153; HANSEN et al. 1983, pp. 3-4; HORVATH et al. 1986, p. 7; LIEBETRAU, BECKER 1992, p. 59; MARTINY, KLOTZ 1990, pp. 79-80).

Using standard applications, however, also has certain **disadvantages**:

❏ Occasional adaptation problems due to mismatch between the software solution and user requirements
❏ Interface problems between various standard software products or between standard software and individually developed software (which is nonetheless necessary)
❏ Poor performance because hardware resource requirements are greater than with individually developed applications
❏ Limited user privileges (sometimes users are not allowed to modify programs)

❑ Dependency on the software manufacturer because programs are not transparent to the user company (source code not available or not documented)
❑ Employee anxiety (employees could worry unnecessarily that certain work processes might become standardized or automated)
(BECKER 1994, p. 154; HORVATH 1986, pp. 7-8; LIEBETRAU, BECKER 1992, p. 59).

We will now discuss standard software and, in particular, standard application software.
Standard software can be differentiated according to different topics. There are two types,

❑ Mathematical-technical software and
❑ Business administration software.

Mathematical-technical software (e.g., method databases or function libraries) generally consists of programs heavily utilizing mathematical functions, statistical methods and operations research methods. **Business administration software** is used to support business administration work processes, (e.g., in Accounting, Human Resources, Production Planning and Control, Material Management or Sales). It has become an important medium for distributing and executing the results of business administration theories because user companies can select from various business concepts (see KLOTZ 1993, p. 19; SCHEER 1990c, pp. 123, 154-163; STAHLKNECHT 1990, p. 401).
When we speak of standard software in the following discussion, we will be referring to business administration application software. These two types can not always be differentiated, however. For example, CAD systems consist of mathematical-technical software, although they most certainly have a business administration aspect, such as when they supply the basic data (bills of materials) for material requirements planning.
Business administration application software can be:

❑ Industry non-specific or
❑ Industry specific

Industry non-specific software is used to carry out business administration tasks that are independent of individual lines of business (e.g., Financial Accounting or Human Resources). **Industry specific software** is primarily used to support industry specific work processes. It is used for the administration of rendering goods and services and the resulting order processing. Some examples of this type of software are production planning and control systems (PPS systems) for manufacturers or merchandise management systems for retailers. It is possible to break down these industries even further and differentiate between lines of business or organization types, such as PPS systems for the textile industry or for plant engineering and construction (see SCHEER 1990c, pp. 145-147; SCHEER 1994a, pp. 398-400; STAHLKNECHT 1990, p. 401; STEINBEISSER, DRÄGER 1989, p. 1; ZENTES, ANDERER 1993, pp. 348-363). The following refers to industry non-specific and industry specific standard software.

Classification of standard software is illustrated in Fig. 1.7. The software classes relevant in this discussion are shaded.

In addition to the above classification, industry non-specific and industry specific standard software can also be differentiated by types of programs, such as:

❑ Specialized programs
❑ Application languages and
❑ Software suites

Specialized programs are used for a very narrow scope of tasks (for instance, plant maintenance or assets accounting). Generally, their business administration and DP functionality is excellent. They are, however, difficult to integrate with existing systems. **Application languages** place various application function "building blocks" at a user's disposal. These building blocks can be assembled according to the individual demands of the company. The programs are flexible, but do not provide the user with very many aids to implement his or her business administration concept. **Software suites** are integrated software systems for a broad range of applications. "Integration" in this context means that the individual programs or modules are linked. Data is transferred automatically.

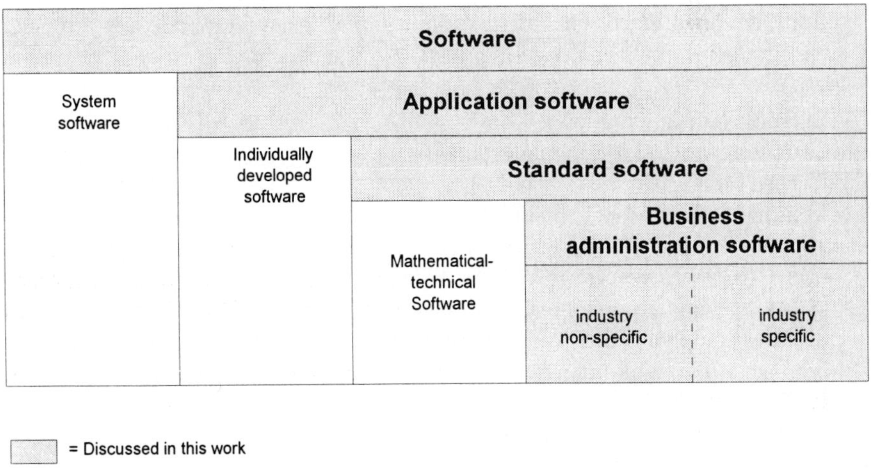

Software				
System software	**Application software**			
	Individually developed software	**Standard software**		
		Mathematical-technical Software	**Business administration software**	
			industry non-specific	industry specific

▢ = Discussed in this work

Fig. 1.7: Classification of software

The interface concept and security functionality are consistent. Today, there is a general trend towards implementing software suites. Modern standard software can sometimes be classified into all three groups: software suites encompassing both application languages and specialized programs (see BALANTZIAN 1992, p. 150; FREY 1990, p. 111; PLATTNER 1993a, pp. 95-106; SCHEER 1990c, pp. 139-142).

Today, standard software systems, especially **ERP** (Enterprise Ressource Planning) systems, are available for most business administration fields, such as:

❑ Finance and Accounting
❑ Cost Accounting
❑ Human Resources Management
❑ Sales / Sales Processing
❑ Purchasing
❑ Production Planning, incl. Material and Capacity Management and Order Release for Manufacturing
❑ Manufacturing Control
❑ Research & Development
❑ Maintenance
❑ Quality Control

(see BECKER et al. 1991, p. 154; MARTINY, KLOTZ 1990, pp. 78-79). The range of standard software products varies for different types of companies. Companies of discrete serial manufacturing have the broadest selection. The standard software offering is narrower for continuous manufacturing or batch production manufacturers, respectively (see SCHEER 1990c, pp. 146-147).

Recently developed standard software prdoucts ("**post ERP** systems") turn away from the mentioned backoffice applications. Therefore they are attunded to engaging customers and driving profits. Typical examples are

❑ Sales force automation
❑ Customer-relationship management
❑ Data mining
❑ Supply Chain Management

(see CALDWELL, STEIN 1998). Especially the **Supply Chain Management** (SCM) systems become more and more important. The functionality is focused on the way companies deal with suppliers, partners and customers to have the right product, at the right price, at the right time, and in the right condition (see STEIN, SWEAT 1998).

1.2.2 Function Orientation in the Development of Standard Software

Standard software, as described above, helps support business administration **work processes**. These work processes are integrated in the **organizational structure** of a company. Previously, organizational structures were almost always function oriented, which is still often is the case even today. This, in turn, leads to **function orientation in standard software** (see BECKER 1994, p. 46; SCHEER 1993b, p. 85).

The role of function orientation in developing standard software is favored by the fact that, in many companies, some organizational functions basically require special versions of a software program. Thus, **standard software** was initially developed only for certain **functions that could easily be standardized**. For example, if a certain market was restricted by Federal regulations, and did not leave any room for different business approaches, a standard solution was appropriate. An individual solution was of little use. Thus, demand for standard software was great (see BECKER 1994, pp. 148-149; SCHEER 1990c, pp. 144-145). Correspondingly, due to the potentially large market, developing standard software was promising for vendors (see SCHEER et al. 1990, p. 91). Situations such as these resulted in the development of function oriented standard software applications, e.g., for Financial Accounting. Financial Accounting is the field in which the largest amount of standard software applications is available today (see KIRSCH et al. 1979, p. 62; LANG 1989, pp. 10-11; RIEDER 1988, p. 82-83). Successively, standard software was developed for **other function areas**, also (see BECKER et al. 1991, pp. 154-155; HANSEN et al. 1983, pp. 38, 39; LANG 1989, pp. 10-11). Function orientation was retained.

As demand for **business process oriented organizational structures** increased, however, these functional software islands became a problem. Work processes linked with each other beyond the initial scope of functional areas needed to be comprehensively supported by standard software, if the negative effect of function orientation was to be avoided (see BECKER 1994, pp. 46-47; WATTEROTT 1993, pp. 93-96). This was an important reason for developing **integrated standard software suites**.

Work processes of various application areas were supported and business administration terminology and theories were consistent (see KLOTZ 1993, p. 19; SCHEER 1993b, pp. 86, 87). Function orientation, however, remained the design paradigm. Software modules were integrated by creating a common data set and by connecting individual functions, although they were not redesigned to be object oriented (e.g., with regard to certain products or product groups). This is known as function integrated standard software (see SCHEER 1992a, pp. 138-139; SCHEER, OETINGER 1992, p. 7).

Modern standard software, such as SAP's R/3 (see PLATTNER 1993a), is said to be object oriented or process oriented, respectively. However, object orientation can only be achieved by adjusting the appropriate parameters (see KELLER, MEINHARDT 1994, p. 5). The software has such rich functionality that various objects (e.g., standard products and variant products) can be edited. The design paradigm is function oriented.

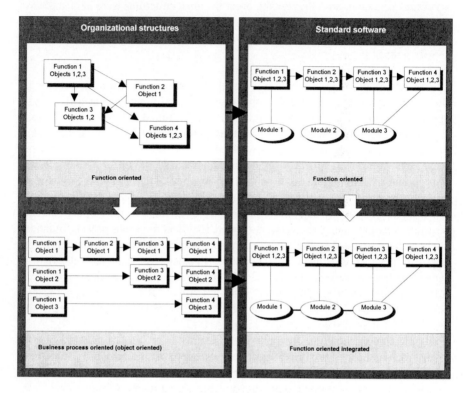

Fig. 1.8: Function oriented development of standard software

Certain approaches of object oriented standard software have been implemented in Supply Chain Management (SCM) systems, in production scheduling systems (part or assembly manufacturing, respectively), in systems supporting the development of discrete products or in cost center control systems (see SCHEER 1994a, pp. 303-307, 604-607, 687-689). However, once again, only sub-processes of organizations are represented. Since the market to be addressed must as large as possible (i.e., companies with various lines of business and various organizational structures), the individual functions must be valid across-the-board (see LUDWIG 1992, p. 1). This, in turn, leads to a **blend of object and function orientation.**

Function oriented development of standard software is illustrated in Fig. 1.8.

Work flow management systems (i.e., standard software products), continuously supporting business processes by managing and controlling events, monitoring functionality and by means of analysis and synthesis tools (see KRICKL 1994b, pp. 18-19), strive to **do away with function orientation** in standard software (see SAP 1994, pp. 5.1 - 5.7). Mainly, they support office work that is organized by personal productivity software (word processing, spreadsheets, etc.), (see SCHEER 1994a, p. 718). Work flow management systems are an aid in using function oriented software in an object oriented manner. They do this by triggering individual functions according to object flows. Work flow management systems are tools for reducing the effect of function orientation in standard software. The original design paradigm of the standard software, however, remains the same.

There are several indications for function orientation in today's standard software: Software vendors specializing in certain functions (see SCHEER 1993b, p. 85), function oriented screens (see KLOTZ 1991, p. 103, 104) or subsequent focus of the software on objects by adjusting system parameters (see KELLER, MEINHARDT 1994, p. 5). When examining modules of software suites used by companies, function oriented development also becomes apparent (see RIEDER 1988, p. 82-86). The software modules correspond to functional areas in organizations. The different members of installations of different software modules demonstrate that standard software modules support individual functions rather than entire business processes.

1.2.3 Characteristics of Today's Standard Software

A central characteristic of today's standard software is its **function oriented design paradigm.** Standard software modules provide business administration functions **across product lines and markets**. Thus, the complexity of the individual modules is still high.

Function orientation in standard software conflicts with the business process oriented development of organizational structures, as described above. However, this conflict is **mitigated by:**

❑ Integration of standard software modules (software suites),
❑ Possible decentralization of software functionality and data storage,
❑ Dynamic adaptability (parametrization) and the
❑ Employee oriented, user friendly concept of standard software.

Modern standard software excels in its high degree of **integration**. Software suites like SAP R/3 are an ideal example therefore (see RIEDER 1988, p. 15-16). This enables a business process oriented view of the various functions (see SCHEER 1993b, p. 86) and standard software support of complete business processes (see KELLER, MEINHARDT 1994, p. 19).

There are several ways of integrating software:

❑ Data integration,
❑ Data structure integration
❑ Function integration or
❑ Module integration

is possible (see BECKER 1991b, p. 166). **Data integration** is the case when data is shared by various departments. This is possible by different software modules using a mutual data base. When **one** data set structure is shared by various contents (e.g., for manufacturing and maintenance orders) and multiple records (e.g., grouping tools to a tool group) use it jointly, this is known as **data structure integration. Function integration** of standard software is the case when two different functions are grouped into a new function. However, function integration is also the case when the result of a certain function triggers the execution of another function, providing certain pre-defined conditions are met. **Module integration**: this means that a software module is used in various areas of the software suite (see BECKER 1991b, p. 166-191).

Integration of various standard software products is possible using **normed interfaces**, e.g., for integrating construction applications (CAD systems) and production planning and control systems (PPS systems) (see SCHEER 1990a, pp. 57-67; SCHOLZ-REITER 1991, pp. 53-83, 132-148, 150-177). This enables an integration of different enterprises (e.g., by exchanging product data or orders with suppliers; see PETRI 1990, pp. 64-104, 170-203; TSCHIRA, ZENCKE 1994, p. 7).

In standard software, the tendency to **decentralize** tasks in process oriented organizational structures is reflected by the concept of **distributed data processing**, especially in software **client/server architectures** (see SCHEER 1994a, pp. 75-76; ZIMMERMANN 1994, p. 68). Software modeled on client/server architectures is characterized by the following features:

❑ Applications are broken up into at least two parts: the "client" and the "server"
❑ The server provides a service
❑ A client uses this service
❑ During the "cooperation" process between the distributed components, there is an "order relationship", triggered by the client, the rest of the time the different components are independent.
❑ Clients and servers communicate with each other via order related messages
❑ It is possible to exchange messages via networks as the delivery medium
❑ A server can assume the role of the client and vice versa.

(see HOUY et al. 1992, pp. 14-15). Client/server architectures enable **optimal distribution of the data processing service** among individual computers and **individual organizational units** (see PLATTNER 1993b, pp. 931-937). From a data processing point of view, it has distinct advantages, such as the ability to leverage special hardware and software. Leveraging existing communication technology such as e-mail and reducing the number of data transfers is also possible (see SCHEER 1994a, p. 75). Small wonder that client/server architectures are the de facto architectural standard in leading-edge standard software products (see BENJAMIN, BLUNT 1993, pp. 76-77).

Modern standard software offers several ways to react to the **dynamics** of organizational structures, reflected in frequent changes of business processes. Without having to modify programs, the software can be tailored to meet the individual needs of an organization. This is known as **customizing** (see STAHLKNECHT 1983, p. 168). By **selecting certain parameters**, a company is able to react to changes in the business environment. Parameters are variables that influence the behavior of standard software (see LUDWIG 1992, p. 1-2). When modeling the business processes with the software, proper adjustments must be made before actually running the standard software. However, this can also be done dynamically, while the software is running (see KELLER, MEINHARDT 1994, p. 5; LUDWIG 1992, pp. 24-25).

Standard software can also be "dynamized" by **modularization**. This makes it possible, at least to some extent, to select only those software components that are actually necessary at a given time. By defining **user exits**, it is possible to complement the standard software with individual applications and to customize it dynamically. This is why complete development environments are available for standard software (see PLATTNER 1993a, p. 106; SCHEER 1990c, p. 147). Dynamic modification of standard software is supported by **IT standardization goals (**e.g., of the operating system). This facilitates switching the system environment (upgrading to more powerful hardware for more complex applications) or adding software modules of various standard software vendors (see FREY 1990, pp. 117-123; LAIDIG 1993, pp. 789-791). Standard software **system updates** facilitate the ability of organizations to continuously adapt to new business developments (see RIEDER 1988, p. 16).

Employee orientation of standard software is apparent in several ways: modern standard software has a **user-friendly and frequently graphical user interface** (see BULLINGER et al. 1993b, p. 941-942). The user interface is the interface between the user and the software. Its purpose is:

❑ To prepare and display information
❑ To control and handle the system
❑ To display help information (concerning data processing and business issues) and
❑ To provide tools for ad hoc querying of information (database queries)

(see OETINGER 1989, p. 31). Standard software interfaces should obviously help the user to carry out his/her work as easily as possible (see PLATTNER 1993b, p.

930). Particularly in lean organizational structures, this enables employees to apply themselves to the work processes in a decentralized, solely responsible manner. This is also facilitated by **standardized interfaces** (see BULLINGER et al. 1993b, pp. 942-950). Standardization enables the use of various standard software systems or several modules of a software suite for various process functions, without forcing users to adapt to different interfaces (see OETINGER 1989, pp. 32-33).

The execution of multiple functions in **on-line mode** and, consequently, instant availability of information, also enhances user-friendliness (see RIEDER 1988, p. 14). Necessary information (e.g., status of a customer order) is immediately available without any additional effort (such as processing lists that have to be generated in batch jobs). Integrating documentation into the standard software **(on-line documentation)** is another important element of employee orientation. Help systems, interactive training programs and appropriate user guides (e.g., user elements, status information and messages) popping up on the screen make system handling much easier (see FREMMER 1992, pp. 97-108).

The key characteristics of modern standard software are illustrated in Fig. 1.9.

The application-independent, data-processing relevant aspects of standard software were not studied. In selecting a software application, certain characteristics in this context, such as the programming languages that were used, are relevant to a certain extent (see LANG 1989, p. 116; MARKMILLER 1989, p. 13). However, they are basically only important for the software manufacturer (developer of the programs). In this work, we will concentrate on standard software from the point of view of the user company.

1.3 Implications for the Implementation of Standard Software

After characterizing the term "Implementation of Standard Software", we will discuss the implications of the conflicting design types of organizational structures and of standard software for the implementation of standard software. Subsequently, we will illustrate the strategic impact of this implementation.

1.3.1 Characterizing and Defining the Term "Implementation of Standard Software"

The **implementation of standard software** can generally be defined as the **sum of all activities** necessary to **effectively utilize** software **in the business environment** of a user company. After implementation, users are able to:

❑ Comprehend and execute the work processes,
❑ To ensure the necessary data quality and
❑ To effectively utilize the information provided by the software

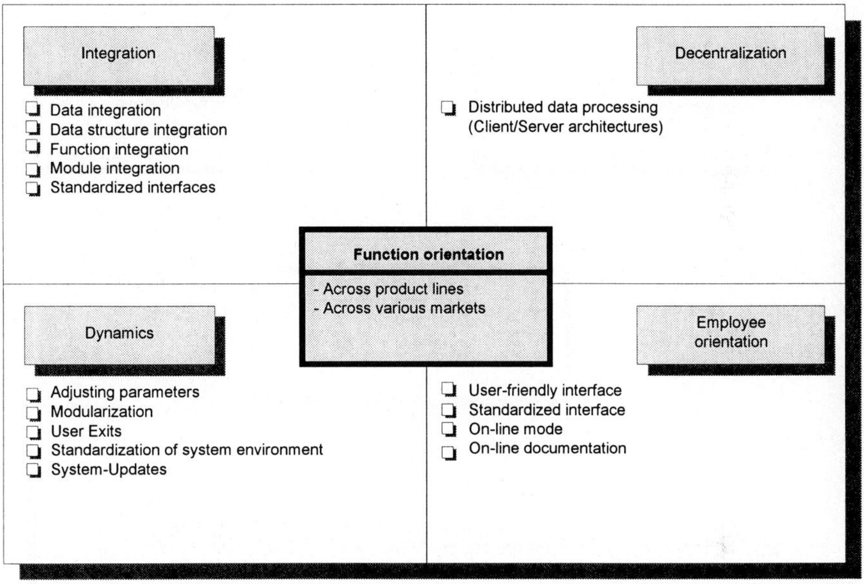

Fig. 1.9: Key characteristics of modern standard software

(see BODENSTAB 1970, p. 64). The software must therefore become an integral part of the enterprise and the changes (e.g., new directives or regulations) brought about by it. Organizational structures and standard software are linked together in the course of implementation. Consequently, in organizational structures, the work processes that are to be executed must be supported by the software (see BECKER 1994, pp. 44-47). This key objective is illustrated in Fig. 1.10.

The "introduction" of software is generally known as "implementation" (see RIEDER 1988, pp. 17-18). In this work we use the term "implementation", and wish to call to attention the different meaning of this word in its pure data processing sense. We do not mean to limit the scope of its content (e.g., to a purely technical installation of the software), as is sometimes customary in organizational theory (see KALKS 1990, pp. 77-78).

When "implementing standard software",

❑ Business / content related activities and the
❑ Corresponding project management

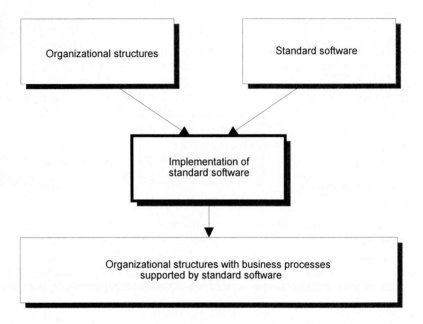

Fig. 1.10: The objective of implementing standard software

can be grouped together (see BARTELS 1993, pp. 13-18; KÖLLE 1990, p. 46; MAYDL 1987, pp. 84-86; RIEDER 1988, p. 18). The process of implementation, i.e., the business / content related implementation process, is determined by **business related activities** (see KÖLLE 1990, pp. 47, 48). **Project management** entails activities for planning the implementation with regards to time, cost, enablement of resources, the sequence of individual activities, monitoring progress of the project and the definition of the person/entity in charge (see FRESE 1993, pp. 448-450; KÖLLE 1990, pp. 48-49; PAGE-JONES 1991, pp. 85-87). The Project Management activities are largely removed from business related issues. The remainder of this discussion will refer to the business related method of implementing standard software. This in turn leads to the appropriate project management.

The implementation can be

❏ Technology centric,
❏ User / user acceptance centric or
❏ Organization centric.

(see HAMACHER 1991, pp. 94-100; JUNKER 1988, pp. 17-21; ROSS 1993, pp. 24-25). In **technology centric** implementations, installing the software is largely regarded as a technological task. The requirements of the users and for the organization are a direct result of the installation of the software (see HAMACHER 1991, pp. 94-95; JUNKER 1988, p. 17). The technology drives the users. **User / user acceptance centric** implementations also take into account that implemented software obtains the desired effect only when accepted by the users. Users present their requests to IT. Consequently, the only software modules implemented are those that are actually necessary for and required by the user. Parallel measures (modifying the organization or employee training) increase user acceptance (see HAMACHER 1991, pp. 96-97; JUNKER 1988, pp. 17-19; RAU 1991, p. 199). **Organization centric** implementations encompass an even larger scope of the entire implementation process. They particularly take into account that the use of modern standard software enables options for modifying the organizational framework of an enterprise. The software can be used as a coordinating mechanism (as enabler) within the organizational structure. During every implementation step, issues involving the process, organizational structure and the users should be considered (see BECKER 1994, pp. 46-47; FRESE 1993, pp. 230-233; FRESE 1994, pp. 132-133; HAMACHER 1991, pp. 98-99; JUNKER 1988, pp. 19-21; KLOTZ 1993, pp. 137-142; RAU 1991, pp. 199-200).

This work is focused on the organizational centric implementation because it is especially appropriate for implementing business administration application software (see FRESE 1994, pp. 132-133; HAMACHER 1991, pp. 100-101; JUNKER 1988, pp. 19-21; ROSS 1993, pp. 24-25; SCHEER, OETINGER 1992, p. 7).

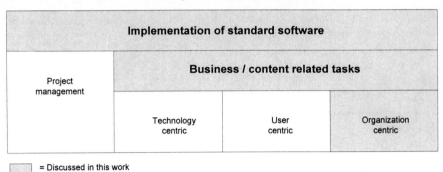

Implementation of standard software			
Project management	Business / content related tasks		
	Technology centric	User centric	Organization centric

☐ = Discussed in this work

Fig. 1.11: Classifying activities in the implementation of software

Fig. 1.11 illustrates the classification of activities for implementing standard software. The focus of the following discussion is shaded.

During the process of implementation, the business content of standard software is, literally, implemented in the organization. Gaps in the software functionality also become apparent. This leads to further development of the standard software. The **multiple relationships between data processing and business administration** become visible when implementing standard software (see SCHEER 1990c, p. 1-4).

1.3.2 Implications of the Conflicting Design Types of Organizational Structures and Standard Software

If the implementation of standard software is organization centric, we must determine whether activities focus on structures in the software -- or on the existing/planned organizational structures of the enterprise. We must establish whether organizational structures will adapt to the software or vice versa. If both the software and organizational structures are developed according to the same design paradigm and according to the same secondary conditions (e.g., to meet strategic objectives), both implementation approaches lead to the same or very similar results. However, the fact that organizational structures and standard software have **different design approaches,** makes adaptation of both structures necessary **during the course of implementation** (see BECKER 1994, p. 46). The strategic objectives of the enterprise should be considered.

A decision in favor of standard software is also a decision in favor of organizational solutions. Work processes, as required by the software, are automatically adapted. Very frequently, the adage " **Structure follows Software**" is applicable (see ÖSTERLE et al. 1991, p. 47). This means that, on the whole, planned organizational structures adapt to the structure called for by the software. If function oriented standard software is implemented according to its structure,

the modules are installed step-by-step. Business administration **functions** for **every object** concerned become operational gradually. This, however, conflicts with the paradigm of business process orientation in developing organizational structures. Herein, engineering activities encompass **every function** that relates to **one object** or one object group, respectively (i.e., a product or a product group). Thus, software oriented implementation results in *function* optimization rather than in process optimization. The result is that planned **process oriented organizational structures are overlapped by function oriented standard software structures.** The strategic objectives of an enterprise, the aim of business process orientation, are therefore only barely met or are not met at all. Fig. 1.12 illustrates this situation.

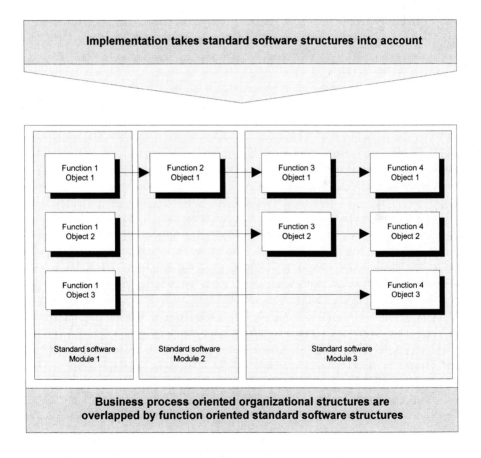

Fig. 1.12. The implications of a standard software oriented implementation

This unintended implementation of function oriented structures can be avoided by a **business process oriented implementation** of function oriented standard software. Instead of a successive, enterprise-wide execution of functions, we have a step-by-step **implementation of business processes**. This means that processes or sub-processes are supported by the software, regardless of the functional structure of the software. The implementation is carried out according to business administration aspects of the organizational development rather than according to data processing aspects of the standard software. The standard software

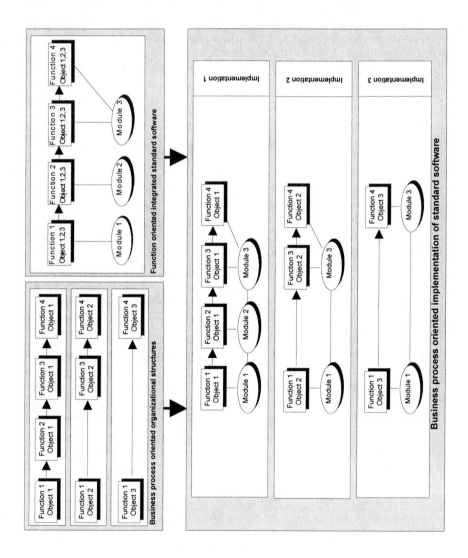

Fig. 1.13. Business process oriented implementation of standard software

implementation is business driven. This ensures that company specific, strategic objectives -- the foundation of organizational structures -- are met.

The purpose of implementing software is to engineer business processes according to a corporate strategy (see JUNKER 1988, pp. 19-21; LAY 1990, pp. 91-92; RAU 1991, pp. 199-200). Fig. 1.13 outlines the basic concept of business process oriented implementation of standard software.

Business process oriented implementation is enabled by the characteristics of the software (integration, decentralization, dynamics and employee orientation). These characteristics are typical of process oriented organizational structures, so that the software can be to implement these organizational concepts.
We are now able to define the implementation of standard software more precisely.
Process oriented implementation of standard software comprises every activity, in order to execute the business processes in question. The objective is optimal support of the strategic objectives of an enterprise.

Therefore,
❑   Appropriate business processes must be defined according to the objectives to be met;
❑   Support of these processes bust be enabled by the software using several modules, if necessary;
❑   The users must be capable of executing the processes by means of the software in a way that ensures meeting the strategic objectives.

The following is a more precise definition of the "business environment", in which the software is to be used (mentioned above in the general definition): "Business processes" must be supported. "Effective use" of the software means optimal support of the company's strategic objectives (see KIRCHMER 1993, p. 136).
Business process oriented implementation of standard software, as defined here, enables optimization of the business processes by means of the software, regardless of the design paradigm of the standard software. This kind of implementation is necessary for today's function oriented standard software. It also makes sense for software that might someday be developed in a process oriented manner. Consequently, workflow management systems support the business process oriented implementation approach.
Implementing standard software becomes an integral part of **process oriented information management**. On the one hand, it enables economical utilization of information as a resource by corporate information systems that are engineered appropriately. On the other hand, the close interrelationship between information management, business processes and the corporate strategy are taken into account (see SCHWARZER 1994, pp. 306-308).

1.3.3 Strategic Significance of the Implementation

The term " strategic" is characterized by three properties: the

❑ Content related focus on important issues (**relevance**), the
❑ Systematic focus on certain essential issues (**simplification**) and an
❑ Effort to carry out everything as soon as possible (**proactivity**).

(see SCHOLZ 1987, pp. 5-6).

Business process implementation of standard software is characterized by two central aspects: the

❑ Business processes to be engineered in the course of implementation and the
❑ Process of implementation per se.

According to the definition, the purpose of the business processes to be engineered is to carry out an overriding task. In turn, the tasks of the enterprise directly or indirectly aim at maintaining or improving the competitive situation (see PORTER 1989a, pp. 59-66), that is, to meet strategic objectives. Business processes form a link between corporate goals and the necessary measures to meet this goal, such as by using IT aids (see FRESE 1994, p. 129; KÜTING 1993, pp. 41-42). Thus, business process oriented implementation of standard software, by which complete **business processes** are optimized, aids in meeting the strategic objectives of an enterprise. Thus, the implementation is **relevant**.

The significance of the results of an implementation requires and rectifies investing in the implementation process per se. Implementation ties up substantial corporate resources, (e.g., personnel or financial assets) for a long period of time, sometimes up to several years. Generally, a company can therefore not afford to have an attempt fail (see ÖSTERLE 1990a, p. 9). Efficient execution of the implementation and, consequently, a head start over the competition, can become an important factor in achieving competitive advantages (see ZANGL 1990, p. 109). This rectifies the **relevance** of the **implementation process**.

Due to the many aspects to be considered, the description of business processes is highly complex (see SCHEER 1993b, p. 87). Implementing standard software can also cause a sea change in a company's business processes. It

❑ Changes many characteristics of an organization, triggering countless internal and external subsequent changes,
❑ Affects many internal and external employees, thus
❑ Making the necessary measures highly innovative.

(see ESSER, KIRSCH 1979, pp. 3-4). This leads to the planned objective of the software implementation being even more complex. During the implementation, we must therefore systematically focus on key issues, that is **simplify**, when mapping the target **business processes**.

The complexity of the business processes to be engineered, and the resulting necessity to simplify their mapping, leads to an elaborate implementation process. This can only be carried out efficiently and economically, if the **implementation process** per se is limited to key issues and is thus **simplified**.

In order to achieve competitive advantages by implementing standard software, market developments should be anticipated and taken into account when engineering the **business processes**. When implementing standard software, **proactivity** is necessary.

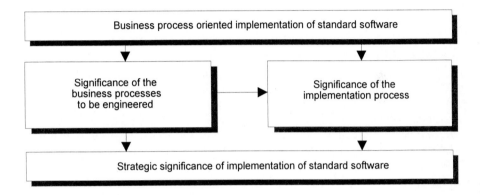

Fig. 1.14: Strategic importance of business process oriented implementation of software

Due to the fact that implementing standard software can take up to several years, the environment (e.g., software functionality or market conditions) can very well change during the implementation process. These changes must be taken into account by **acting proactively** during the whole **implementation process**, ensuring focused utilization of resources.

The business processes to be engineered when implementing the software, as well as the implementation process per se, prove the **strategic importance** of **implementing business process oriented standard software**. This is illustrated in Fig. 1.14.

At times, the potential of achieving a competitive advantage by means of standard software is challenged by the argument that "standard solutions" can not differentiate competitors (see BECKER 1994, p. 155; KÜTING 1993, p. 133). This is refuted by examples showing that appropriate use of standard software can very well improve the competitive situation of companies (see DAHLHEIM 1993, p. 34; FÜLLER 1990, p. 47; LAMETER et al. 1994, p. 63; SCHRÖDER 1993, p. 32). This differentiation is achieved by tailoring the software to the requirements of the particular company and by early implementation.

1.4 Objective and Structure of this Work

It is the **objective** of this work to develop a **procedure model** for *business process oriented *i*mplementation of* standard software* (BIS)**, in order to meet **strategic objectives** (precise description of all steps in the implementation approach). The model must be sufficiently detailed, in order to make its use practical. The various design approaches of organizational structures and standard software, namely process and function orientation, are overcome.

BIS links elements of strategic information system planning with elements of tactical and operational approaches, respectively. On the one hand, comparable to strategic information system planning, it serves to execute the strategic objectives set by corporate management and/or enables the definition of these objectives (see NEU 1991, p. 43). On the other hand, it must carry out tactical and operational tasks (see RIEDER 1988, p. 18). This positioning of the implementation of standard software within information system planning is illustrated in Fig. 1.15.

In a first draft, BIS begins **designing** central **business processes relevant** for achieving strategic objectives. Organization, function, data and detailed process models are then added to the resulting process models, enabling the focused execution of the business processes. In Phase 2 of BIS, the business processes become sufficiently detailed to meet the central requirements defined in Phase 1. At the same time, the **business administration concepts of the standard software** are utilized as much as possible, in order to obtain an effective and efficient solution. In Phase 3 of BIS, the detailed concept of the business processes is **executed**.

For every step in the implementation phases,

❑ The goals are explained,
❑ The business / content related procedure is defined and
❑ Possible support by methods and IT tools is described.

The **goals** define which results must be achieved in a given implementation phase, in order to proceed with the next steps. They set a guideline for each individual activity. The business / content related **procedure** describes what must be done in each implementation step, in order to achieve the desired objectives. The result is a process model of the implementation. **Support by methods and IT tools** shows how the previously defined activities can be executed. The decisive factor here is to show **one** possibility (not all possibilities) of executing the activities and to prove whether the defined procedure can be executed.

The procedures are explained by examples from real implementation projects. When studying possible DP support of these procedures, the growing role of IT tools for planning and executing information systems is taken into account (see KRAUS, KRAEMER 1993; SCHEER 1991b; SCHÜLE, SCHUMANN 1992).

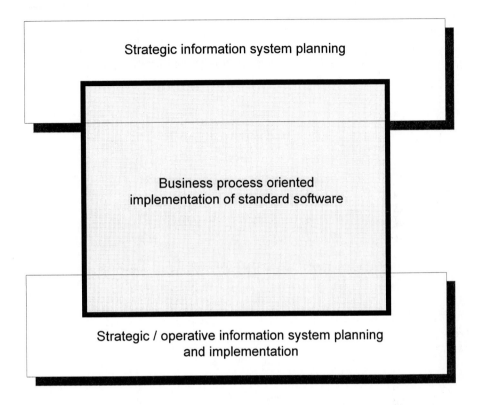

Fig. 1.15: Positioning BIS in information system planning

Based on the fundamental discussion regarding business process oriented development of organizational structures and based on the resulting implications for implementing standard software in **Chapter 1**, we will develop a BIS procedure model in **Chapter 2**. Using the results of Chapter 1, we will define requirements for the implementation of standard software. These requirements will be the foundation for judging today's approaches in implementing standard software. The requirements for implementing and judging these approaches are the starting point for the development of a BIS procedure model.

In **Chapters 3, 4 and 5**, we will describe the various phases of BIS: The strategy based business process optimization concept (BPO concept), the deduction of the standard software based BPO concept and, finally, the BPO implementation. Every phase ends with the definition of the framework controls

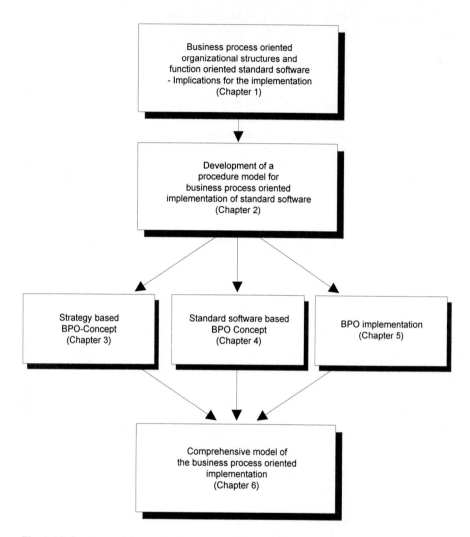

Fig. 1.16: Structure of the work

for the next implementation phase, the last one ending with the actual operation of the software.

Chapter 6 provides an overview of the total BIS procedure model. The detail process model that was developed is aggregated. Furthermore, we will summarize how BIS meets the requirements defined in Chapter 2. In conclusion, we will look ahead to BIS development opportunities.

The structure of this work is illustrated in Fig. 1.16.

2 Development of a Procedure Model for Business Process Oriented Implementation of Standard Software

We will now develop a procedure model for BIS, and a framework for a detailed discussion of the implementation phases in the following chapters.

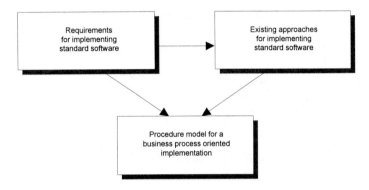

Fig. 2.1: Structure of Chapter 2

To begin with, we will discuss the requirements for implementing standard software. These requirements lay the foundation for assessing selected approaches of information system planning. Considering the demands for implementation and what we have learned from these approaches, we will develop the BIS procedure model. The structure of Chapter 2 is illustrated in Fig. 2.1.

2.1 Requirements for Implementing Standard Software

The requirements for implementing standard software result from

❑ Adjusting the characteristics of business process oriented organizational structures and function oriented standard software and
❑ General aspects of software implementation, as taken from professional publications.

The structure of requirements illustrated in Fig. 2.2 is based on the classification of organizational structures or standard software, respectively, as depicted above.

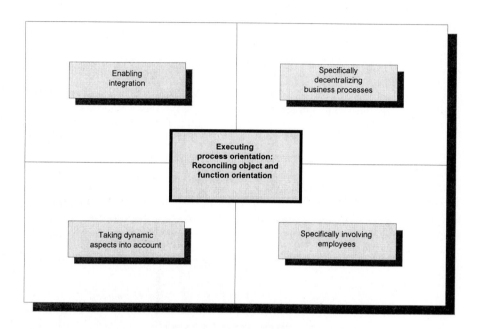

Fig. 2.2: Structure of the requirements for implementing standard software

Basic requirements for creating the necessary factors for business process orientated implementation are compiled in the

❏ "Executing Business Process Orientation"

group. In order to implement business process oriented structures, requirements that specifically utilize characteristics of standard software are classified in the following groups:

❏ "Enabling Integration",
❏ "Specifically Decentralizing Business Processes",
❏ "Taking Dynamic Aspects into Account " and
❏ "Specifically Involving Employees".

In order to avoid redundancies, requirements that could technically appear in several groups are mentioned only once in the dominating group. The requirement groups are interdependent because every requirement is important for engineering business processes. Regarding requirements to execute business process orientation, i.e., reconciling object and function orientation of organizational structures or standard software, respectively, we will explain how these change when standard software becomes more business process oriented (e.g., when using workflow management systems).

2.1.1 Executing Business Process Orientation

The basis of every BIS activity is the **definition of company specific business processes**. This reflection on and structure of the enterprise in its entirety ensures that   individual activities within the software implementation process are coordinated and focus on corporate strategic goals. Therefore, in the implementation process, the processes must be initially defined. Central process structures characterizing the process must also be defined, as well as the organization, functions, data and details. In order to avoid any function orientation necessitated by the standard software, processes must be determined independently of the standard software product. Defining the processes independently of the data processing aspects guarantees implementations that are based on business criteria and that actually execute business processes. Furthermore, this enables implementations that are independent of technological developments over a long period of time (see KAUFMANN 1993, pp. 21-23; SCHÄFER 1990, pp. 50-51; SCHEER 1990b, pp. 15-18). Processes must be determined **taking strategic goals into account**, especially the company's competitive strategy (see SCHÄFER 1990, pp. 29-30; WILDEMANN 1987, pp. 158-165). This enables a strategy driven implementation, i.e., a goal oriented utilization of the necessary means is ensured. When defining business processes, sub-divisions of a company are determined so they can be supported by standard software in individual projects. This makes the process less complex.

When implementing business process oriented software, this software independent process definition is also necessary, e.g., for ensuring the focus of the strategy.

If the business processes are already defined, one must determine in which sequence and to which extent they should be supported by standard software. The extent of propagation of the software in the enterprise, the **"direction of diffusion"** must be determined (see WILDEMANN 1987, pp. 154-156). It is possible for the same modules to be used in several different places, such as when dispatch handling is implemented in a process for standard products and in one for variant products, also. The demand for information technology (hardware and software) should thus be defined accordingly (see HEINRICH, BURGHOLZER 1990, p. 9).

Cross-module implementation is easier with business process oriented software because the individual modules are already predetermined for use in a certain process. However, the basic requirement of defining the "direction of diffusion" for the standard software to be implemented remains the same.

When implementing, the target business processes should be **simultaneously detailed and precisely specified** (see SCHÄFER 1990, p. 51; WATTEROTT 1993, pp. 61-63). A successive definition is necessary of **what** should be done to optimize the business processes (detailing) and **how** this is to be carried out by means of standard software and accompanying measures (i.e., a specification), such as creating new departments. The **business administration concept of standard software** should systematically be taken into account (see BECKER 1994, p. 148). A simultaneous approach is important because a software driven, prematurely precise specification can jeopardize the execution of business process orientation. On the other hand, purely organization driven and business administration oriented detailing leads to a loss in efficiency (see KIRCHMER 1993, pp. 140-141). Customizing standard software is an integral part of the implementation process and should be carried out on the coarsest level of detailing and specification.

For business process oriented software, simultaneous detailing and precise specification is also necessary. However, software-appropriate, precise specifications of target business processes, specifically customizing, are less complex because the individual software modules are, at a minimum, partially focused on the business processes that need to be supported.

The more similar the business administration content of the standard software and the requirements of the enterprise become, the less time-consuming executing specific steps becomes, also (see RIEDER 1988, pp. 66-70). If discrepancies cannot be avoided, **software enhancements** or **modifications** should be defined during the implementation process. This becomes necessary in order to complete the business processes according to strategic goals (see SCHRÖDER 1993, p. 32). Migration, especially modification of standard software, should only be carried out in exceptional cases. It can make installing new software releases more time-consuming because they must also be taken into account (see HÜTTENHEIM 1990, p. 142; PIERCE 1987, p. P5). Thus, business processes should be implemented in accordance with the "standard" that is called for.

As a rule, these requirements should be considered when implementing standard software. With function oriented software, the probability of having to modify is greater than with business process oriented software (see BAUMANN, GERBER 1990, p. 59). Specific business process requirements lead to a corresponding modification of functional modules. However, these modules are also required in other processes. Other requirements can also be essential, which in turn leads to additional modifications.

If business processes pertaining to information and material flow are implemented during BIS, the **material and information flow** must be **reconciled** during the implementation process (see BECKER, ROSEMANN 1993, pp. 33-36). This ensures that processes affected by the implementation of standard software are optimized and that sub-optimal as-is-conditions (caused by the material flow requirements) are not cemented in place.

A holistic approach in implementing, starting with defining the business processes and followed by successive detailing and specific steps, requires appropriate **method support** (see HEINRICH, BURGHOLZER 1990, p. 9; WILDEMANN 1990, p. 23). This reduces the possibility of random results and the risk of errors caused by the high degree of problem complexity. Efficiency and effectiveness are thus improved.

As a rule, this is valid for implementing standard software on a large scale. Due to varying design principles of organizational structures and standard software, implementations become more complex and make method support even more important.

Reconciling Object and Function Orientation

❏ Define business processes independently of a particular software product (software independent), in accordance with the strategic goals

❏ Determine the extent of propagation of the standard software in the enterprise ("direction of diffusion")

❏ Simultaneously detail and specify the business processes, utilizing the business administration concepts of the standard software

❏ Determine and define the necessary software enhancements and modifications

❏ Reconcile materials and information flows

❏ Make problems less complex by using methods appropriately

❏ Determine an implementation strategy in order to coordinate the individual tasks

Fig. 2.3: Requirements for executing business process orientation

---

Defining individual business processes creates a basis for defining implementation sub-projects. However, these must be coordinated. This leads to a synergistic effect, utilizes dependencies between the processes and also prevents overreaching the financial or human resource potential of the enterprise. Moreover, technological requirements, such as the availability of standard software modules or their use in multiple processes, must also be considered (see HEINRICH, BURGHOLZER 1990, pp. 327-328). The resulting coordination requirements must be defined in the **implementation strategy** (see WILDEMANN 1990, p. 21).

Such an implementation strategy is necessary, independently of the design principles of the software. However, due to the technological interdependencies of processes (such as multiple use of identical modules in various processes), coordination requirements are greater for business process oriented implementation of function oriented standard software.

The requirements for executing business process orientation are illustrated in Fig. 2.3.

2.1.2 Enabling Integration

Integration characteristics, primarily regarding the integration of data and functions, are important characteristics of business process oriented organizational structures and of modern standard software. During the integration process, **integration characteristics** of the software should be used, in order to **implement efficient business processes**. This can occur by creating appropriate positions where certain tasks (e.g., R&D), referring to defined objects (e.g., products), can be carried out in a holistic manner (see KLOTZ 1993, pp. 95-112, 137-142). Cross-enterprise integration relationships, as are used by just-in-time concepts, should be considered when implementing standard software (see SCHEER 1992a, p. 145).

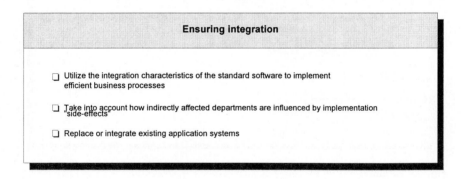

Ensuring integration

❏ Utilize the integration characteristics of the standard software to implement efficient business processes

❏ Take into account how indirectly affected departments are influenced by implementation "side-effects"

❏ Replace or integrate existing application systems

Fig. 2.4: Requirements ensuring integration

Integration relationships exist beyond processes, too. **Business processes** can also be **networked**. For example, the necessary basic data must be entered and maintained as a mandatory requirement for executing the "MRP-Process". Examples of these basic data are: bills of materials, routing and material masters. The maintenance of this data can be carried out in a second process. Coordination tasks can be accomplished in common processes, linked to multiple other processes (see SCHEER 1992a, p. 14). Thus, one should always consider that an implementation in one department can lead to "side-effects" in another department (see WILDEMANN 1987, pp. 156-158).

When standard software is implemented, **application systems** are generally already in place. These must either be **replaced** in the course of implementation, or **linked** or **integrated** with the new standard software (see HEINRICH; BURGHOLZER 1990, p. 320). Thus, the standard software must be coupled with the existing IT landscape. This also comprises migrating existing digital data to the standard software or developing interfaces to the existing systems.

Requirements for ensuring the integration are recapped in Fig. 2.4.

2.1.3 Specifically Decentralizing Work Processes

In order to specifically decentralize enterprise tasks when implementing standard software, defined **business processes** or sub-processes must be **assigned to organizational units.** In this context, the degree of independence, freedom for decision-making and responsibility of the individual units must be defined (see BULLINGER et al. 1993a, pp. 122-123; FRESE 1994, p. 130; SCHEER 1992a, pp. 144-145). Specific steps must be carried out by defining decentralized organizational units, such as physically grouping units that are separated at the present time.

Specifically decentralizing business processes

❏ Allocate business processes to specific organizational units

❏ Ensure coordination of decentralized units

❏ Take company size and industry characteristics into account

❏ Ensure an IT structure that reflects the organizational structure

---

Fig. 2.5 Requirements for specifically decentralizing work processes

Decentralized units, e.g., various manufacturing "islands", usually call for a superior **controlling instance** (see SCHEER 1992a, p.146), to be defined and executed in the course of implementation. The **size of the enterprise** and its respective **industry** should also be **considered** in this context (see RIEDER 1988, p. 61). In large corporations, it is decisive to create decentralized units. In smaller business this is not particularly necessary. A company's industry can influence organizational measures. For example, in a consumer goods company, a decentralized shipping department (in various regions), enabling faster service for retailers, is important. This is hardly the case in a company in the capital equipment industry, where a shipping department is most probably not responsible for a competitive advantage.

When implementing standard software, an appropriate **IT infrastructure** must be set up. When creating decentralized units, decentralized availability of the data processing system must also be ensured (see HEINRICH, BURGHOLZER 1990, p. 236). Thus, appropriate hardware and networking facilities for client/server architectures must be planned and implemented. This should be carried out in close collaboration with the IT infrastructure already existing in the company, in order to enable a solution that is as low cost and cutting-edge as possible.

The requirements for specifically decentralizing business processes are illustrated in Fig. 2.5.

2.1.4 Taking Dynamic Aspects into Account

Implementing standard software can take several months -- even years. Within this time-frame, business processes can be moved from the as-is situation to the target situation by

❑ **Continuously modifying** software support of the current processes (e.g., introducing many interim solutions),
❑ **Implementing step-by-step** (e.g., by introducing some interim steps) or
❑ **Implementing ad hoc** (e.g., by completely executing of target business processes)

(see HEINRICH, BURGHOLZER 1990, pp. 329-330; RAU 1991, pp. 200-201; WILDEMANN 1987, pp. 151-152). Due to dynamic developments in the global marketplace, affecting business processes, and continuous development of standard software, **combining the above mentioned approaches** makes sense. On the one hand, in order to waste as little time as possible, business processes must be quickly migrated ("ad hoc") to the target status. On the other hand, new developments must continuously be considered. It could be necessary to execute defined interim solutions, such as when certain software releases are only available successively or when business capacities (human resources, capital, etc.) require this. The approach taken should reflect the requirements of the particular company (see SIEPE 1991, p. 24).

In between quantum innovation leaps, business processes are continuously improved ("kaizen") or developed further, step-by-step (see IMAI 1993, pp. 47-61). Thus, implementation activities do not cease, once the standard software is up and running. Which phases of standard software implementation reactivate which sub-process, must be constantly monitored.

Work processes can be migrated from the as-is to the target status, i.e., standard software goes live by means of

❑ Parallel migration or
❑ Key date migration.

Parallel migration means that the new work processes are being tested while existing ones are still running, i.e., existing application systems are not switched off when the new standard software is up and running. In **key date migration**, the as-is status is terminated at a pre-determined time (or a certain event) and the target status is installed (see HEINRICH; BURGHOLZER 1990, pp. 328-329). Parallel migration reduces risks (e.g., program or customizing errors can be corrected during parallel tests without affecting day-to-day business). On the other hand, key date migration avoids double work. Depending on how important the business processes to be executed and the existing environmental factors (such as competitive pressures) are, **an optimal choice** should be made; or both methods should be **combined**, respectively.

Engineering business processes in BIS leads to organizational migration of work processes, but also to migration in IT support. This calls for **organizational** and **software related measures**. These can be combined as follows:

❑ Organizational measures before software related measures,
❑ Software related measures before organizational measures.
❑ These measures should be executed simultaneously

(see WILDEMANN 1990, pp. 200-206). For reasons of efficiency, during implementation, the measures **should be carried out simultaneously** (see MATTHEIS 1993, p. 222-223).

The success of implementing standard software can be assessed in two levels, according to the strategic importance of the implementation:

❑   The success of the implementation itself and
❑   The success of the standard software that has been implemented.

The **success of the implementation** refers to target criteria of the implementation process, such as

❑ Duration of the project,
❑ Time-consumption for internal employees,
❑ Time-consumption for external employees,
❑ Whether the employees are content with the new system.

Taking dynamic aspects into account
❏ Ensure an optimal combination of continuous, step-by-step and ad hoc migration from an as-is to a target status
❏ Ensure an optimal combination of parallel migration and key data migration
❏ Parallel implementation of organizational and software related measures
❏ Ensure profitability of the implementation process and of the results of the implementation

Fig. 2.6: Requirements for taking dynamic aspects into account

Profitability of the **implementation process** is a central aspect. **The success of the new standard software** is reflected by whether the strategic goals for the software have been met (see RIEDER 1988, pp. 59-61). **Profitability as a result** of implementation is also a key factor. BIS must ensure both aspects.

Fig. 2.6 illustrates the requirements for taking the dynamic aspects into account.

2.1.5 Specifically Involving Employees in the Implementation Process

Involving employees in the process of implementing standard software can be accomplished by several means. We can distinguish between a

❏ Participative approach and a
❏ "Gate keeping" approach

(see RIEDER 1988, p. 63). In a **participative implementation** approach, the employees in question are included in the whole implementation process and, thus, in the decisions to be made. This does make implementing more strenuous and more time-consuming, but has the distinct advantage of resulting in general acceptance of the implementation results. The **"gate keeping"** approach aims to keep the implementation process short and simple by including as few people as possible in implementation activities. However, this can lessen employee acceptance of the results, losing time that had been gained earlier (see RIEDER 1988, pp. 63-65). Large-scale implementation projects can be carried out more efficiently with the participative approach (see RIEDER 1988, p. 164). BIS should focus on this fact. When implementing standard software in small scale areas (such as when doing a prototype), the implementation process can be

accelerated by the "gate keeping" process (see MATTHEIS 1993, p. 218). Therefore, in BIS, "gate keeping" elements should be **specifically included.**
Executing business processes by means of BIS is only possible when employees are in a position to carry out the new work processes. This predetermines the appropriate qualification of the employees. Qualification can be regarded as the sum of all skills and knowledge necessary to

❑ Address the requirement issues of the work situation at hand,
❑ Actively take part in improving the work situation and to
❑ Integrate one's own work in the corporate environment or business world, respectively.

(see KNETSCH 1987, p. 35).
Regarding BIS, employee qualification regarding the

❑ Business administration effects of software implementation and
❑ Handling of the standard software,

must be ensured. **Business administration qualification** is essential because process orientation (or the integration connected with it) leads to an increase in the total scope of tasks, changing the quality of the work. For example, after implementation, a manufacturing control employee is responsible for controlling a whole manufacturing "island" and its various work processes, and no longer for a group of identical machines in one single work process.

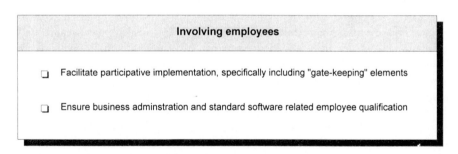

Fig. 2.7: Requirements when specifically involving employees in the implementation process

Routine activities, such as maintaining filing cards, are replaced by administrational-operational or coordinating tasks, e.g., maintaining parameters in material masters (see WILDEMANN 1990, pp. 220-223). **Software related qualification** ensures that changed business administration contents can be implemented by utilizing the software appropriately (see WILDEMANN 1990, pp. 223-229). Qualification requirements brought about by BIS, for example, could in turn require a review of employees' compensation terms (see WILDEMANN 1990, pp. 230-232).

Fig. 2.7 depicts the requirements for specifically involving employees in the implementation process.

2.2 Existing Approaches for Implementing Standard Software

We will now discuss existing approaches for implementing standard software and judge them according to the requirements of the implementation. Approaches for implementing standard software can be found in

❑ Strategic information system planning, in
❑ Tactical and operational information system planning and in
❑ Explicitly standard software oriented approaches of information system planning.

Here, we are also taking planning and executing computer integration manufacturing (CIM) into account because CIM plays a key role in implementing standard software (see HOPP 1990, p. 30; SCHEER 1990a, pp. 141-142).

The requirements of implementing standard software affect the characteristics of strategic, tactical and operational planning (see BROMBACHER 1991, pp. 113-118; WATTEROTT 1993, pp. 13-16). Thus, all three planning levels will be discussed. Tactical and operational planning, however, will not be discussed with regard to the various approaches of information system planning, because both planning levels are generally addressed by the same or similar methods. In addition to general approaches of information system planning that entail the implementation of standard software as an indirect task, we will explicitly discuss approaches addressing standard software implementation.

The approaches for information system planning to be discussed were grouped according to the characteristics of strategic, tactical and operational planning, respectively (see WATTEROTT 1993, pp. 13-16). Of the various approaches for **strategic information planning** (see GÖRGEL 1991; HUBER, GUMSHEIMER 1991; MEYERSIEK, JUNG 1989; NEU 1991; WATTEROTT 1993; WILDEMANN 1990), we will employ the approach of **Wildemann** as an example which studies the development of implementation strategies in the computer integrated manufacturing (CIM) environment. Wildemann's work addresses various aspects of CIM implementation, but focuses on a strategic point of view. Organizational topics, which play a key role in business process oriented implementation, are discussed in detail. As a example for the **tactical and**

operational information system planning approach (see BANOS, MALBOSC 1990; DAENZER 1989; HEINRICH 1994; HEINRICH, BURGHOLZER 1990; KAUFMANN 1993; POCSAY 1991; RIEDER 1988), we will select **Heinrich and Burgholzer's** approach of system planning, because it addresses various issues of standard software implementation. The approach of **SAP AG** for **implementing SAP R/3 software** (see JOST 1993a and 1993b; KELLER, MEINHARDT 1994a and 1994b; SAP 1993) will be examined as an example for **standard software oriented information system planning** (see BOLL 1993; JÄGER et al. 1993, pp. 425-427; RIEDER 1988, pp. 17-20; SAP 1992). SAP's approach refers to SAP R/3 software and thus to a modern and increasingly popular standard software product (see HATTKE 1994, p. 2, 16; APFEL 1994). As a key element, this approach focuses on business processes (see KELLER, MEINHARDT 1994a, pp. 4-5). It can therefore be generally applied for standard software oriented implementation approaches. IT support of this approach (see JOST 1993a, p. 10; KELLER, MEINHARDT 1994a, p. 5) illustrates an additional aspect that is not the case with the two other planning approaches.

Procedure models for implementing software, referring to specialized areas, such as CAD implementation (see KNETSCH 1987; REICHEL 1985; SCHÄFER 1990), will not be studied in detail because they do not correspond to the holistic approach selected for implementation (engineering all business processes). This is also true for approaches addressing individual implementation aspects, such as IS related approaches (see LUDWIG 1992) or issues pertaining to project management (see BARTELS 1993).

2.2.1 Strategic Approach of Information System Planning

Wildemann's phase concept for developing CIM implementation strategies was selected as an example of implementing standard software according to the concept of strategic information system planning (see WILDEMANN 1990). Planning encompasses **five phases** (see WILDEMANN 1990, pp. 237-243):

Phase One analyzes the initial situation. For this reason, it is necessary to first take stock of the CIM modules (software modules) in use. The characteristics of the as-is situation are as follows:

❑ CIM modules (standard software modules)
❑ Organizational structure,
❑ Availability of qualified planners and
❑ Financial potential

(see WILDEMANN 1990, pp. 23-26).

Based on the "effectivity potential" determined, such as the effects of the market, productivity and cost, as well as the investment to be expected, a target concept is designed. This entails the following characteristics:

❑ Time of execution,
❑ Degree of integration of the system,
❑ Execution steps,
❑ The potential degree of investment and
❑ The effects to be expected of the CIM implementation

(see WILDEMANN 1990, pp. 26-79). By comparing as-is and target situations, the **technological gap** to be closed by the implementation can be determined. This should be specified in **Phase Two** of the implementation. Now, the

❑ Module gap and the
❑ Integration gap

must be studied individually.

The **module gap** refers to CIM modules (technology) not present at this time, such as PPS systems or robot driven transportation systems (see WILDEMANN 1990, pp. 88-94). Analyzing the **integration gap** (collaboration of the CIM modules) refers to

− Material flow (from the supplier to the customer),
− Order processing, accompanying the material flow as information flow,
− Indirect functions (such as quality assurance or maintenance) and
− External integration (customer/supplier)

(see WILDEMANN 1990, pp. 95-139).

In addition to studying the technology used,

❑ Organizational gaps (organizational deficiencies, such as sequential work processes instead of parallel work processes),
❑ Qualification gaps and
❑ Argumentation gaps

should be described. In this context, argumentation gaps refer to the economic evaluation of CIM, requiring instruments of strategic investment planning as a preparation for making investment decisions (see WILDEMANN 1990, pp. 237-239).

In **Phase Three** of the implementation process, the technical conceptual framework will be developed. A basic decision must be made for either

❑ Full integration or
❑ Partial integration.

With full integration, all activities for carrying out specific business processes are linked by data processing methods. With partial integration, "integration islands" are created on purpose. The former ensures a better overview. However it is frequently the latter that provides the full benefits (see WILDEMANN 1990, pp. 140-146).

Next, we must determine whether the CIM system to be implemented should be decided upon by

❑ Evolutionary progress of the existing IS applications or by
❑ Creating a new infrastructure.

(see WILDEMANN 1990, pp. 146-150).
Next, the direction of integration must be determined. It can either be

❑ Horizontal (within a function area) or
❑ Vertical (within a product group).

For holistic execution of business processes, the vertical procedure is usually necessary (see WILDEMANN 1990, pp. 150-154).

Next, the essential integration steps must be determined in a step-by-step conceptual design. To this end, the following aspects should be examined:

❑ Simplify processes by segmenting them,
❑ Draft specific manufacturing strategies,
❑ Introduce flexible automation in certain areas,
❑ Implement paperless manufacturing and procurement,
❑ Integrate individual elements into one total conceptual design and
❑ Assess the CIM conceptual design holistically

(see WILDEMANN 1990, pp. 154-158).

In **Phase Four** of the implementation process, the time of implementation is determined. The following variations are possible:

❑ Early introduction – the underlying technology is not yet feasible,
❑ Early introduction – the technology is feasible,
❑ Late introduction – the technology is not feasible,
❑ Late introduction – the technology is feasible.

A comprehensive chance-risk assessment determined that early introduction of a particular type of CIM technology generally ensures the greatest efficiency (see WILDEMANN 1990, pp. 159-181).

Next, the speed of integration should be determined. We can distinguish between

❏ Continuous modification of the existing system in many steps,
❏ Step-by-step implementation according to a pre-determined plan or
❏ Ad hoc implementation in one single investment.

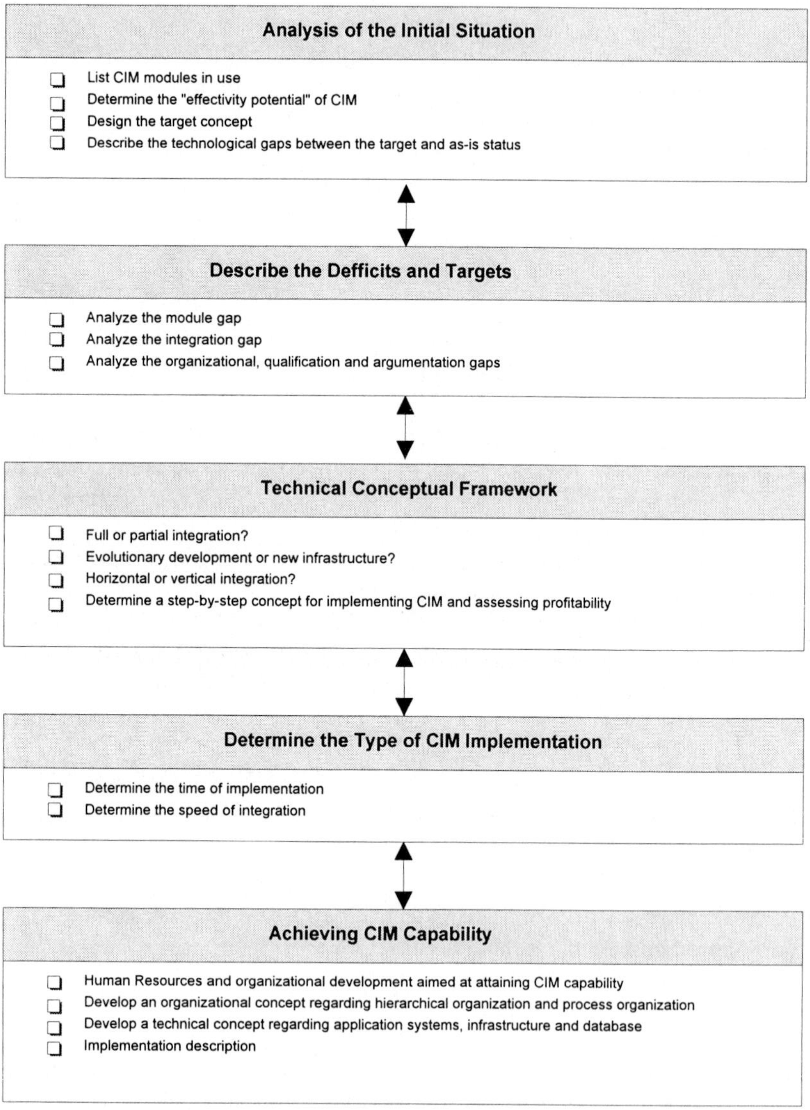

Analysis of the Initial Situation

❏   List CIM modules in use
❏   Determine the "effectivity potential" of CIM
❏   Design the target concept
❏   Describe the technological gaps between the target and as-is status

Describe the Defficits and Targets

❏   Analyze the module gap
❏   Analyze the integration gap
❏   Analyze the organizational, qualification and argumentation gaps

Technical Conceptual Framework

❏   Full or partial integration?
❏   Evolutionary development or new infrastructure?
❏   Horizontal or vertical integration?
❏   Determine a step-by-step concept for implementing CIM and assessing profitability

Determine the Type of CIM Implementation

❏   Determine the time of implementation
❏   Determine the speed of integration

Achieving CIM Capability

❏   Human Resources and organizational development aimed at attaining CIM capability
❏   Develop an organizational concept regarding hierarchical organization and process organization
❏   Develop a technical concept regarding application systems, infrastructure and database
❏   Implementation description

Fig. 2.8: Phase concept according to Wildemann for planning CIM implementation strategies

Quick integration generally leads to implementation of IT systems of the same generation, reducing the expense of integration. In slower procedures, the flexibility of the organization or of the employees, respectively, is less challenged (see WILDEMANN 1990, pp. 182-197).

In order to avoid any resistance from employees or in any organizational form, the implementation process calls for

❑ Training of the personnel and for
❑ Organizational development.

(see WILDEMANN 1990, p. 198-232). This ensures the CIM capability of the enterprise. Technological and organizational development must be simultaneous and well coordinated, if the desired goal is to be reached. The employees in question should be trained as soon as possible because they will be responsible for entire business processes rather than just for individual functions. This also increases the scope of their tasks (WIDEMANN 1990, pp. 198-232).

The phase concept for planning CIM implementation strategies according to Wildemann is depicted in Fig. 2.8.

2.2.2 Tactical / Operational Approach for Information System Planning

As an example for implementing standard software in tactical and operational information system planning, we will study Heinrich and Burgholzer's approach for system planning (see HEINRICH 1994; HEINRICH, BURGHOLZER 1990). Here, a **five phase concept** is also used. Furthermore, **cross-phase activities**, such as testing and documentation, also occur (see HEINRICH 1994, pp. 39-46). For every phase, we will first describe the **procedure**, then the **methods** and **tools** to be used.

In **Phase One**, the preliminary study, we

❑ Determine the business goals,
❑ Define the conceptual goals,
❑ Design the primary conceptual design and, thus,
❑ Elaborate the project plan.

Considering overlying planning goals, we will first deduct the business goals. These determine functions, services and interfaces with the information and communication system to be implemented. The conceptual goals determine the quality characteristics of the planning process and planning result. Considering the business and conceptual goals, alternative system concepts are designed. The optimal concept is selected as a primary conceptual design. The project plan determines the requirements of a project for implementing the primary conceptual design and defines the necessary technical, personnel, financial and time related resources (see HEINRICH 1994, pp. 239-328).

Phase Two comprises the **detailed study**: Here, we

❑ Study the as-is status,
❑ Analyze the as-is status,
❑ Optimize the as-is status and
❑ Adjust the primary conceptual design.

The as-is concept of the information and communication system is studied in the area delineated by the primary conceptual design. This is carried out as detailed as is necessary for system development. The results of this study are then analyzed to determine the strengths and weaknesses of the as-is status. During the optimization process of the as-is status, measures are determined and taken. This leads to a rapid improvement of issues that can be corrected on a short-term basis. Subsequently, the primary conceptual design is adjusted, based on the study of the as-is status. Special emphasis is placed on strengths and weaknesses that have been determined (see HEINRICH 1994, pp. 329-394).

Phase Three refers to the **rough project draft.** Here, we need to carry out the following tasks:

❑ Classify the entire system into sub-projects,
❑ Create a system design within the sub-projects,
❑ Determine the technical requirements,
❑ Select the appropriate systems.

Initially, the entire system described in the primary conceptual design is grouped into sub-projects, enabling a continuously methodical procedure. Using appropriate design methods and adhering to known design principles, the information and communication systems, respectively, are designed. The sub-systems are then regrouped into an entire system and refitted to the information infrastructure. This lays the foundation for determining the quantitative and qualitative hardware and software requirements. During the process of selecting the system, the system classification and system design results for determining which system technology is to be used, are documented in functional specifications. The next steps are a tender, assessing the various offers and evaluating alternatives. Then the winning hardware and software suppliers are selected and the contracts are signed (see HEINRICH, BURGHOLZER 1990, pp. 7-175).

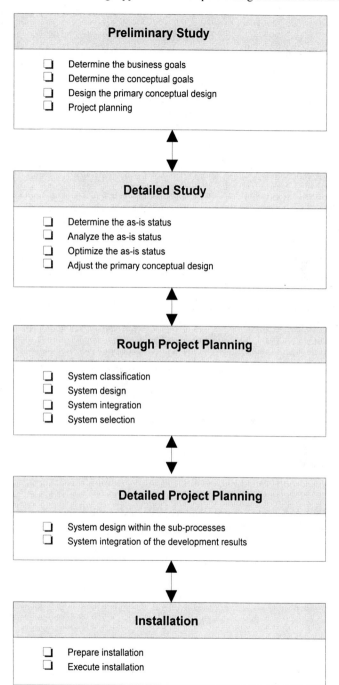

Fig. 2.9: Phase concept according to Heinrich/Burgholzer

Phase Four deals with the **detailed project stage**. It addresses the issues of

❑ System design and
❑ System integration.

During the system design phase, the information and communication systems are designed in the sub-projects that are already defined. To this end, appropriate design methods and tools are used. In addition to the design of individual software, this also comprises the procurement of standard software (see HEINRICH, BURGHOLZER 1990, p. 194). During system integration, the results of the sub-project design are combined in application systems. If necessary, multiple application systems are integrated to form complete information and communication systems. It can also become necessary to integrate existing systems. In the detailed project stage, logical models resulting from the rough draft are transformed into physical models (see HEINRICH, BURGHOLZER 1990, pp. 179-316).

Phase Five comprises the **installation**. We can distinguish between

❑ Preparing for the installation and
❑ Executing the installation.

As a rule, the installation can only begin, once the detailed project stage for the application system in question has been concluded and the necessary preparatory measures have been carried out (see HEINRICH, BURGHOLZER 1990, pp. 321-322).

In installation process, we can distinguish between

❑ Complete migration and step-by-step migration,
❑ Key date migration and parallel migration, as well as between
❑ Immediate migration and migration within a certain time frame

The pros and cons of each alternative are an aid in selecting the proper procedure (see HEINRICH, BURGHOLZER 1990, pp. 326-330).

Preparing for the installation refers to

❑ Human resources,
❑ Organizational,
❑ Spatial,
❑ Equipment,
❑ Programming and
❑ Data

technical aspects (see HEINRICH, BURGHOLZER 1990, pp. 332-337).

Executing the installation comprises

❑ Carrying out appropriate tests, the
❑ Beginning of processing,
❑ Evaluating and adjusting features and functions of the application system,
❑ Turning the system over to the users, and addressing final issues

(see HEINRICH, BURGHOLZER 1990, pp. 339-343).
Fig. 2.9 illustrates the phase concept according to Heinrich/Burgholzer.

2.2.3 Standard Software Oriented Approach towards Information System Planning

We will regard SAP AG's procedure of implementing its SAP R/3 software as a standard software oriented approach towards information system planning (see JOST 1993a and 1993b; KELLER, MEINHARDT 1994a and 1994b; SAP 1993). The procedure comprises **four phases of developing a requirements definition** (see KELLER, MEINHARDT 1994b, pp. 85-87). They are complemented by the **customizing**, i.e., **Phase Five** (see KELLER, MEINHARDT 1994a, p. 36; SAP 1993, p. 1). In addition to method support, **data processing tool support** is available, e.g. by the ARIS Toolset. It contains the SAP R/3 reference models describing the business administration content of the standard software in form of information models (see IDS 1994a; JOST 1993a, pp. 11-19; KELLER, MEINHARDT 1994a, pp. 6-22, 38).

Phase One begins with a study of the **corporate situation**. This rough as-is analysis begins with the definition of the goals, in which

❑ Target of the project, the
❑ According function areas and
❑ Responsible organizational units

are allocated.
Then,

❑ Process execution,
❑ Information flow relationships / data clusters, the
❑ Scope of functionality and
❑ Organizational structures

are documented.

The documentation of business processes in the existing process organization is executed by referring to the R/3 reference model. This facilitates target and as-is reconciling at a later date. By studying information flow relationships, information object exchanges between function areas become apparent. The information objects are described by data clusters. When assessing the scope of functionality, the functions executed in the enterprise's as-is situation are entered in a static structure (function trees). The last step is displaying the organizational structure (see JOST 1993a, pp. 11-16; JOST 1993b, pp. 33-59; KELLER, MEINHARDT 1994a, pp. 22-25; KELLER, MEINHARDT 1994b, pp. 86). If no significant results are to be expected from studying the current corporate situation, one can also start with Phase Two, i.e., by creating the requirements model directly (see KELLER, MEINHARDT 1994b, pp. 87, 88).

Phase Two comprises developing the **requirements model**. Here, we discuss the

❑ Process view (event - function - series), the
❑ Function view (function trees, among other things), the
❑ Information flow view (information flowing into and emanating from a function), the
❑ Data cluster view (aggregated data elements) and the
❑ Organization view (organization charts).

Relevant excerpts of R/3 function models, illustrating business administration functionality of the software in these various views, are selected and modified according to specific company requirements. Information models that do not yet exist, but are still necessary, are supplemented by stock taking. The main focus in creating requirements models is on the process view. It combines the function, data cluster and organization views and describes the process logic by means of event-function-series (see JOST 1993a, pp. 16-19, JOST 1994b, pp. 59-163; KELLER, MEINHARDT 1994a, p. 26-35; KELLER, MEINHARDT 1994b, p. 87).

In **Phase Three**, we determine the **course of action**. In reconciling target and actual data, appropriate

❑ Process validation,
❑ Function validation,
❑ Information flow validation,
❑ Data cluster validation and, finally,
❑ Organization validation

are carried out. In this context, deficiencies regarding existing IT support and any integration gaps are pointed out.
Any organizational inadequacies and missing functions are determined.

With regards to business process reengineering resulting from the implementation of R/3, the following changes become necessary: changes in the

- ❑ Existing organizational structure,
- ❑ Organizational responsibilities for executing the process,
- ❑ Existing process steps, their run times and process costs and the
- ❑ Information flow relationships between function areas.

We must now determine whether the R/3 functionality is sufficient, or whether additional, individual programs might be necessary (see JOST 1993a, pp. 13-16; JOST 1993b, pp. 163-175; KELLER, MEINHARDT 1994a, pp. 35-36; KELLER, MEINHARDT 1994b, p. 87).

In **Phase Four**, the **implementation sequence** is determined. By means of

- ❑ Modularization and
- ❑ Prioritizing

of the current conceptual design, the implementation sequence of R/3 application modules is determined (see JOST 1993b, pp. 175-200; KELLER, MEINHARDT 1994b, pp. 87).

Customizing is carried out in **Phase Five**. The results from modifying the R/3 reference models in Phase Two are used (see KELLER, MEINHARDT 1994a, p. 36; KELLER, MEINHARDT 1994b, pp. 87, 88). The customizing procedure model encompasses the following steps:

- ❑ Organization and conceptual design,
- ❑ Detailing and execution,
- ❑ Preparing for going live
- ❑ Going live

(see SAP 1993, p. iii, iv).

During organization and conceptual design,

- ❑ Requirements are analyzed,
- ❑ Project assignments are detailed,
- ❑ Project standards are laid down, a
- ❑ Time table is scheduled, the
- ❑ System is installed,
- ❑ Training classes are planned and held,
- ❑ Users and system administrators become skilled in SAP functionality,
- ❑ Functions, processes and responsibilities are determined,
- ❑ Interfaces are designed and a
- ❑ System infrastructure is planned

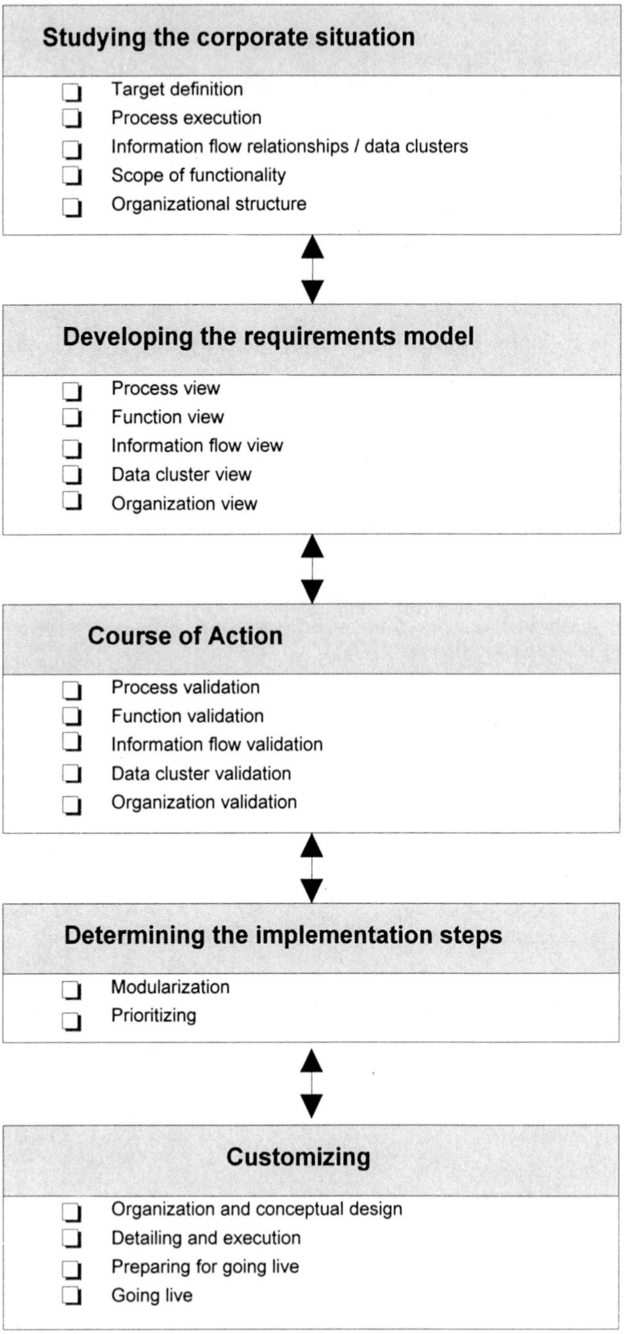

Studying the corporate situation

- ❏ Target definition
- ❏ Process execution
- ❏ Information flow relationships / data clusters
- ❏ Scope of functionality
- ❏ Organizational structure

Developing the requirements model

- ❏ Process view
- ❏ Function view
- ❏ Information flow view
- ❏ Data cluster view
- ❏ Organization view

Course of Action

- ❏ Process validation
- ❏ Function validation
- ❏ Information flow validation
- ❏ Data cluster validation
- ❏ Organization validation

Determining the implementation steps

- ❏ Modularization
- ❏ Prioritizing

Customizing

- ❏ Organization and conceptual design
- ❏ Detailing and execution
- ❏ Preparing for going live
- ❏ Going live

Fig. 2.10: Phase concept of SAP AG for implementing SAP R/3 software

(see SAP 1993, pp. 2-10).

After assuring the quality of this concept, the following steps are carried out during the detailing and execution phases:

❏ Organizational structures are modeled,
❏ Primary data are determined,
❏ Processes and periodical processes are modeled,
❏ Interfaces are created,
❏ Forms, reports and appropriate authorization are determined

(see SAP 1993, pp. 11-18).
Next, the quality of the resulting prototype of the configured standard software is checked and the following activities regarding preparing for going live are carried out:

❏ A date for going live is planned,
❏ User documentation is completed, the
❏ Production environment is set up,
❏ Technical system administration is organized,
❏ Reorganization and archiving are determined,
❏ Users are trained, an
❏ Integration test is carried out, the
❏ System load is analyzed,
❏ Data are transferred to the production system and
❏ Data are maintained and entered manually

(see SAP 1993, pp. 19-26).
After a quality check of the production system, it can go live. Subsequently,

❏ technical and
❏ organizational fine-tuning

of the SAP R/3 standard software is necessary (see SAP 1993, pp. 27).
Fig. 2.10 depicts SAP AG's phase concept for implementing SAP R/3 software.

New structures and extensions of SAP's approach, such as the AcceleratedSAP (ASAP) approach (see e.g. SAP 1997), are not presented now because they will not influence the following conclusions.

2.2.4 Evaluating the Various Approaches

The approaches described by Wildemann, Heinrich/Burgholzer and SAP AG are evaluated according to the requirements for implementing standard software. Thus, the evaluation is structured according to these requirements:

We will first examine how the procedures described meet the requirements as pertaining to **reconciling** of **object** and **function orientation**. During the design of the target concept in Phase One of the procedure model, Wildemann **defines business processes independently of software products** and according to corporate strategic goals. This is complemented by describing any inadequacies and formulating the goal. The initially technical procedure is enhanced by organizational issues in Phase Five. Heinrich and Burgholzer design a neutral primary conceptual design in Phase One of their procedure. However, the strategic goals of the enterprise, especially its competitive strategy, are not explicitly included. In the SAP approach, a neutral description of the business processes is basically omitted. From the very beginning, the conceptual design is based on SAP R/3 specific reference models, i.e., the business administration content of the standard software. Regarding the technical conceptual design, Wildemann explicitly discusses the "direction of diffusion" of the software technologies to be used. The other approaches review this only indirectly, by creating sub-systems. Wildemann does not **simultaneously detail** and **specify** the conceptual design. He focuses on the strategic approach. Heinrich and Burgholzer offer various approaches during their detailed project stages and during the installation phase. These approaches, however, are basically not focused on the implementation of standard software. They clearly focus on the conceptual and technical aspects of individual software development. SAP's approach ensures simultaneous detailing and specification by means of R/3 reference models. However, a neutral initial solution, one that also has to be specified, is lacking. In the SAP procedure, **software enhancements** and modifications are specifically deducted and defined by determining the course of action. Only Wildemann adjusts **material and information flows** while describing the deficits of the as-is situation in the technical conceptual framework. Heinrich and Burgholzer, as well as SAP, extensively address the issue of **less problem complexity** by the systematic usage of conceptual methods. Wildemann discusses this topic in a general manner by explaining the necessity of a method. For Wildemann, developing an **implementation strategy** plays a key role in creating the technical conceptual framework and determining the type of CIM implementation. The same is true for Heinrich and Burgholzer, who discuss this topic in project planning in their preliminary study. In the SAP approach, the definition of an implementation strategy is just briefly touched upon.

An assessment of the various procedures regarding the requirements for ensuring **integration** leads to the following results. For Wildemann and SAP, the use of **integration characteristics** of the **standard software** to be used plays a key role. This aspect is less important for Heinrich and Burgholzer. This standard software - specific issue is neglected in favor of reviewing appropriate activities in individual software development. Wildemann examines the effect of integration on **indirectly affected departments** in the description of deficits and in the technical conceptual framework. The other approaches do not explicitly discuss this issue. All three planning approaches discuss the replacement and **integration of existing software**.

The requirements for specifically **decentralizing work processes** are met as follows by the procedures we have studied: Wildemann and SAP explicitly **allocate** business processes to **organizational units**. For Heinrich and Burgholzer, this organizational issue is less important. Thus, these authors do not explicitly discuss ensuring the **coordination of decentralized units**.

The planning approaches of Wildemann and SAP do ensure this coordination. Wildemann discusses these coordination requirements in detail in the technical conceptual framework and also when he describes activities necessary to attain CIM capability. The approaches of Wildemann and SAP include the **size of the enterprise** and the respective **industry** in information system planning. For Heinrich and Burgholzer, ensuring an appropriate **IT infrastructure** in an installation plays a key role. Wildemann does not discuss this issue at all, while SAP only touches upon it (in the customizing phase of the SAP procedure).

Regarding the requirements for taking **dynamic aspects** into account, we assess the planning approaches as follows. Wildemann, as well as Heinrich and Burgholzer, discuss combining **continuous, step-by-step** and **ad hoc migration.** However, Wildemann does this in much greater detail. Only Heinrich and Burgholzer examine the issues revolving around **key date migration** and **parallel migration**. All three approaches ensure **parallel migration** of **organizational** and **technical (IS) measures**. All planning approaches also take into account that **profitability** of the implementation and that the results of the implementation must be ensured. SAP stresses this aspect by means of its R/3 reference models and the ARIS Toolset, both of which enable a profitable implementation and a high standard of implementation results. Wildemann focuses on profitability issues with regard to the results of implementing CIM. To this end, he uses methods of strategic investment planning. Heinrich and Burgholzer only touch upon profitability aspects.

In this last step, we will examine how the requirements regarding the **inclusion of employees** are met. None of the approaches studied examines the possible combination of **participative** and **gate keeping** approaches. All three procedures take the necessary **business administration** and **software related qualification** of future standard software users into account. Wildemann and SAP's planning approach point out the major importance of this qualification aspect.

Requirements / Implementation Approach	By Wildemann	By Heinrich/ Burgholzer	By SAP
Reconciling object orientation / function orientation			
Neutral Definition of business processes / strategic goals	●	○	-
Determination of "directions of diffusion"	●	○	○
Simultaneous detailing and specifying	-	○	○
Deriving / defining software enhancements / modifications	-	-	●
Adjusting material flow / information flow	●	-	-
Reducing problem capacity by using methodology	○	●	●
Implementation strategy	●	●	○
Ensuring the implementation			
Utilizing the software's integration characteristics	●	○	●
Taking impact on indirect areas into account	●	-	-
Replacing / integrating existing software	●	●	●
Specifically decentralizing business processes			
Allocating business processes and functions to business units	●	-	●
Ensuring coordination of decentralized units	●	-	○
Taking size and industry of company into account	●	-	●
Ensuring appropriate IS infrastructure	-	●	○
Dynamic aspects			
Optimal combination of continuous, step-by-step or ad hoc migration	●	○	-
Optimal combination between key date migration / parallel migration	-	●	●
Parallel migration organization / software measures	●	●	-
Profitability	○	○	●
Invoiving employees			
Combination of participative and gate keeeping implementation	-	-	-
Business administration and software qualification	●	○	●
Legend			
fully complies ● partially complies ○ does not comply -			

Fig. 2.11: Evaluating approaches for implementing standard software

Fig. 2.11 comprises the evaluation of these approaches for implementing standard software.

Wildemann's strategic approach focuses on the question of **what** should be done. Various migration aspects, such as simultaneous detailing and specification, are less important in this approach. Wildemann ensures the strategic importance of the implementation. On the other hand, Heinrich and Burgholzer's and SAP's approaches stress operational implementation, i.e., they do not discuss **what**, but rather **how** things should be done. Heinrich and Burgholzer show how to integrate implementation with holistic system planning. He generally addresses issues concerning individual software development in more detail than standard software issues. On the other hand, SAP's procedure aims more at the implementation of standard software. Company specific, software independent aspects are barely addressed, however.

Considering strategic considerations (according to Wildemann's procedure), BIS should now offer a holistic approach of information system planning (according to Heinrich and Burgholzer's procedure) and also stress aspects reflecting standard software (according to SAP).

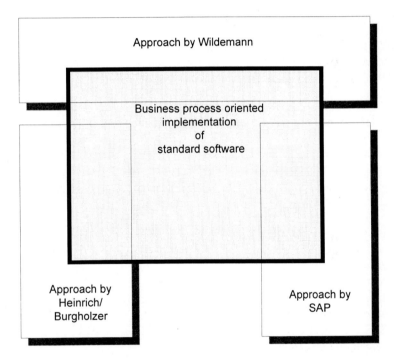

Fig. 2.12: Positioning of business process oriented implementation

In the three planning approaches studied, any missing or only partially discussed aspects, such as simultaneous detailing and specification during implementation, should be added to BIS. BIS thus closes the gap between the procedure for information system planning and tactical / operational installation of standard software. This positioning is depicted in Fig. 2.12.

2.3 Developing a Procedure Model for Business Process Oriented Implementation

The BIS procedure model is based on Scheer's Architecture of Integrated Information Systems (ARIS; see SCHEER 1990b). An information system architecture is supposed to describe an information system's elements and the procedure for its implementation in a general manner (see ÖSTERLE et al. 1991, pp. 26, 69; SCHEER 1990b, pp. 1-3). Such an architecture can be used as a framework for the implementation of information systems by using standard software. In this context, ARIS is especially well suited because it stresses the importance of the organization as an independent information system view and explicitly examines the correlation of various information system views (organization, data, functions) – parameters that actually determine the business process (see SCHEER 1990b, pp. 13-15).

We will subsequently illustrate the ARIS Architecture as a framework for procedures. Based on the positioning of the standard software implementation in the architecture, we will deduct a procedure model for BIS

2.3.1 Using the ARIS Architecture as a Framework for Procedures

Scheer's Architecture of Integrated Information Systems (ARIS) is based on the analysis of process chains, such as the entire order processing process – from order acceptance to fulfillment. The elements of the process chain model are structured as follows:

❑ Functions (time-consuming activities, such as order acceptance),
❑ Events (initial and final events define the start and end of a process / function, such as the arrival of a customer order or feedback from a manufacturing order),
❑ Environmental condition of the task (the function) to be executed (information needed to control a process, e.g., warehouse stock, reflected in data values),
❑ Users and organizational units (e.g., departments), as well as
❑ IT operating resources.

These are structured and classified in the following views: the

❑ **Data view** (events and environmental conditions), the
❑ **Function view** (processes or functions), the
❑ **Organization view** (users and organization units) and the
❑ **Resource view** (IT operating resources).

The relationships between the various views are positioned in the

❑ Control view

(see SCHEER 1990b, pp. 13-15).
The resource view is especially diversified (CPUs, networks, programs), yet from a business point of view, it also lays down relatively unimportant secondary conditions for the other information system views. Therefore, this information system view is not discussed explicitly, but rather reviewed along with the other views that are described according to their IT context. This results in a phase model for the data, organization, function and control view:

❑ In the **Requirements Definition (business concept)**, the information system to be implemented is described and structured in such a way that it can be used as a starting point for a specific implementation. The business content to be described takes up the bulk of this phase.
❑ In the **Design Specification**, the requirements definition (business concept) is transformed into IT terminology.
❑ Based on the design specification, the next step is technical **Implementation Description**, i.e., adapting the concept to specific hardware and software components.

Recent extension of the ARIS Architecture (see SCHEER 1998a and SCHEER 1998b) are not discussed here because they are not significant for the following explanations.

Elaborating an **initial business solution** is mandatory before carrying out these three planning phases. To this end, every information system view is examined in context so the overall benefit of the information system becomes apparent. These studies review the initial business situation, respectively (as-is analysis)
Operations and maintenance follow the implementation phase. However, the phase will not be examined further (see SCHEER 1990b, pp. 15-19).
The architecture of ARIS is illustrated in Fig. 2.13.

2.3.2 Positioning the Implementation of Standard Software within the ARIS Architecture

We must first examine which information system views need to be considered when implementing standard software:
Standard software provides a

❑ Function repository (function view) and
❑ Structures of master and transitory data (data view). It applies
❑ Organizational controls (organization view) and determines the
❑ Collaboration of functions, data and the organization (control view).

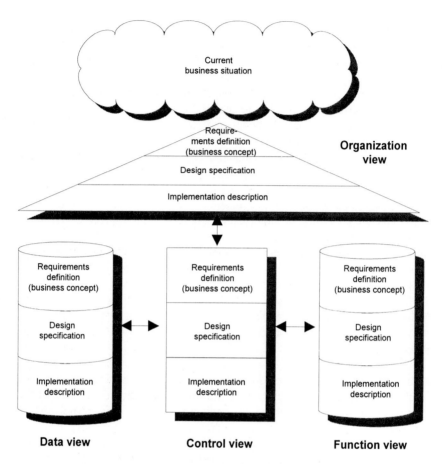

Fig. 2.13: ARIS Architecture according to Scheer (see SCHEER 1990b, pp. 13-19)

By the use of standard software, functions can be carried out based on the appropriate data. Organizational controls are applied by "standard software organizational units" (see KELLER, MEINHARDT 1994a, p. 18), to which certain tasks (such as the execution of functions) are linked. Collaboration of the various information system views becomes apparent by the fact that standard software functions process certain data structures. They are also carried out by defined standard software organizational units according to certain process logic directed by the software.

Thus, standard software controls every information system view. During software implementation, this applies to every information system view. In order to engineer business processes, and according to standard software requirements, the implementation of standard software determines

❑ **Who may execute**
❑ **Which functions**
❑ **With which data and according to**
❑ **Which processing logic.**

Thus, business processes must be described completely. This can only be ensured by examining every information system view.

When implementing standard software, **every information system view** must be considered. The **control view** is the **focal point** because it basically ensures the focused collaboration of every information system view with the goal of executing optimized business processes.

Fig. 2.14 illustrates the positioning of standard software implementation in the information system views of the ARIS Architecture.

In order to plan and implement a business process, the company elaborates a requirements definition (business concept). In the IT concept, this draft will include exact IT product specifications. During implementation, the IT concept is implemented with specific IT resources. However, the user company is not the only entity to undergo these three phases. It is also the way software manufacturers draw up conceptual designs and implement standard software. The entire development of standard software is based on business concepts that are described in the requirements definition (business concept) of the standard software and then executed in the IT concept and implementation. The requirements definition (business concept) of standard software determines the variations of supporting business processes by means of the software (see BECKER 1994, pp. 153-155).

All **three phases** of the ARIS Architecture, i.e., requirements definition (business concept), IS concept and implementation, are relevant for implementing standard software because information systems are designed and implemented by means of standard software. However, in the standard software implementation, it is possible to emphasize activities in the **requirements definition (business concept) level**. This is due to the fact that, in the IS concept and implementation levels, it is possible to draw upon development results of the software manufacturer. The requirements definition (business concept) of standard software is decisive because it impacts the engineering of future business processes of the user company (see KELLER, MEINHARDT 1994a, pp. 4-5; KENGELBACHER 1990, pp. 143-144; ÖSTERLE 1990, pp. 22). The business options provided by the software should be optimally utilized in accordance with the strategic goals of the enterprise. If the standard software is to be customized or enhanced, interfaces developed, etc., then the IS concept and implementation phases must be carried out during the standard software implementation in the user-company.

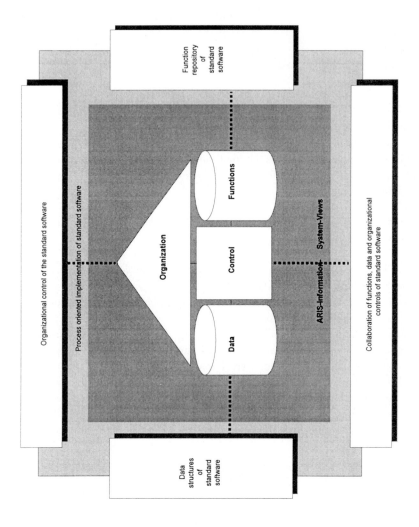

Fig. 2.14:Positioning the implementation of standard software in ARIS information system views

Fig. 2.15 demonstrates the positioning of standard software implementation in the ARIS Phase Concept.

The phase of elaborating the initial business solution, specifically the analysis of the initial situation (as-is analysis), will not be examined. We are assuming that the general benefit information systems, that should actually be shown in this phase, is obvious because it actually triggers the implementation of standard software. Multiple procedure models carrying out as-is analyses are available today (see BALANTZIAN 1992, pp. 71-88; BANOS, MALBOSC 1990, pp. 18-39; JOST 1993b, pp. 27-175; NEU 1991, pp. 47-111; SCHÄFER 1990, pp. 134-151; SCHEER 1990b, pp. 55-61; WATTEROTT 1993, pp. 71-128).

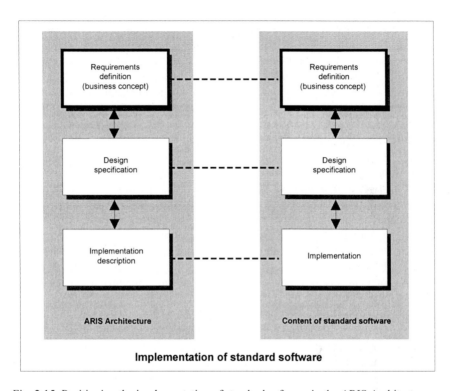

Fig. 2.15: Positioning the implementation of standard software in the ARIS Architecture

2.3.3 Deducting the Procedure Model

The positioning of the standard software implementation in the ARIS Architecture will now be utilized to deduct the BIS procedure model (see KIRCHMER 1993, pp. 137-142).

With regard to the requirements definition phase (business concept) of implementing standard software, two central issues should be addressed. In order to ensure the execution of a company's strategic goals, the industry and company specific situation of the user company should be considered, independent of the standard software. Secondly, the requirements definition (business concept) of the standard software, as described above, should be included in the implementation activities. This is necessary to ensure optimal utilization of the software. This is why the **requirements definition (business concept) phase** of the ARIS Architecture is divided into **two parts**.

The first phase ensures that **industry- and company specific** requirements are considered when the business processes are engineered. To this end, the appropriate business processes must be defined by means of information models, and specifics must be determined. This occurs independently of the standard software to be used, in a **strategy based BPO concept**. Utilization of standard software at a later time is only considered, inasmuch as the information models to be created attain as many degrees of freedom as possible for standard software detailing. Therefore, the models of a strategy based BPO concept should be kept as rough as possible.

The strategy based BPO concept is detailed according to the **requirements definition (business concept) of the standard software**. This means that business requirements of the strategy based BPO concept are detailed according to the business content of the standard software, resulting in the **standard software based BPO concept**. The detail models resulting here are so specific that they can be implemented according to the standard software to be implemented. They should be based on the requirements definition (business concept) level of the ARIS Architecture because neither IS conceptual nor implementation issues are applicable.

The requirements definition (business concept) of the software manufacturer is the **reference model** of the software. Reference models are characterized by information content well beyond an individual issue, qualified, structured and thus easily adaptable to company specific situations (see JOST 1993b, p. 12; SCHEER 1994a, SCHÜLE 1994, p. 19). According to the respective content, we can distinguish between

❑ Industry specific reference models and
❑ Standard software reference models.

Industry specific reference models can be used to support the elaboration of the strategy based BPO concepts.

In the data processing and implementation levels, measures for implementing business processes by means of standard software are deducted from the strategy and standard software based BPO concept. This BIS phase is called **BPO implementation**. Typical activities are conceptual design and implementation of interfaces for data transfer or for linking third-party software to the software that is to be implemented. Other examples are implementing individual auxiliary programs or carrying out customizing activities. Due to their reduced volume during standard software implementation, IS conceptual activities and implementing are grouped together into one BIS phase.

The strategy based and software based BPO concept and BPO implementation phases apply to every ARIS information system view, as shown above. The main focus of BIS is on the control view (see above). Thus, the control view should be explicitly addressed in every BIS phase. Organization, data and function views should be addressed individually, if this reduction of complexity leads to optimized results of the implementation or to an optimized implementation process.

The BIS procedure model and the positioning of BIS between the standard software user and manufacturer is depicted in Fig. 2.16

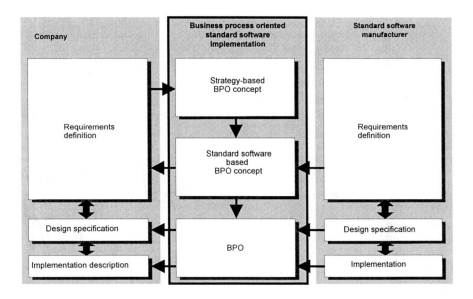

Fig. 2.16: Procedure model of business process oriented implementation

In the following chapters, we will describe in detail the individual phases of business process oriented implementation. Every procedure step will be grouped into a process model.

| Function | Event/ result | "AND/OR" links" | EXCLUSIVE / OR links | relationship |

Fig. 2.17: Symbols displaying event-driven process chains (EPCs)

By Chapter Five, the entire BIS will be modeled as a process. BIS will be displayed in event-driven process chains (EPC), in which functions are triggered by one or multiple events, i.e., actual states of information objects. One or multiple events are the result of the execution of a function (see KELLER et al. 1992, pp. 10-14; SCHEER 1994a, pp. 49-53).

Thus, processes can be represented as functions in a chronological sequence, i.e., according to their dynamic behavior (see KELLER, MEINHARDT 1994a, p. 5). The symbols displaying EPCs are illustrated in Fig. 2.17. The individual sub-process models are linked by using the same events in different sub-processes.

The explanation of procedure and IT tool support is based on the functionality of the ARIS Toolset. This, in turn, is based on the ARIS Architecture, from which the BIS procedure model was deducted. Therefore, we can expect IT support that is best linked to BIS requirements.

3 Strategy Based BPO Concept

In defining strategy based BPO concepts, we must ensure that **company** and **vertical market specific** requirements – such as are necessary to implement **strategic goals** -- are taken into account when engineering business processes. The resulting guidelines for later phases of BIS ensure that additional BIS tasks focus on the strategic goals of the enterprise and that these are implemented successively.

In general, the strategy based BPO concept is **independent of any particular standard software product**. Thus, there is a low **degree of detailing**. The **degree of detailing** should be sufficiently general as to permit standard software product specific details at a later point in time. This reduces the need to reconcile between the requirements definition (business concept) of the software application and the strategy based BPO concept. Strategy based BPO concepts are only detailed if this required for implementing strategic goals.

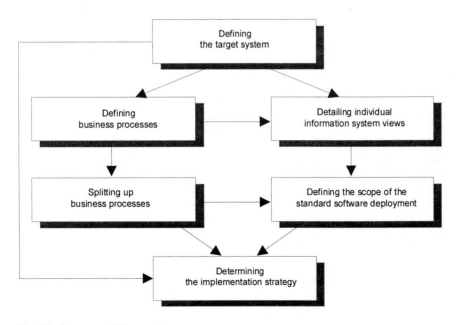

Fig. 3.1: Structure of Chapter 3

The strategy based BPO concept is comparable to the basic conceptual design described by Heinrich (see HEINRICH 1994, pp. 268-274). However, it stresses the strategic significance of implementing standard software, rather than scrutinizing technology. Thus, it refers to the strategic focus as discussed in Wildemann's target conceptual design (see WILDEMANN 1990, pp. 26-28).

The strategy based BPO concept can be defined in **six steps**:

❑ Defining the target system (business goals)
❑ Defining all business processes in question as a total information model,
❑ Detailing individual information system views
❑ Splitting up the total information model into sub-models, each one describing individual processes (splitting up business processes)
❑ Defining the scope of the standard software deployment
❑ Defining the implementation strategy

The goal, procedure, appropriate supporting method and IS tool are described for every step of defining the strategy based BPO concept.

The structure of Chapter 3 is illustrated in Fig. 3.1.

3.1 Defining the Target System

In planning the information system, the target system (the business goals) can be defined as one of the tasks of the as-is analysis of the enterprise (see HEINRICH, BURGHOLZER, pp. 179-184; KELLER, MEINHARDT 1994a, p. 22; SCHEER 1991b, p. 63). Yet some individual goals can only be specified or quantified, respectively, once the results of the as-is analysis are known. The target system acts as an "interface" between as-is analysis and the target conceptual design. In BIS, this interface function and the significance of the target system for ensuring a strategy driven implementation of standard software justify defining the target system first, when establishing strategy based BPO (see NEU 1991, pp. 112-114).

3.1.1 Goal

The goal of defining the target system (the business goals) is to create a common basis for **aligning** and **prioritizing implementation tasks**. This ensures a strategy and business driven implementation of the standard software, which is especially important for the implementation of mission critical systems, e.g. for the Supply Chain Management (SCM). All ensuing tasks should be designed to support the target system. Thus, the tasks are actually driven by the target system.

This ensures strategic harmony (see SCHOLZ 1987, pp. 61-68), i.e., compatibility of the implementation tasks within the context of the enterprise strategy.

Using the term "system" is sensible because individual goals and their relationships must be defined.

3.1.2 Procedure

Generally, **profit maximization** is the "bottom line" **goal** of profit oriented companies. Additional goals are used to ensure profit maximization by transforming it into operational figures (see GOLDRATT, COX 1990, p. 66; NEU 1991, pp. 15-16). The goals can be interconnected in a network. A sub-goal can support several superior goals (see SCHEER 1994a, pp. 63-64). Any number of goal levels can be defined.

In order to implement BIS, the target system should be determined in **three individual steps**, by:

❑ Defining a competitive strategy,
❑ Deriving critical success factors,
❑ Deriving operational goals.

Taking the competitive strategy into account ensures a strategic focus of the target system. Operational goals serve to control and monitor the success of conceptual design and implementation measures. Critical success factors link competitive and operational goals.

The starting point of defining the target system is the **competitive and strategic focus** of the enterprise (see HUBER, GUMSHEIMER 1991, pp. 30-31; MAIER-ROTHE, p. 149; NEU 1991, pp. 115-118; WATTEROTT 1993, pp. 71-72; WILDEMANN 1987, pp. 158-165; WILDEMANN 1990, pp. 48-50. In this context, we can define three various basic strategies:

❑ Differentiation,
❑ Cost leadership and
❑ Focusing, e.g., concentrating on niche markets

(see PORTER 1990, p. 62). **Differentiation strategies** aim at creating a unique position for the company within the marketplace. Competitive advantages by **cost leadership** presuppose significant cost advantages within the particular vertical market. **Focusing** strategies result in a company concentrating on a certain corner of the market, such as a certain buyer group, a certain product area within the market, or a geographically limited market. Within this market segment, differentiation strategy, cost leadership or a combination of all are implemented (see PORTER 1990, pp. 62-69). Defining the basic business of a company is the cornerstone of a company's competitive strategy. All this external information is necessary input for BIS.

Critical success factors are derived from the competitive strategy. They depict which results must be achieved by all means to implement the competitive strategy (see ROCKART 1982, p. 17). Every critical success factor should be applied to the competitive strategy and, therefore, to the entire organization. In nine different consulting projects in manufacturing companies carried out by the author, it was determined that critical success factors generally derive by specifying the following aspects:

❑ Increasing flexibility,
❑ Increasing quality and
❑ Reducing costs.

In order to **increase flexibility**, the following dimensions can be defined:

❑ Time dimensions (e.g., reducing the duration of an order process)
❑ Volume dimensions / quantities (e.g., delivering small and also large amounts of product),
❑ Product characteristics (e.g., delivering customer specific variants) or
❑ Other dimensions (e.g., detailed information available for the customer due to more transparent order processing).

The quality of the

❑ Product (as in long product life), of the
❑ Added benefits of the product (as in after sales service) or
❑ Other (as in brand image)

can be improved.

Cost reduction can be achieved regarding

❑ Personnel costs,
❑ Operating resources,
❑ Material costs or
❑ Other costs (such as investing in inventory).

According to these guidelines, the dimensions described in publications can be adapted to company specific requirements (see JOST 1993b, pp. 193-197; WATTEROTT 1993, p. 79). The potential success factors illustrated in Fig. 3.2 can be **modeled** to determine the critical success factors of any company.

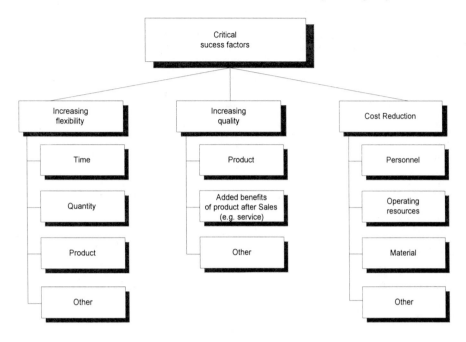

Fig. 3.2: Model for determining critical success factors

Critical success factors are a cornerstone for defining **goals** (see SCHEER 1990b, p. 63; SPANG 1993, p. 105). Goals are characterized by the

❑ Substance of the goal (such as increasing capacity load),
❑ Extent of the goal (such as " by 20%") and
❑ Period of the goal (such as "within one year")

(see SPANG 1993, pp. 103-105). Such a goal can support one or several success factors. Relationships between goals result from focusing on identical or different success factors. For example, the goal "Reduce process time of a customer order by 30% in the next two years" could derive from the success factor "Reduce processing time". Likewise, the former can support the success factor "Improve customer service" because short delivery times can also be considered to be a kind of service. On the other hand, individual goals can conflict with each other, such as "Reduce manufacturing processing time by 20%" and "Reduce manufacturing costs by 30%".

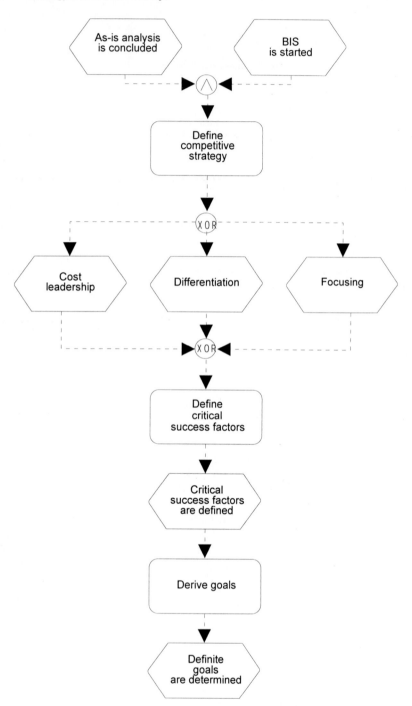

Fig. 3.3 Procedure for establishing a target system

This conflict should be resolved in BIS by appropriate conceptual design and implementation measures. Goals can be quantified by comparing as-is data from the initial situation with industry specific measures or measure systems (benchmarking) (see KÜTING 1983, p. 237). Industry specific measures are available from various associations (see RICHTER, PFLIEGER 1991).

Technically, any number of goals can be defined and then structured in any number of levels (see SCHEER 1990b, pp. 63-64). In order to simplify the target system, however, this should be limited (see WATTEROTT 1993, p. 80).

All implementation tasks should be defined according to the goals, and thus according to the critical success factors. This ensures that the competitive strategy is supported, in turn optimizing the competitive situation of the as-is work processes of the enterprise. If specific goals for implementing relevant areas of the enterprise are not defined, the necessary issues can be prioritized and focused on in BIS, for example, based on success factors (see ROCKART 1982, pp. 19-20). Admittedly, this does complicate monitoring the success of the new system. Implementation projects carried out by the author in companies ranging from 150 to 6,000 employees, typically have between five and ten success factors. Between five and fifteen goals should be defined for companies of this size. This finding is confirmed by empirical studies (see WATTEROTT 1993, p. 80). In larger corporations, an increase in the number of goals can be expected, because a larger amount of corporate divisions with specific success factors are affected.

Fig. 3.3 illustrates the procedure for establishing the target system.

3.1.3 Supporting Methods and IT Tools

Target systems can be depicted in structural diagrams (see SCHEER 1990b, pp. 63-64, SPANG 1993, p. 105). The elements of the target system, i.e., competitive strategy, critical success factors and goals, respectively, are then put into focus with one another. The symbols for illustrating structural diagrams are depicted in Fig. 3.4.

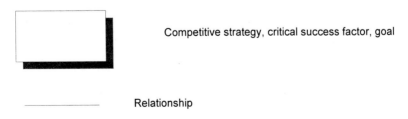

Competitive strategy, critical success factor, goal

Relationship

Fig. 3.4: Symbols illustrating structural diagrams

Fig. 3.5 illustrates an example of a target system, based on an implementation project of the author in a mechanical engineering company with 4,000 employees. We would like to point out that this enterprise most certainly selected a differentiation strategy, but still defined cost as a critical success factor. This of course stems from the fact that even "unique" products can not be sold at any price desired, forcing companies to observe cost issues.

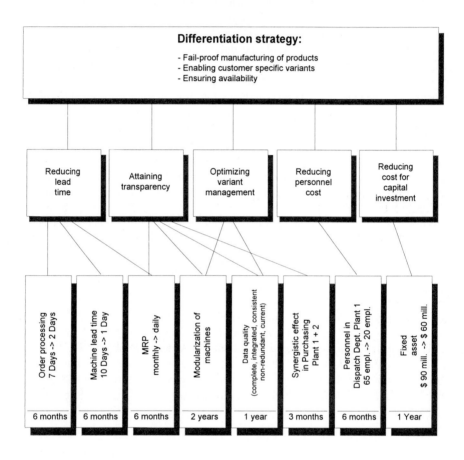

Fig. 3.5: Example of a target system

Due to the small amount of data necessary when establishing target systems, the use of less formal illustration methods is possible. Thus, the target system could be represented as a table and the necessary relationship could be annotated verbally. Based on the experience of the author, a IT tool is not necessary to depict the target system (see KELLER, MEINHARDT 1994a, p. 22).

However, as-is values of the enterprise, as are necessary for quantifying critical success factors, can be determined by means of software tools, such as with the index analysis of the ARIS Toolset (see IDS 1994b, p. 2.-70 - 2.-115). This is sensible when the required pieces of information can not be provided directly.

Computer Aided Team software systems (CATs) can be used to define the target system efficiently. They are especially useful when a large amount of employees in the enterprise must cooperate to ensure a consensus. IT Tools, such as group systems, are useful for

❑ Coming up with,
❑ Organizing and
❑ Selecting ideas.

Empirical studies show that the time required to come up with ideas (here: with regard to the target system) can be reduced by up to 90% (see KRCMAR 1993, pp. 5-9).

3.2 Defining Business Processes

Step Two in establishing a strategy based BPO concept is defining the business processes.

3.2.1 Goal

When defining business processes, all (according to the project scope) relevant **processes** of the enterprise should be defined. The degree of detail should be sufficiently high to define the structure of the business processes, i.e. the interrelationship of the individual enterprise tasks, but low enough not to confine the engineering of the standard software based BPO concept more than is necessary.

The processes must be **comprehensive** and the networking aspects of business processes must be taken into account. This ensures that the enterprise is viewed and modeled as an entire system. This also guarantees that the effects of the implementation on **indirectly affected departments of the enterprise** are taken into account. On the other hand, **processes beyond the enterprise** can be included in the entire conceptual design and their requirements can be included (see DAVIDOW, MALONE 1993, pp. 14-17).

The business processes in an information model are the starting point for all other tasks in BIS. These aim at detailing or specifying the processes, taking the target system into account.

The definition of business processes reflects the desired target status, rather than the as-is process. Radical changes (see HAMMER, CHAMPY 1994, p. 49) can be introduced, and hesitant adaptation can and must be avoided (see NOLAN et al. 1993, pp. 2-3).

3.2.2 Procedure

Business processes are defined in **four steps:**

❑ Acquiring a reference model pertinent to the vertical market segment,
❑ Defining the functions in a company specific manner,
❑ Defining the process logic in a company specific manner,
❑ Adding company specific business processes or sub-processes.

Step One is to create a **process reference model** pertinent to the **vertical market segment**. Using reference models ensures that

❑ None of the relevant processes are overlooked,
❑ Approaches typical for the vertical market are taken into account,
❑ Neither sub-optimal as-is processes nor
❑ Possibly non-appropriate standard software structures are modeled.

Reference models pertinent to vertical markets can also include typical business processes beyond the enterprise. Vertical market reference models ensure simple and company specific adaptability because

❑ Vertical market specific terminology is used,
❑ Fundamental structures for enterprises in certain vertical markets (such as discrete manufacturing and assembly in mechanical engineering, or continuous-flow production in the paper industry)

are taken into account. Vertical market reference models can be purchased in consulting companies (see BROMBACHER et al. 1993, p. 185; KIRCHMER, LAMETER 1994, pp. 505-507; ÖSTERLE et al. 1991, p. 71).

The vertical market specific, but company independent reference model will now be used to establish a company specific initial solution. To this end, we must study the

❑ Functions of the process model and
❑ the functions' process logic.

Process logic is a result of events triggering functions or being triggered by functions.

Initially, we should start with a **company specific definition** of the **functions.** For every function in the reference model, we must check whether products or product groups exist or will exist, for which the execution of this function would be necessary. If this is not the case, the function with its relationships can be removed from the reference model. If the function is required, we must define whether it should be used

❑ For certain products / product groups individually or as
❑ A central coordinator for all products.

Defining a coordination function is necessary when it serves to reach defined goals (such as larger purchase volumes and, thus, lower material costs when centrally planning the purchase of initial materials of several product groups). When a function is allocated to products or product groups, it is already allocated to the business processes of the appropriate divisions or identified as a coordinating common function (see SCHEER 1994a, pp. 22-27).

Functions are elements of general business processes, yet they also represent (can be described as) object oriented processes, i.e. **processes or sub-processes**, respectively (see BROMBACHER 1991, p. 126; SCHEER 1990b, p. 65). They are detailed and specified in later phases of BIS.

Simultaneously with the company specific adaptation of the functions of the reference process model, **process logic** linked with it should also be adapted. To this end, events included in the reference model should be studied, as to whether they exist in the specific enterprise.

In Step Four, the company specific process model should now be **completed**. **Functions and events not existing** in the reference model, but that are required by the company, are missing in this information model. The missing information objects are determined by studying the

❑ Product spectrum and the
❑ Target system.

When assessing the **product spectrum,** one must examine whether products exist that had previously not been allocated to any other functions, or at best, had been allocated to relatively few functions compared to other products. Then the functions (pertaining to the as-is situation) relating to these products can be included in the process model. At the same time, the necessary process logic must be completed.

Studying the **target system** takes advantage of the close correlation between functions and goals. A function can be defined as the process affecting an object, and supporting one or multiple goals (see SCHEER 1990b, p. 63). Thus, functions and corresponding process logic necessary for implementing the goals, but not yet included in the present process model, must be completed.

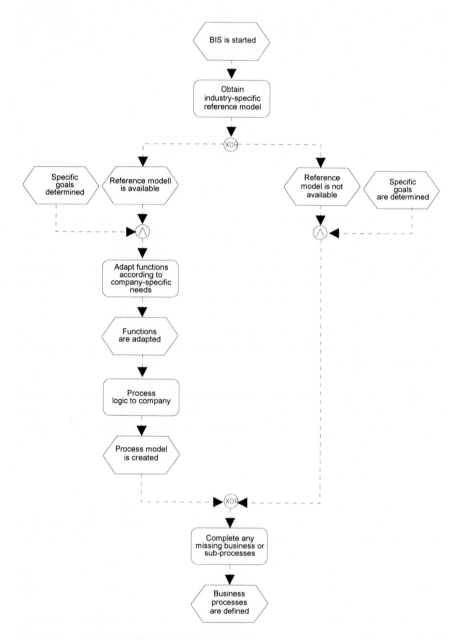

Fig. 3.6: Procedure for defining business processes

The business process model previously completed must be assessed regarding its logical consistency, possibly leading to completion of the process logic. Elements missing in the processes defined here are less significant because they are neither directly relevant for the goal nor do they have an effect on the products. Furthermore, they are of little significance for the vertical market because they were not included in the corresponding vertical market reference model.

The **processes** defined here are **optimized** from the initial situation because they

❑ Conform to vertical market reference models and, thus, also conform to ideal processes within the vertical market. They have also been
❑ Examined and completed regarding the target system.

They can be radically different from the as-is situation.

If vertical market specific reference models are not available, all the business processes must be defined, as described in Step Four. This leads to a loss in efficiency and effectiveness.

When defining business processes, they should be described in a simple manner, limited to linking functions by appropriate time-related process logic (see KELLER, MEINHARDT 1994, pp. 4-5; SCHEER 1994a, pp. 49-52). The degree of detailing should be general, ensuring an enterprise-wide view with as little effort as possible. This general level of detailing can also be achieved by limiting the number of functions to be studied, as is customary in the SADT or IDEF0 methods (see ERKES 1989, p. 63; HEINRICH 1994, p. 110). When examining general reference models, such as Scheer's extended Y-CIM model (see SCHEER 1990a, p. 2-3) or the Y-CIM model, expanded to include commercial functionality (see SCHEER 1994a, p. 85-87), it becomes apparent that manufacturing companies can be described with as little as 20-30 functions. However, practical work carried out by the author in seven implementation projects in three different vertical markets has shown that 30-50 functions are more suitable to define the key business processes of a company (see BROMBACHER et al. 1993, p. 179). In manufacturing companies, these business processes generally include:

❑ Order processing and shipping
❑ Manufacturing program planning and MRP
❑ External procurement
❑ Warehouse management
❑ Time- and capacity management
❑ Release and processing of production orders
❑ Maintenance, tool and device manufacturing, technology planning
❑ Customer service

❑ Waste management
❑ Marketing
❑ Research and development (R&D)
❑ Development of routings / preparation of manufacturing
❑ Quality assurance
❑ Financial accounting
❑ Cost accounting and performance analysis; controlling
❑ Human resources
❑ Information management

(see PORTER 1989a, pp. 59-66; SCHEER 1994a, pp. 85-88).
The procedure for defining business processes is illustrated in Fig. 3.6.

3.2.3 Supporting Methods and IT Tools

The business processes can be modeled according to the event driven process chains (EPCs) already described. EPCs are not only used to describe BIS processes, but are also used within BIS. If the names of functions or events are not sufficient to uniquely define their content, appropriate terminology definitions must be allocated.

Fig. 3.7 depicts an expert of generally defined business processes of an mechanical engineering company with a staff of 2,000 employees. A vertical market specific aspect would, for example, entail different processing of customer orders depending on the degree of standardization of the products in demand. In the example of the mechanical engineering company, uncomplicated standard products are processed immediately, straight out of the warehouse. Customer orders trigger Shipping. Variants of the standard products are assembled according to the customer order. Special orders, perhaps requiring customer specific parts, are initially processed by Engineering. In the course of BIS, this logic should be supported by the new standard software product.

In various implementation projects carried out by the author, it has sometimes proven useful to skip an explicit illustration of individual events. At a high level of detail, these events are frequently meaningless. For example, the result of "Release manufacturing order" could be the "Manufacturing order is released" event. Events such as these inflate the amount of elements actually necessary for illustrating the process (usually by a factor of 2 to 3, based on the author's experience), without providing any additional information. The process model becomes cluttered. When depicting process logic, functions should be directly connected by arrows. The events between the arrows are obvious. Thus, functions are sorted in a procedure sequence (see SCHEER 1990b, pp. 70-74). For these illustrations, value added chain diagrams can be used (see KIRSCH 1994, pp. 4.4.-22 - 4.4.-23).

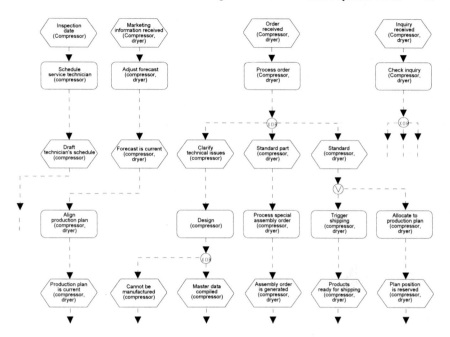

Fig. 3.7: An example of how to define a business process

EPCs and value added chain diagrams can be modeled by means of the ARIS Toolset (see IDS 1994c, p. 4.-1 - 4.-80; KIRCHMER 1998a, p. 66; KIRSCH 1994, p. 4.4.-3 - 4.4.-14, 4.4.-22 - 4.4.-23). Here, software support is sensible despite the relatively small data volume because systematic detailing of the models (in the following phases of the BIS) is simplified. In the following phases of BIS, detail processes can be included in the hierarchy (see IDS 1994c, p. 5.22) and precisely allocated to the business processes thus defined. This ensures a consistent implementation of the business processes.

3.3 Detailing Individual Information System Views

In Step Three of establishing a strategy based BPO concept, we will discuss detailing individual information system views.

3.3.1 Goal

The goal of detailing individual information system views is to model **enterprise specifics** -- relevant to maintaining a competitive edge -- as detailed as necessary. These are then systematically specified and implemented in the following BIS phases. Subsequently, the planned implementation of the new standard software supports the differentiation characteristics of the enterprise. In this manner, BIS is used to maintain and achieve **competitive advantages**, helping to achieve strategic goals (see SCHRÖDER 1993, p. 32).

The number of enterprise specifics should be kept to a minimum, reducing the need for reconciling the resulting business administration requirements definition (business concept), standard software and the detail models of the strategy based BPO concept. This not only reduces the planning effort, but also eliminates the potential need for enhancing or modifying the standard software.

If, in the course of BIS, these detailed aspects should lead to enhancements of the standard software or even make the deployment of standard software debatable, then the specifications defined here serve as a starting point either for individual enhancement or complete individual development of a software solution.

3.3.2 Procedure

Detailing individual information system views involves up to **eight steps**:

❑ Establishing the product model, (and for a market model)
❑ Establishing a function level concept, (accountability model)
❑ Determining the functions or sub-processes still to be specified,
❑ Determining the kind of models to be designed,
❑ Modeling the organizational view,
❑ Modeling the data view,
❑ Modeling the function view,
❑ Modeling the control view,
❑ Merging the models.

Step One is to establish a **product model**. Products can be goods or services (see KIRCHMER 1996, pp. 268-270). This describes the central product characteristics of the enterprise, driving the business processes. The structure of the products and the added services associated with the products (such as service after sales) usually characterize key differentiators of a company. Product characteristics and their being modeled in the new standard software are significant factors when designing business processes (see GOLDHAR 1989, p. 263; GRÖNER 1991, pp. 39-41; LOOS 1992, p. 14). Relationships between products and product components (such as assemblies sold as individual products, but also as components of products) are key to relationships between processes. For this reason, it is important to illustrate the products and their relationships transparently. All this is modeled in the ARIS Architecture's **data view**.

The products of the company, as well as the central product components influencing the purchasing decision of potential customers, are determined. The relationships of the resulting data elements are added. Primarily, their business administration and logical relationships are modeled. Elements relating to engineering and technical aspects are secondary. For example, for a company dealing in plant engineering and construction, the product model should include engineering and customer service, if appropriate. Strategically significant elements of the plant are also key. By means of the product model, it is possible to check for completeness of the business processes (every element of the model must be processed in at least one process). The product model can be complemented by a market model (see KIRCHMER 1995, pp. 268-270, KIRCHMER 1998b). This is necessary when market characteristics drive the processes, e.g., in retail.

At the beginning of Step Two of detailing individual system views, an **organizational level concept** is established. This is the hierarchical organizational guideline for executing business processes, i.e., the **organizational view** is a focal point. The organizational basic structure is the cornerstone for centralizing or decentralizing tasks and corresponding business processes at any later point in time.

Given the low degree of detail in business process models, a detailed definition of the hierarchical organization is not possible at this stage of BIS. **Level concepts** are more appropriate for the general structuring necessary here (see SCHEER 1990a, pp. 127-130; SCHEER 1990b; pp. 110-111). These concepts determine the hierarchical organizational structure of an enterprise without specifying particular organizational units, such as are typical in an org chart. In order to establish company specific organizational levels, we must differentiate between structures

❑ Referring to manufacturing of the products (goods and services) enabling the company's market position, and structures,
❑ Referring to the sales/distribution of these products.

The **levels should be defined** in such a way, as to let a department in a superior level coordinate one or more units in a subordinate level (see SCHEER 1990a, p. 127).
Typical levels for the manufacturing structure are

❑ Product area levels
❑ Operation levels
❑ Company area levels
❑ Operating resource group levels
❑ Operating resource levels and
❑ Operating resource component levels.

Typical levels for the sales and distribution structure are

❑ Regional sales offices
❑ Sales offices and
❑ Staff in the field (sales representatives)

Efforts in manufacturing and sales and distribution, respectively, are coordinated by

❑ Corporate (headquarters)

(see SCHEER 1990a, p. 127).

Based on personal experience of the author in seven implementation projects in companies with a staff of between 150 and 6,000 employees, the manufacturing and sales/distribution aspects, respectively, can be defined in three to four levels (see LAMETER et al., pp. 59-60).

Positioning the functions to be executed by business processes (see definition of business processes) in organizational levels leads to the **function level concept** (accountability model). The criteria and coordinating characteristics are provided by the following aspects:

❑ Functions in the same organizational level pertain to the same time period. For example, the manufacturing functions "Manufacturing program planning for one month" or "Detailed manufacturing planning for one week" could be allocated to two different levels. The same could be true for functions pertaining to the sales and distribution functions "Create forecasts for the year" or "Monthly forecast".
❑ The relevant data for the functions in one level must be of the same actuality, e.g., monthly data or weekly data.
❑ The data volume created by the functions in the same level must be roughly the same size. For example, the number of products; the number of parts to be manufactured; the sales volume of products in a certain region; the sales volume of products per customer in a certain region.

(see SCHEER 1990a, pp. 128-130).

The function level concept links function views and organizational views, leading to a specification of the **control view** (see SCHEER 1990b, pp. 110-111). This defines the general hierarchy organizational positioning of the functions and, thus, the corresponding business processes, determining the appropriate degree of centralization or decentralization, respectively. The existence of multiple functions at corporate headquarters suggests a centrally run organization. Distributed functions in subordinate organizational levels lead to decentralization effects. In the following phases of BIS, the function level concept is used to allocate implementation tasks to the various organizational units. The procedure for establishing a function level concept is depicted in Fig. 3.8.

In the next step of detailing individual information system views, we must determine **functions or sub-processes**, respectively, which need to be **specified** further. This is achieved by examining the functions regarding their

❏ Relevance for achieving the target system **and** the
❏ Planned company specific design

(see SCHRÖDER 1993, p. 32; DAHLHEIM 1993, p. 34).

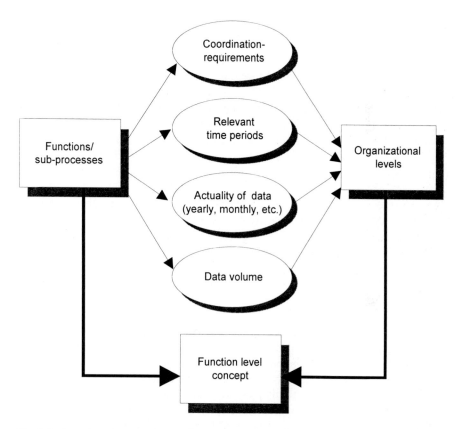

Fig. 3.8: Procedure for establishing a function level concept

It should be noted that a company specific design of business processes in an as-is situation should not be automatically included in detailed information models. This could prevent a standardization of work processes which would otherwise be sensible from an efficiency point of view (see BOLL 1993, p. 418).

Functions of the business processes are graded as "high", "medium" or "low", according to their **significance** in helping achieve the **target system**. This also depends on the results of the as-is analysis and management's evaluation. Based on personal experience of the author, this general evaluation is sufficient for defining the functions that must be detailed.

Now the functions are evaluated regarding the previously planned **company specific design.** To this end, we must examine the

❑ Products relevant for the function (see product model), the
❑ Positioning of functions in function levels, the
❑ Relevant data (from initial or final events of the functions),
❑ General company rules and the
❑ As-is situation of the company.

For example, the particulars of the **products** relevant for a function can require specific detail functions for order processing.

The necessary specifics of various company locations, allocated to individual levels, can derive from the **function levels.** Thus, increasingly global competition (see PORTER 1989b, p. 38) requires international business activities, company locations abroad and the appropriate design of business processes.

This leads to special requirements resulting from

❑ Specific communication issues between operational units (such as language barriers, different time zones, different measures and currencies),
❑ Heterogeneous markets (such as requirements for international marketing),
❑ Personnel aspects (such as differing qualifications and mentality of employees),
❑ Business issues (such as long payment periods due to poor financial conditions) and
❑ Legal requirements

(see OLIFF et al. 1989, pp. 42-54; SPANG 1991, pp. 39-41). For example, monitoring payments in Italian or Spanish subsidiaries, given these countries' traditionally long payment periods, could lead to a significant competitive edge. A factor such as this would have to be included in the concept.

Company specific **data structures**, such as modeling retraceable dates of a manufacturing order, could require the specific design of a sub-process.

General **company rules**, such as KAIZEN, Lean Production or TQM (see IMAI 1993; WOMACK et al. 1992) can require sub-processes to be specifically designed..

Company specific issues regarding the company's **as-is situation** might be maintained and must therefore also be defined.

Evaluating functions with regard to their significance in helping achieve the target system and the previously defined company specifics, results in a "**Target - Specifics Matrix**" (see Fig. 3.9). Functions or sub-processes significant in achieving the goals of the target system, and that must be designed company specifically, must be specified in detail. Even if they are only moderately significant in helping achieve the goal, the functions to be carried out according to company specifics should be characterized more precisely. In the course of BIS, for reasons of efficiency, other functions or sub-processes should be detailed in the standard software based BPO concept.

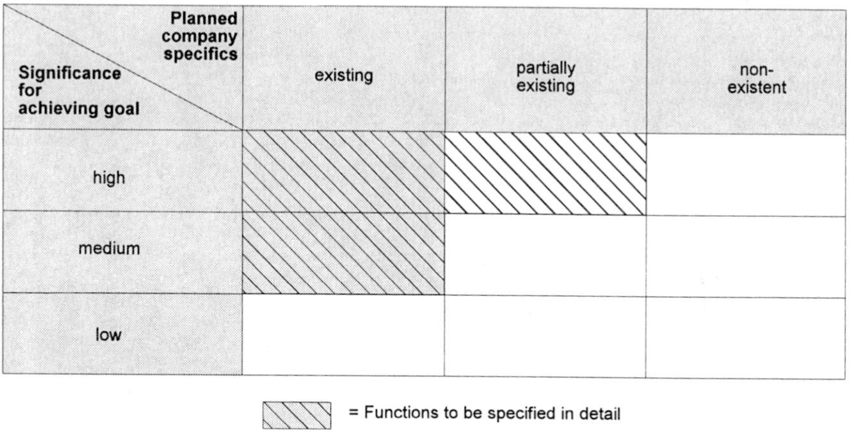

Significance for achieving goal \\ Planned company specifics	existing	partially existing	non-existent
high	▨	▨	
medium	▨		
low			

▨ = Functions to be specified in detail

Fig. 3.9: Target - specifics matrix

The functions or sub-processes that were determined, must now be specified by information models, according to the ARIS information system views. The **model types** must now be defined. We can differentiate between

❑ Organizational models (hierarchical organizations),
❑ Data models,
❑ Function models and
❑ Control models.

The views to be modeled result from the company specifics that were previously determined. The issues must be established in the data, function, organizational or control models (process models), respectively, giving the sub-process in question the desired company specific character.

If decentralization is an issue, this can lead to detailing of the organizational view and the control view (allocation of functions to organizational units). For example, if the information relationship between a customer order and a manufacturing order is significant for the execution of an order related assembly, then it should be detailed according to the data view. Simulation functionality in manufacturing control can require function oriented detailing. It can also be necessary to specify process logic in process models, such as when modeling specific parallelization of sub-processes that originally had been sequential (see

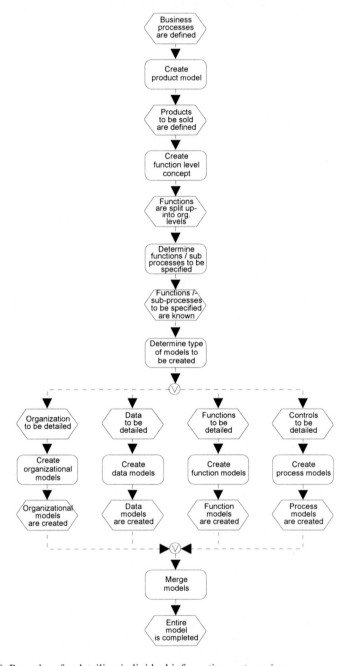

Fig. 3.10: Procedure for detailing individual information system views

STEINMETZ 1992, pp. 200-203). It is generally not necessary to detail in a purely functional manner because the differentiators usually result from functions dependent upon content and time, not from the isolated design of the function itself.

The last step in detailing individual information system views involves **merging** the resulting **information models** according to the business processes. **Their consistency and completeness must be ensured.** Every model is allocated to one or more business processes. Individual models relating to a business process and possibly created by different persons, must be kept consistent. For example, the data model of the customer order must take the specifics defined in the product model into account.

The procedure for detailing individual information system views is illustrated in Fig. 3.10.

3.3.3 Supporting Methods and IT Tools

Describing **data models** is a challenging task in methodology. Data models can be modeled in **entity relationship models (ERM)** (see CHEN 1976, SCHEER 1994a, pp. 31-35). Practical applications are simplified by various enhancements (see LOOS 1992, pp. 17-43; SCHEER 1994a, pp. 35-47).

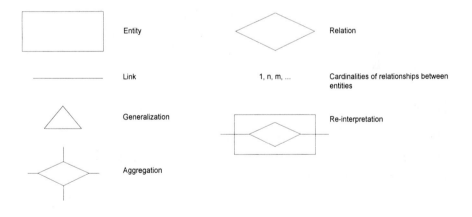

Fig. 3.11: Symbols describing enhanced entity relationship models (eERM)

Element types, e.g., "customer" or "product" are put into context with each other, as in "customer buys product". Interrelationships are detailed by cardinalities. For example, a customer buys exactly one type of "product", but the same type of product is also needed by multiple customers. *Generalizations* are useful enhancements (" customer" and " supplier" are generalized to " partner").

Other sensible enhancements are: *reinterpretations* (the " buys" relationship is used as an independent element type. In the context of " order", it is linked with other element types) or *aggregations* (relationship between more than two element types). In the strategy based BPO concept, attributes for individual element types (see SCHEER 1994a, p. 33) can be omitted, given the low degree of detailing (see BROMBACHER et al. 1993, pp. 179-180). The symbols for depicting enhanced entity relationship models (eERM) are illustrated in Fig. 3.11.

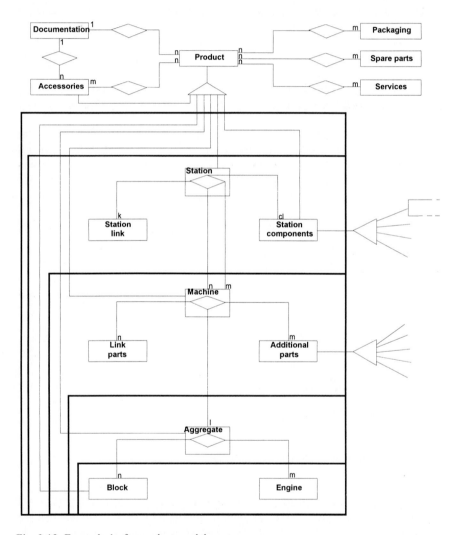

Fig. 3.12: Example 1 of a product model

Figs. 3.12. and 3.13 give examples for product models. Fig. 3.12 illustrates an excerpt of a product model stemming from a company in the plant engineering and construction business. The aggregation block, an individual product in its own right, and the motor form an aggregate. The motor is also for sale as a product and can be installed in large factories, for example. The addition of several additional parts results in a complete machine. Several machines can be linked to form a machine station. Additional services, like spare parts or documentation are also available. This complex, multiple tier product structure influences all logistical processes. Every customer and manufacturing order must be engineered and processed in this manner.

Fig. 3.13 depicts an excerpt of the product model of a automotive supplier in the industrial ceramics industry. It demonstrates that these products are structured much more simply. "Logs" are made from the raw material. They are then processed into "pieces", from which "substrates" are manufactured. Substrates can be refined even further. Substrates and refined substrates are sold as products. The main issue here is that the manufacture of these products must be traceable by means of "traceability information". This is greatly significant for the sub-process of manufacturing order processing.

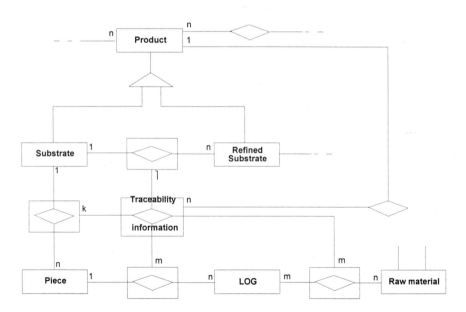

Fig. 3.13: Example 2 of a product model

Fig. 3.14 depicts a part of a data model of the "customer order – assembly order" relationship in a mechanical engineering company. The key issue is that bill of material items and operations are defined to specifically suit customer orders. The master data thus defined is the cornerstone for assembly orders specified to customer orders. This is of great significance for increasing the flexibility of an enterprise.

Organizational levels and **function levels,** on which the former are based, can be defined **without any formal methods** (see SCHEER 1990b, pp. 90-92, pp. 110-111). This is possible due to the small number of elements to be processed, namely five to ten organizational levels and approx. 30 - 50 functions. Allocating locations to the levels increases the data volume only minimally.

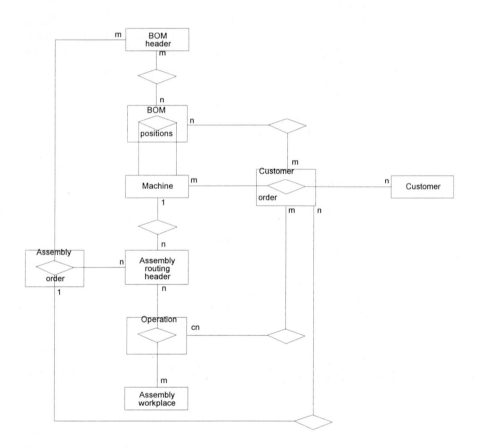

Fig. 3.14: Example of a data model

Fig. 3.15 illustrates a function level concept of a mechanical engineering company with a staff of approx. 2,000 employees. Key issues are decentralized processing of standard orders for dryers by the field staff and the shift of quality assurance tasks to the level of the manufacturing process. In order to ensure corporate identity, user documentation of all products is produced centrally, at the corporate office. However, according to the demands of the individual international subsidiaries, documentation for compressors and dryers is enhanced locally.

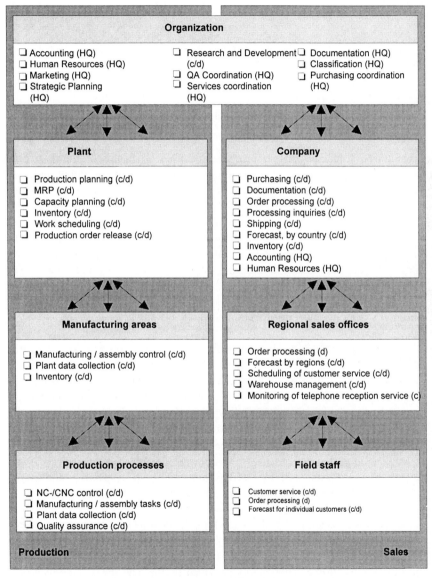

c = Kompressor, D = Dryer, HQ = Headquarters

Fig. 3.15: Example of a function level concept

Detailed **organizational models** can be illustrated by means of organizational charts (see SCHEER 1994a, pp. 28-29). This puts organizational units into focus with one another. Thus, **organizational charts** can also be considered as a kind of structure diagram. The symbols for illustrating organizational charts are shown in Fig. 3.16. Examples of organizational charts are given in Chapter One.

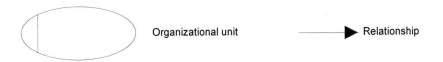

Fig. 3.16: Symbols illustrating organizational charts

Models of the **control view** can be specified by means of **detail process models**. The required data elements or responsible organizational units are allocated to the functions included in the process, if required for stressing company specifics (see SCHEER 1994a, pp. 53-54). This can be illustrated by the EPCs described in Chapter 3.2.3, to give an example. Fig. 3.17 shows an excerpt of the detail process model in a mechanical engineering company. It specifies the machine configuration specified to customer orders. This is carried out in two steps. First, the "top", then the "frame" fitting to it, are configured. The frame is either mounted at the factory or at the customer site. The two tier product configuration defined here is key to improving the company's ability to respond to customer wishes and thus must be implemented in BIS.

Function models can be illustrated by means of function trees (see SCHEER 1990b, pp. 64-69; SCHEER 1994a, pp. 19-20). This puts the functions in the structure diagrams into focus with one another. The symbols used to illustrate function trees are shown in Fig. 3.18. Functions in function trees can be grouped according to various criteria. The following are frequently used criteria:

❑ The same objects are processed (object oriented),
❑ They are allocated to a process (process oriented) and
❑ They have the same activity (activity oriented, as in "Change manufacturing order"; or "Change customer order" into function tree "Change order")

(see KIRSCH 1994, p. 4.1.-4 - 4.1.-7). Fig. 3.19 shows an excerpt of a process oriented function tree in a mechanical engineering company. It compiles the functions necessary for configuring products. This illustration simplifies the task of reconciling with the functionality provided by the new standard software at a later date.

appropriate function of the existing process model. Data models refer to corresponding events. By referring to the business process functions in question (illustrated in the control view), organizational models are allocated to the processes (see IDS 1994d, p. 2.-30 - 2.-32).

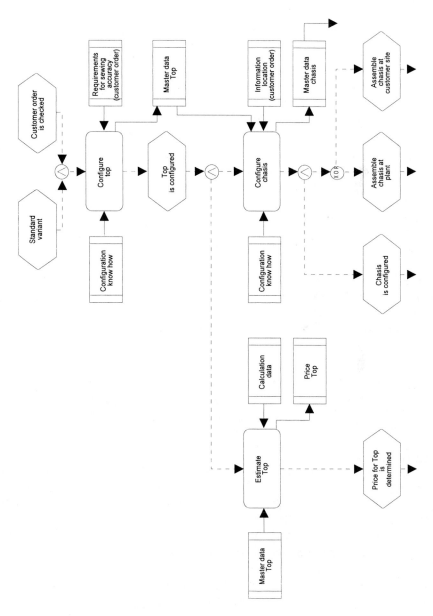

Fig. 3.17: Example of a detailed process model

Fig. 3.17: Example of a detailed process model

In turn, individual sub-models can be designed in a hierarchical manner. Fig. 3.20 illustrates the allocation of sub-models to business processes.

Fig. 3.18: Symbols for illustrating function trees

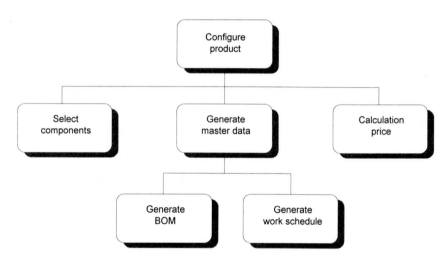

Fig. 3.19: Example of a function model

Organizational, data, function and process models, respectively, can be modeled by means of the ARIS Toolset (see IDS 1994c, p. 5.-20 - 5.-80; KIRSCH 1994, p. 4.1.-2 - 4.1.-8, 4.2.-1 - 4.2.-4.2.-24, 4.3.-1 - 4.3.-6, 4.4.-1 - 4.4.-18). The links between sub-models and business processes can also be modeled in the ARIS Toolset (see IDS 1994d, p. 2.-30 - 2.-32). IT support of BIS is especially significant because this ensures that the sub-models previously designed can be efficiently and effectively managed, by means of navigation functionality within the tool (see IDS 1994e). Pinpoint access from business processes is also possible. In later phases of BIS, this will simplify the deployment of the models.

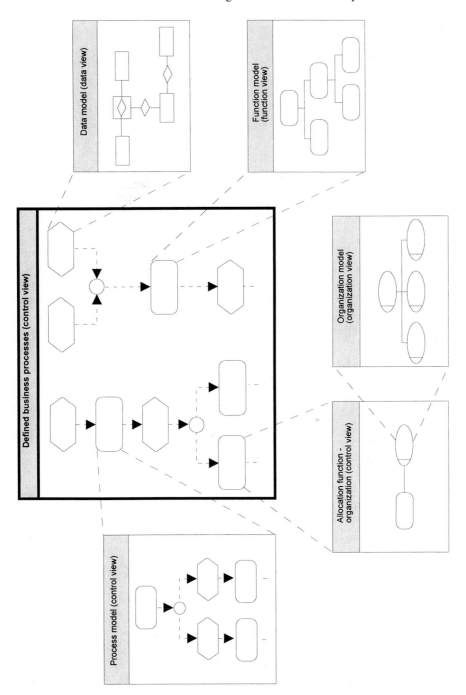

Fig. 3.20: Allocating sub-models to the business processes

3.4 Splitting Up Business Processes

Step Four in establishing a strategy based BPO concept comprises splitting up business processes, thus creating manageable units that can be efficiently processed in later phases of BIS.

3.4.1 Goal

The goal of splitting up business processes is to **reduce complexity** in later phases of BIS (see HEINRICH, BURGHOLZER 1990, p. 14; WILDEMANN 1990, p. 142) by defining manageable process excerpts. IT oriented criteria for creating sub-systems, such as defining data, transport or security systems, respectively, (see HEINRICH, BURGHOLZER 1990, p. 14-16), can be omitted. This classification lays the groundwork for individual development, but is not focused solely on the implementation of standard software. The standard applications are already available and have definite requirements regarding the IT oriented sub-systems. Thus, **business administration criteria** are well suited for splitting up business processes. The processes should be segmented in an organizational manner (see WILDEMANN 1990, p. 142). Functions and sub-processes that are closely linked according to their information content are grouped together (see WATTEROTT 1993, pp. 129-131).

When splitting up business processes, the resulting **sub-processes** should be sufficiently **manageable**, so as to ensure additional efficient processing. **Business process orientation** and corresponding **object orientation** must also be ensured. This guarantees the creation of business process oriented organizational units, according to the sub-processes (see BECKER 1991a, pp. 141-142, KELLER 1993, pp. 166-168).

3.4.2 Procedure

Business processes are split up within **five steps**:

❑ Split up business processes according to the products handled within the processes,
❑ Define additional objects to split up the processes,
❑ Delimitate sub-processes,
❑ Detail and/or enhance the objects that are used to split the processes
❑ Detail the structure of the sub-processes.

Initially, the **business processes are split up according to the products handled within the process,** providing the basis for the creation of individual divisions (see FRESE 1993, pp. 173-174; WILDEMANN 1990, p. 142). This

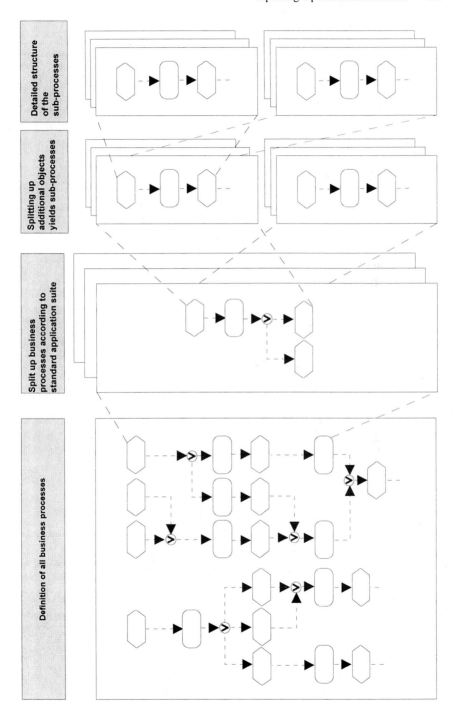

Fig. 3.21: Splitting up business processes

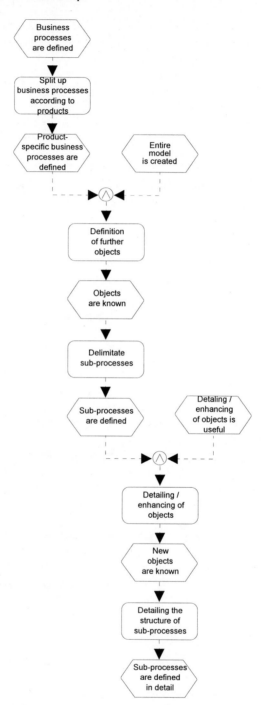

Fig. 3.22: Procedure of splitting up business processes

transforms business processes, previously defined for multiple products or product groups, into product specific processes. These processes split is possible because the products in question are already allocated to the individual functions of the business processes (see process definition). Functions to be executed centrally should be included in all the product specific business processes, in order to ensure proper specification of the coordination tasks in later BIS phases.

In the second step, the resulting **business processes** can be **split up** based on more detailed objects handled in the process. In technical fields, such as research and development, or manufacturing and assembly, parts and assemblies, i.e., product components, can be split up used to define sub processes (see WATTEROTT 1993, p. 131; WILDEMANN 1990, p. 142). These objects can be found in product models or bills of material. Appropriate objects should also be determined for other departments in the enterprise. The following objects are typical candidates:

❑ Finished products,
❑ Parts and assemblies manufactured in-house,
❑ Raw materials
❑ Bought-in parts
❑ Operating resources,
❑ Tools,
❑ Employees or
❑ Documents,

i.e., important information objects of the enterprise (see SCHEER 1994a, pp. 711-715). Along these objects, business processes can be split up into sub-processes, identical objects being pre-dominant within a sub-process. This creates sub-processes in technical areas -- such as manufacturing islands (see MASSBERG 1993, pp. 17-22) -- as well as in business administration planning units, such as order processing departments for special order types (see BECKER 1991a, pp. 141-142; WILDEMANN 1990, pp. 140-144).

In order to **define the sub-processes**, the driving objects are allocated to every function and every event of the business processes. Event-function sequences referring to the same objects are grouped into sub-processes. The next sub-process commences with the next new object. This produces multiple sub-processes, referring to the same objects. Thus, an event-function sequence describing the process -- from customer order processing, via manufacturing program planning and MRP, to the release of the manufacturing order -- can be split up into the "customer order processing - manufacturing program planning" sub-process, pertaining to final products. The other sub-process would be "MRP - release of the manufacturing order", focusing on assemblies, parts and raw materials. Sub-processes in Assembly and Shipping would pertain to the final products.

Based on personal experience of the author in implementation projects in various vertical markets and in companies with a staff of 150 to 6,000 employees, up to 60 sub-processes can be defined. However, these are frequently very similar and only include a few functions. In these cases, for reasons of efficiency, multiple sub-processes can be grouped in "process clusters". An example would be grouping all sub-processes pertaining to tools and operating resources.

These **sub-processes** can be **split up** even further. This is the case when the individual functions of the driving objects are detailed or enhanced, in order to make the sub-processes sufficiently homogeneous. To this end, the sub-processes, or the functions included therein, should be examined, in order to ascertain whether it makes business sense to detail the objects. Typical criteria for detailing the above objects are as follows:

❑ Regions or customer groups for finished products (see KIESER, KUBICEK 1992, pp. 88-95),
❑ Degree of standardization of finished products (LAMETER et al. 1994, p. 59) and
❑ Requirements for the processing technology regarding raw materials, parts and assemblies (see MASSBERG pp. 19-22).

If enhancement or detailing of the object spectrum is necessary, the detailed and enhanced objects of corresponding functions or events of the sub-processes must be split up. Thus, the function "Customer Service" could be transformed into "Customer service of clients in the construction industry" or "Customer service of clients in the manufacturing industry".

Business processes are split into three levels, according to object orientation. The structure of this split is illustrated in Fig. 3.21.

The entire procedure of how to split up business processes is depicted in Fig. 3.22.

3.4.3 Supporting Methods and IT Tools

Due to the fact that the sub-processes created here are formed by **splitting up** the **business processes**, the **EPC method** mentioned above can be maintained. The sub-processes can be modeled as copies of excerpts of the business processes. These are then detailed further in subsequent BIS phases.

Fig. 3.23 shows an excerpt of the sub-processes of a company in the plant engineering and construction business with a staff of 6,000 employees. The events and functions shown here refer to medium size and small machines. The business processes for the "large system" product group are treated separately, like in a division organization. The first sub-process -- from the "customer order has arrived" event to the "manufacturing program changed" event – refers to the finished product. The sub-process triggered by the "manufacturing program changed" and "time period arrived" events refers to parts and assemblies manufactured in-house.

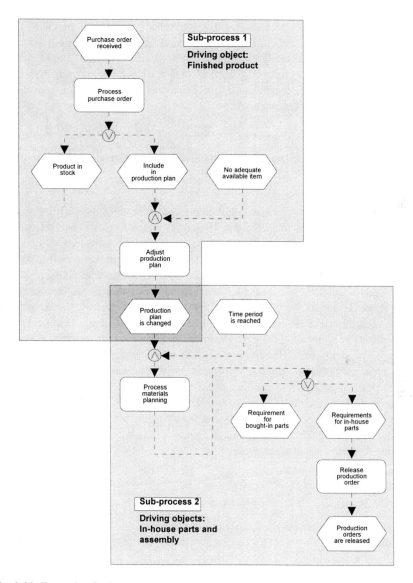

Fig. 3.23: Example of sub-processes

Final events of a sub-process, such as "manufacturing program changed", are included in the connecting sub-process as initial events. In this manner, networks between the sub-processes are taken into account. Distributed over time, the sub-processes can be processed in later phases of the standard software implementation.

The sub-processes are modeled in the ARIS Toolset, simplifying additional processing in later BIS phases. Using "reference copies" to model the sub-processes is useful. In this copy mode, object instances, i.e., the sub-processes to be created, refer to the already existing object definitions (see IDS 1994c, p. 5.43 - 5.45, 5.57-5.58). This referencing ensures that any changes in the sub-processes are also carried over to the business processes and vice versa. The allocation of detail models is also maintained.

3.5 Defining the Scope of the Standard Software Deployment

Step Five of the strategy based BPO concept is the definition of the scope of the standard software deployment. Standard software can be selected by reconciling enterprise requirements with several standard software products. This is frequently regarded as an important step in planning and deploying standard software, and for this reason is discussed in detail in various books (see FRANK 1980; LANG 1989; MARKMILLER 1989). However, due to a concentration of application vendors down to only a few suppliers in recent years, the significance of the selection process has dwindled (see HORVATH et al. 1986, pp. 8-11; SCHEER 1991b, p. 9). Strategic decisions in favor of or against a standard software product can frequently be made according to general supplier characteristics, such as previous experience with that supplier, their reputation, market position or general product characteristics, as well as their mid-term or long-term aspects (see MÜLLER 1990, p. 36, WATTEROTT 1993, pp. 96-99). When reconciling business processes and standard software, one should focus on defining the scope of the standard software deployment, rather than on just selecting a particular software product per se.

3.5.1 Goal

In defining the scope of the standard software deployment, the goal is to **determine** which sub-processes can be supported by the new **standard software**. Therefore, we must define

❑ Whether and where the deployment of the standard software is generally possible and sensible, and determine
❑ Whether strategic company specifics are addressed by the new standard software.

This determines the scope of additional implementation tasks and trigger can substantial development of individual software which might become necessary (see SCHRÖDER 1993, p. 32).

Reconciling can correct a strategic decision for or against a specific standard software product. Therefore, creating a strategy based BPO concept can be regarded as a component of the software selection.

3.5.2 Procedure

Defining the scope of the standard software deployment is a **three step** process:

❑ Reconciling the business processes in question with the information models of the standard application,
❑ Reconciling the detailed information models with the information models of the standard application,
❑ Evaluating the results of this reconciling.

The first step is to **reconcile** the business processes with the functionality of the standard software. To this end, the information models of the **business processes** and of the **standard software** must be compared and any differences determined. Models of the object oriented sub-processes are used take the specific characteristics of the processes into account. Material requirements planning for complex machines (potentially yet to be configured) differs from a comparable function for simple, mass-produced products. If **reference models** are available for the new **standard software** (see KELLER, MEINHARDT 1994a, pp. 6-18), then these reference process models should be used to examine the software. If this is not the case, appropriate standard software models based on the software product information should be designed. For this first step, it is sufficient to describe the software by functions and process logic, according to the sub-processes.

If the reference models of the standard software are available, reconciling the models will be complicated by

❑ Differing degrees of detail and the
❑ Use of different terminology.

Usually, a common base model, to which the business process model and standard software model refer, does not exist. Therefore, the models' terminology and structure do not coincide. Initially, this means that a basic prerequisite for comparing the two models is not met (see JOST 1993b, p. 164). However, since business processes in the strategy based BPO concept are described very generally, every single function and the events linked with it can be allocated to the corresponding elements of the standard software process model by existing terminology definitions (for the business process models or the models of the standard software, respectively). These definitions are used as a common base model. Due to the differing model structures, either multiple elements of the standard software model, single elements or none at all can be allocated to every element of the business process model. The result is, how well the standard software **supports** the **business processes**. This is defined in a general scale of detailing, corresponding to the business process models. The process of reconciling business processes and the standard software is illustrated in Fig. 3.24.

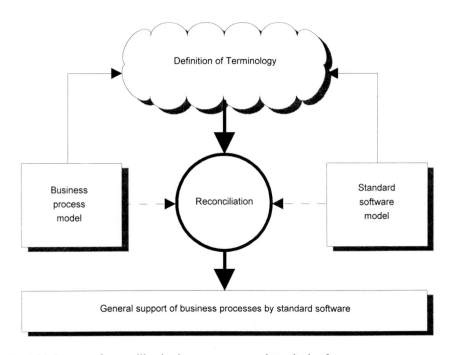

Fig. 3.24: Process of reconciling business processes and standard software

Detail information models, designed for individual information system views and representing strategically significant issues, must be **reconciled** with the information models of the standard software. The procedure is comparable to reconciling business process models. This task is occasionally more complex due to the higher degree of detailing. However, since only a few of the central aspects of the business processes are usually modeled in detail, reconciling is considerably less complex than designing and evaluating large functional specifications to select a standard software product (see LANG 1989). This determines **how well the** standard software **supports the strategic issues (degree of support).** If necessary, the results of this reconciling can be used as the basis for defining company specific enhancement of the standard software. These enhancements are justified by the significance of the process excerpts in question.

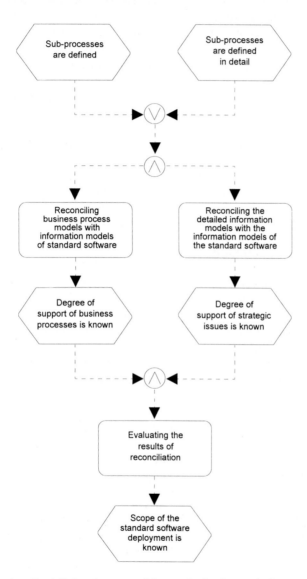

Fig. 3.25: Procedure for defining the scope of the standard software deployment

The last step in defining the scope of the standard software deployment is **evaluating the results of reconciling**. Due to the general degree of detail this can only be general in scope and can only recommend whether and for which sub-processes deployment of this particular standard software is possible, which would make closer examination worthwhile. Sub-processes poorly supported by the standard software - or not at all - should be implemented by other means, such as by implementing a different application or appropriate organizational measures. The key issue in deciding whether to deploy standard software or not, is whether existing object structures, such as products, can be modeled. If the data structures are not suited for this, deployment of this application is probably not useful (see BROMBACHER 1991, pp. 122-124).

If several competing standard software products are being considered, a decision regarding which software to deploy in later BIS phases can be made, according to the results of reconciling. One key prerequisite for implementing business process oriented organizational structures by means of BIS is support of every aspect of the business processes by the standard software, not just optimal support of a few functional areas.

The procedure of defining the scope of the standard software deployment is depicted in Fig. 3.25.

3.5.3 Supporting Methods and IT Tools

In order to simplify reconciling with company specific information models, standard software information models should be described with the same procedures. Thus, process models should be modeled using EPCs, data models using a homogeneous ERM method, function models using function trees and organizational models using org charts. If the standard software information models and enterprise information models at hand are depicted in different kinds of models (such as if standard software reference models are modeled according to a different method), the differing model methods should be migrated into a common model method. This can be accomplished by examining the corresponding meta information models, enabling a complete information system view (SCHEER 1990b, pp. 55-197).

Information models can be **compared** automatically by means of the **ARIS Toolset** (see IDS 1994b, p. 2.-116 - 2.-150). To this end, it is necessary to link the two models (see IDS 1994b, p. 2.-119), providing them with a common base model. Given that the information models created in the strategic BPO concept are independent of any application products, they must be allocated manually. Due to the differing structure of the models this is at best quite complex, if not impossible. This explains why comparing models **interactively** (using the appropriate ARIS Toolset functionality) is more efficient. ARIS Toolset's functionality and information models ensure easy navigation (see IDS 1994e), making it easy to locate the elements one wishes to compare. In company specific information models, standard software is capable of storing models as attributes (see IDS 1994c, p. 5.-32 - 5.-42), enabling tool supported evaluation.

3.6 Determining the Implementation Strategy

The last step in establishing a strategy based BPO concept is to define the implementation strategy.

3.6.1 Goal

The goal of defining the implementation strategy is to define **how** the enterprise will navigate from the **as-is situation** to the **to be situation**, as described in the strategy based BPO concept, within a certain amount of time (see JOST 1993b, p. 175; WILDEMANN 1987, p. 144), and thus **achieving** strategic **goals**. Therefore, we must now sketch a general guideline regarding contents and a time-frame for the following BIS steps.

The following procedure must focus on the possibilities of the enterprise to conduct such an implementation project. This means that at any given time during the implementation process, the competitive edge of the company must be maintained. Personnel, organizational, financial and technological restrictions must be taken into account. At the same time, the competitive situation, as defined by the target system, must be improved (see JOST 1993b, pp. 179-180; WILDEMANN 1987, p. 144). The risk of potentially exceeding restrictions or not meeting goals must be minimized (see NEU 1991, p. 215).

Given these restrictions and in order to minimize risks, strategic BPO concepts and their enterprise-wide consequences must be implemented step by step. These steps must include interdependencies of individual tasks, covering all possible aspects and potential networking. The sequence of additional conceptual designs and implementation steps of BIS should ensure implementation of the target system as quickly as possible (see JOST 1993b, pp. 175-177; WILDEMANN 1987, pp. 144-145).

The following issues should be addressed in the implementation strategy: the

- ❑ Time of implementation, the
- ❑ Type of implementation (continuous, step by step or ad hoc),
- ❑ Scope and time of purchasing the standard software (and hardware, if necessary), the
- ❑ „Direction of diffusion" (how to " spread" the software into the enterprise)
- ❑ Integrating the standard software with the existing environment,
- ❑ Organizational and personnel requirements

(see WILDEMANN 1987, p. 144).

Implementation strategies should be company specific. Due to generally differing initial situations, enterprise independent implementation strategies are not feasible (see JOST 1993b, p. 177).

Implementation strategies should be defined with an adjustable time schedule, to be able to react to changing guidelines. These "rolling" plans are necessary because of the duration of implementations (see JOST 1993b, p. 177; ÖSTERLE 1990a, p. 9). Implementation strategies must interface with project management which sets the framework for the structure and time schedule of the project.

3.6.2 Procedure

Implementation strategies are established in **three steps:**

❑ Determining the guideline of the application software,
❑ Prioritizing sub-processes and
❑ Scheduling implementation tasks for the sub-processes.

Initially, an **application software guideline** must be defined, determining which application software product will be used in the future. This includes the new (selected) standard software, but also additional software solutions or already implemented software.
We must define

❑ Which existing application software product will continue to be used and
❑ Which additional software will be implemented.

Thus, we must take

❑ Standard software products and
❑ Necessary individual software development

into account.
In order to define the application software guideline, one should first determine whether the existing software should still be used. This mainly affects sub-processes only minimally supported by the new standard software, if at all. One should ascertain whether the new software supports these sub-processes and whether the old applications are still suitable for use.

This is accomplished by studying the old software product's

❑ Micro-suitability, determining whether its functionality, efficiency and reliability are sufficient to support individual functions, and its
❑ Macro-suitability, determining whether it makes business sense to link the old software with the entire business process (via interfaces) and

❑ Future market prospects, pertaining to its software concept (such as the programming languages it uses) and its manufacturer

(see WATTEROTT 1993, pp. 93-96). When implementing standard application suites like SAP /3, linking third party applications is frequently quite complex. Thus, third party systems (either bought-in or in-house developed) are frequently not macro-suitable (see SCHEER 1990c, p. 142).

The software to be implemented must be defined. This is carried out by allocating specific standard software products or modules (according to the definition of the scope of the standard software deployment) or individual third party applications for the sub-processes in question. If need be, general application software specification (without mentioning a specific brand name of the software such as "sales information systems") must be used, which can then be specified at a later time.

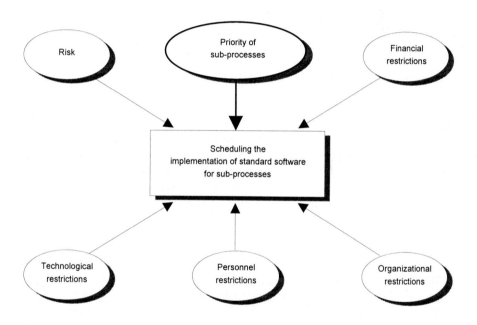

Fig. 3.26: Influencing factors for scheduling implementation tasks

In preparation for scheduling further implementation tasks, **sub-processes** should be **prioritized** as to their contribution in achieving the goal. The contribution of each sub-process for the target system should be defined. Its potential usefulness, as determined in the as-is analysis, can be rated, although subjective evaluation of management and other experts are also necessary. Sub-processes must be examined individually and in the context of the entire process.

Determining priorities of the target system ensures that the effects of BIS regarding the company's competitive edge will schedule the time-frame of successive implementation tasks. **Executing strategic goals** is **key**, which in turn drives the implementation schedule. Based on personal experience of the author, not every sub-process is assigned different priorities. Moreover, there are "priority groups", in which the individual sub-processes can be sequenced, according to additional criteria.

The last step is to **schedule** successive implementation activities. In addition to prioritizing sub-processes, the following influential factors should be considered:

❑ The risk of not reaching certain goals,

❑ Financial restrictions, such as for purchasing the necessary software or hardware enhancements,
❑ Technological restrictions, such as availability of standard software modules,
❑ Personnel restrictions, i.e., taking quantitative and qualitative availability of human resources into account, and
❑ Organizational restrictions, such as guidelines delaying or preventing process oriented integration of departments. For example, carrying out business processes in various subsidiaries of an enterprise, where each subsidiary has a different owner with his own personal agenda

(see JOST 1993, pp. 179-187; NEU 1991, pp. 213-216). The influencing factors mentioned above are illustrated in Fig. 3.26.

Using these influencing factors and taking the priorities for individual sub-processes into account, the **earliest starting time** for successive phases of BIS can be defined. Due to multiple influencing factors, allocating sub-processes and **execution periods** is highly complex (see NEU 1991, p. 219; KÖLLE 1990, p. 47). One should differentiate between the time necessary to

❑ Establish the standard software based BPO concept and to
❑ Implement BPO.

The **minimum time required** to design a sub-process according to the standard software is a result of the time required to detail the information models. Ideally, the necessary implementation measures (e.g., technical activities, like customizing) can be carried out simultaneously. Estimates are made based on the standard software reference model. The excerpt of the reference model must be analyzed and, if necessary, adapted to suit company specifics. The **maximum time required** is determined by the urgency of the optimization measures, i.e., their influence on the competitive edge of the company. Actual duration incorporates the mentioned influencing factors with the previous schedule.

Indicators regarding a realistic assessment of implementation periods are available from the experience gained from implementing appropriate standard software products. The following implementation periods have been compiled, based on personal experience of the author in five different implementation projects with SAP R/2 and SAP R/3 software in multiple vertical markets and in companies with a staff of 1,000 to 6,000 employees, and according to reports on similar projects (see GERBECKS 1994, p. 13; LAMETER 1994, p. 12; SCHRÖDER 1994; STAMP 1994). These are valid for the business processes mentioned above and for sub-processes (for a team or object group, respectively, of five persons, working on the implementation full-time):

❑ Customer order processing and shipping: 8 - 15 months
❑ Manufacturing program and material requirements planning: 12 - 18 months,
❑ External procurement: 6 - 10 months,
❑ Warehouse management: 6 - 10 months,
❑ Time and capacity planning: 12 - 24 months,
❑ Production order release and processing: 12 - 18 months,
❑ Maintenance: 6 - 8 months,
❑ Customer service 10 - 15 months,
❑ Work scheduling: 3 - 6 months,
❑ Financial accounting and assets accounting: 3 - 6 months,
❑ Cost accounting / performance analysis; controlling: 8 - 15 months and
❑ Human resources: 8 - 12 months.

The substantial variances demonstrate the substantial effect of various enterprise and vertical market specific issues. These figures can be fine-tuned by consultancies and software companies in specific implementation projects, where company specific characteristics, such as product standardization, product structure or manufacturing type, are a given (see JOST 1993, p. 37).

Continuous, step by step or ad hoc implementation of standard software in the company divisions leads to simultaneous or sequential implementation periods for each sub-process in the business process. The type of implementation is detailed in the migration plan which will be defined in the next BIS phase.
Scheduled implementation tasks

❑ Provide indicators regarding the appropriate time of purchase of the standard software, depending on the implementation of the sub-processes,
❑ Provide the necessary information regarding integration of the new standard software with the existing IS environment,
❑ Determine the "direction of diffusion" of the standard software, depending on the implementation of the sub-processes,
❑ Determine general requirements for the necessary hardware and
❑ Provide information regarding qualitative and quantitative personnel requirements
(see NEU 1991, pp. 192-211).

If the **influencing factors** of the implementation strategy are changed, the individual steps should be examined to see if any modifications are necessary. Modifications can pertain to prioritization, software guidelines or scheduling. If the target system needs to be adapted to a changing competitive situation, the prioritization of the sub-processes must be modified, also. Releasing new standard software modules can require a corresponding modification of the standard software guidelines. A shift in the release plan of the software vendor or funding issues at the end user company can require a modification of the schedule.

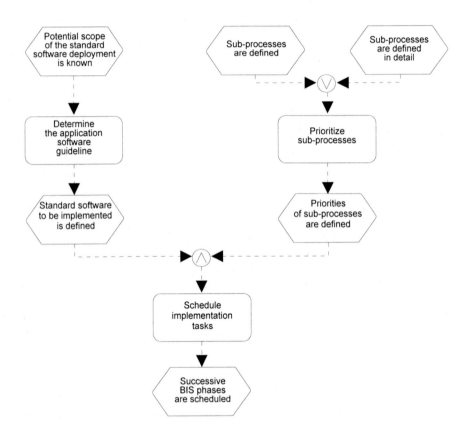

Fig.. 3.27: Procedure for establishing an implementation strategy

The procedure for establishing an implementation strategy is illustrated in Fig. 3.27.

3.6.3 Supporting Methods and IT Tools

Application system guidelines are created by allocating the application software to the corresponding sub-processes. **Illustrating** them in **tables** is sufficient. With today's trend toward implementing entire standard application suites (see BRENNER 1990, p. 10; SCHEER 1990c, p. 142), the various modules of a particular software vendor are frequently used to support a sub-process. **Application software details** can be **allocated** to the **sub-processes** by using the **ARIS Toolset** (see KIRSCH 1994, p. 4.1.-9 - 4.1.-16). This ensures access to all the information in the Toolset that is relevant to the process.

Short name of the sub-process	Applications system
Customer order processing (compressors)	SD, PS
Customer order processing (dryer)	SD
MRP (in-house / bought-in parts)	MM, PP
Production order processing (parts, assemblies)	PP, MM
Production order processing (compressors)	PP, QM, MM, SD
Production order processing (dryer)	PP, QM, MM, SD

Fig. 3.28: Example of application system guidelines

Fig. 3.28 illustrates an example of an excerpt of the application system guidelines in a mechanical engineering company with a staff of approx. 2,000 employees. SAP R/3 modules are allocated to the sub-processes.

Sub-processes can be prioritized by means of an effectivity analysis (see HEINRICH 1994, p. 162-173). In this context, the

❑ Individual goals of the target system are evaluated, the
❑ Sub-processes are evaluated according to their significance for achieving the goal, then the
❑ Effectivity values are calculated

(see JOST 1993b, pp. 177-179). Sufficient evaluation can be achieved even without formal methods because, based on the experience of the author, management drives desired developments by setting priorities. This is also true with regard to financial, personnel, organizational restrictions and risk assessment. Technological restrictions, such as availability of individual software modules, are communicated by the standard software vendor.

Scheduled implementation tasks can be illustrated in **tables** or **Gantt charts** (see PAGE-JONES 1991, pp. 91-94). Fig. 3.29 depicts an excerpt of scheduled implementation tasks regarding sub-processes of a mechanical engineering company with a staff of 2,000 employees. Each sub-process differentiates between the tasks of standard software based BPO concept and BPO implementation. The application software systems or modules are depicted in the application system guidelines.

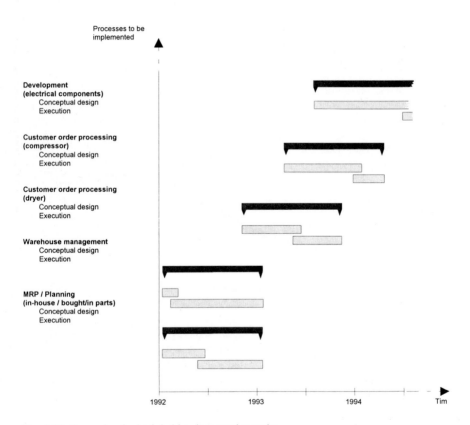

Fig. 3.29: Example of scheduled implementation tasks

Special IT tool support is not required to create application system guidelines or carry out an efficiency analysis. IS supported documentation, such as a word processing system and a spreadsheet program, would be useful for editing purposes. Scheduling should be done using a project management system (see MICROSOFT 1992), enabling detailing of the implementation tasks at a later point in time.

4 Standard Software Based BPO Concept

Standard software based BPO concepts **detail** the strategy based BPO concept **according to** the requirements definition (business concept) of the **standard software**. This creates a business goal oriented framework for the business process design and implementation based on the standard software. The sub-processes are processed according to the implementation strategy.

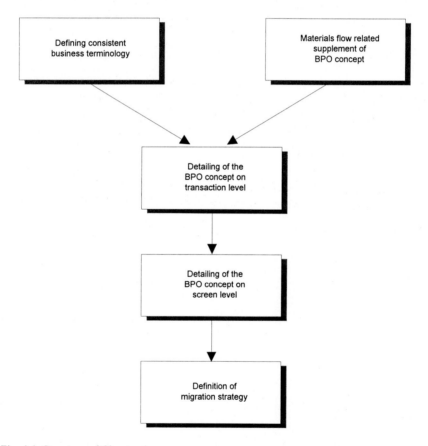

Fig. 4.1: Structure of Chapter 4

The **detail models** resulting from the standard software based BPO concept are sufficiently **specific** to be implemented by means of the **standard software**. However, they are still positioned on the requirements definition (business concept) level of the ARIS Architecture because IS design and/or implementation issues are less significant, if not totally irrelevant in that phase of BIS. It is immaterial whether the standard software is split up into individual modules or with which programming language the software was designed. The **degree in which** the standard software based BPO concept is **detailed** correlates to the structure of the business contents of the **standard software**. These business contents of the standard software are classified in transactions and in individual dialog steps characterized by screens (see SCHEER 1994a, p. 61). Thus, there are two detail levels in the standard software based BPO concept: the **transactional level** and the **screen level.**

The standard software based BPO concept is comparable to the target concept approach of SAP for implementing standard software (see KELLER, MEINHARDT 1994a, p. 26). The BPO concept however ensures systematic implementation of the strategic goals, which is not the case with the SAP approach.

The standard software based BPO concept consists of **five steps**:

❑ Defining consistent, enterprise-wide business terminology,
❑ Supplementing the BPO concept with material flow information,
❑ Detailing the BPO concept on the transactional level,
❑ Detailing the BPO concept on the screen level and
❑ Defining the migration plan.

The respective goal and procedure, as well as method and IT tool support (if applicable) must be defined for each step of the standard software based BPO concept.

The structure of Chapter Four is depicted in Fig. 4.1.

4.1 Defining Consistent Business Terminology

Step One in establishing a software based BPO concept is to define a consistent business terminology.

4.1.1 Goal

The goal of defining a consistent business terminology is to define **enterprise-wide business terms**. Simplifying communication within the enterprise and beyond, this "common language" simplifies successive conceptual design and implementation activities, as well as operational processing of business processes after going live with the standard software

The business terminology required by the standard software lays the groundwork for business term definitions. It replaces various company specific synonyms, homonyms, overlapping of and deviations from existing terms (see ENDL, FRITZ 1992, p. 39). Implementing standard software systematically standardizes the terms used in the company. Using these business terms has the following effect:

❑ Understanding the business contents of the standard software becomes easier,
❑ Communication with the standard software vendor is simplified,
❑ Misinterpretations within the company -- and between the company and its partners (customers or suppliers) – can be avoided,
❑ Time-consuming, frequent discussions regarding company specific business term definitions are reduced.

Business terminology should be sufficiently formalized to ensure efficient and effective dissemination around the enterprise, although the degree of formalization of the business term model should be low enough to enable quick comprehension of the modeling method and, thus, of the terminology per se. On the other hand, the representation of terms should be sufficiently formalized to avoid misinterpretations, making it unnecessary to scrutinize verbal descriptions.

The relationships between business terms in the new standard software and current company specific terms should be specifically addressed to properly position the new terms.

4.1.2 Procedure

Consistent business terminology is defined in **three steps**:

❑ Determining standard software based business terms,
❑ Supplementing the relationships between the business terms,
❑ Allocating company specific terms.

The terms are defined for business processes or sub-processes to be implemented according to the implementation strategy are defined. Based on the business process oriented approach of the BIS, step by step the terms are defined for every area of the enterprise.

The business terms to be examined refer to the information objects in the business processes. Therefore, the business term models should be positioned in the **data view** of the ARIS Architecture.

The first step in defining consistent business term definitions is to **determine** relevant standard software based **business terms**. This is based on the allocation of software modules to corresponding sub-processes, one of the tasks in the development of the implementation strategy. The business terms relevant for these modules can be defined by a

❑ Standard software reference model containing a business term model or data model, or by
❑ Standard software product descriptions, such as product documentation.

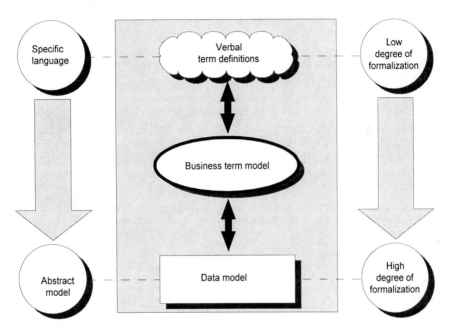

Fig. 4.2: Positioning the business term model

If the business terms are not self-explanatory, they must be defined in detail. If business term models have already been established for other sub-processes by means of BIS, the new terms need only be supplemented or existing definitions expanded, respectively.

The **business terms** are put into **relation** with one another. This is also done by means of the standard software reference model or the product description, leading to the **business term model**.

Experience gained in various modeling and standard software implementation projects indicates that, in order to transparently illustrate the business links relevant to users, it is sufficient to show the existence of a relationship between two objects. It is usually not necessary to specify relationships in detail, as in a data model, the main reason for this being that business terms are generally abstracted much less than data elements in a data model. For example, the "manufacturing order" or "customer order" business terms are used, although the abstract term "order" could be included in the data model. Business term models are **more specified** and **less formalized** than data models. Yet they structure business reality in a more abstract and formalized way than purely verbal term definitions (see Fig. 4.2).

Existing **company specific business terms** are now allocated to the terms of the business term model. This connects the standard software based common terminology, still to be implemented, with the as-is situation, facilitating migration at a later point in time from the as-is to the target situation.

The allocation between as-is and target business terms does not need to be unique. An as-is business term can be allocated to multiple standard software terms and vice versa (see Fig. 4.3). Unique allocations can lead to differences in contents, which in turn can be included in the definitions of the terms. For example, the terms "manufacturing order" or "work order", used synonymously in the as-is situation, can be allocated to the standard software business term

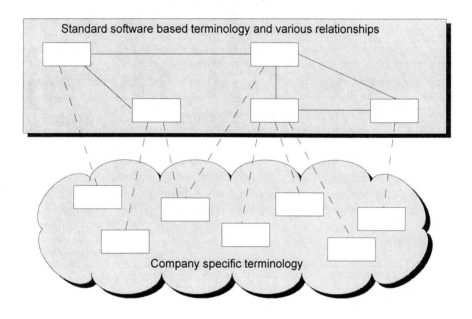

Fig. 4.3: Allocating company specific business terms to standard software based business terms

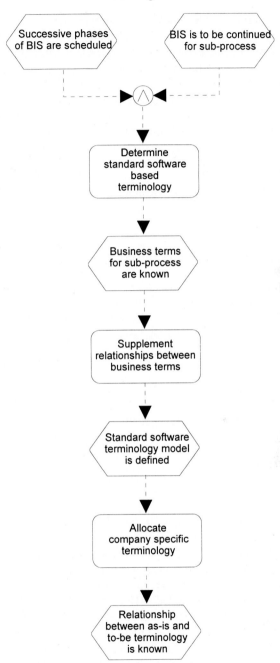

Fig. 4.4: Procedure for defining a consistent enterprise-wide business terminology

"manufacturing order". The as-is term "customer order" can be split up in the standard software based terms "scheduled order" (for products to be delivered from the manufacturer to the customer by a certain date) and the term "third-party order" (products of manufacturer A to be delivered to the customer via manufacturer B).

As-is business terms should not be allocated to standard software based business terms until the relationships between the standard software terms have been supplemented. Relationship details make target terms easier to understand, facilitating efficient allocation of the as-is terms.

The procedure for defining consistent business term definitions is illustrated in Fig. 4.4.

4.1.3 Supporting Methods and IT Tools

Business term definitions can be represented in special **business term models**. Business terms can be linked to one another and classified in a hierarchy (see KIRSCH 1994, p. 4.2.-24 - 4.2.-25). Detailed definitions should be attached to the various terms. Fig. 4.5 depicts the symbols illustrating business term models. Business terms models can be elaborated within the ARIS Toolset.

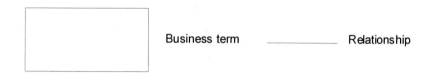

Fig. 4.5: Symbols for illustrating business term models

An excerpt of the business term model in a SAP R/3 based "Material requirements planning" sub-process of a company in the mechanical engineering industry is depicted in Fig. 4.6. A planned order refers to actual requirements for materials. If a planned order refers to bought-in parts, it leads to a purchase order request; if not, it leads to a production order. The material requested by the manufacturing order is reserved. This reservation can refer to other manufacturing orders if manufacturing orders are still open for these materials. Otherwise, it will refer to purchase orders (for bought-in parts). The purchase order results from a purchase order request. The term "production order" replaces company specific terms, such as "manufacturing order", "assembly order" or "work order". This avoids current differentiation between production orders. The company specific term "order" is defined very generally, since it means both "purchase order request" and the actual "purchase order". This is where more differentiated business terms will be used at a later point in time. There are no synonyms for the business terms "planned order" and "reservation".

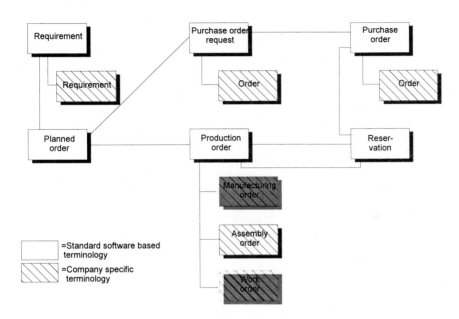

Fig. 4.6: Example of a business term model

4.2 Material Flow Related Supplement of the BPO Concept

Step Two in establishing a standard software based BPO concept is to supplement the BPO concept with material flow information. This is especially important for the implementation of "post ERP" systems, such as SCM) systems.

4.2.1 Goal

The goal of supplementing the BPO concept with material flow information is to systematically include in BIS **requirements** for designing business processes, resulting from the correlation between **material flow** and **information flow**. This results in reconciling material flow and information flow, ensuring across-the-board optimization of the business processes, while current or planned material flow conditions are met. The close link between material flow and information flow in industrial enterprises makes it necessary in BIS to examine both of these aspects, in order to design the business processes called for by the target system (see BECKER, ROSEMANN 1993, pp. 33-36; WILDEMANN 1990, pp. 95-99). In this context, the

❑ Requirements of material flow regarding the new information systems should be taken into account, as well as the
❑ Functionality provided by the standard software for optimizing material flow.

Planning for and implementing material flow are not the focus of BIS.
The BPO concept should be supplemented regarding

❑ Improvement of the existing material flow,
❑ Material flow planning to enhance existing buildings and office space and
❑ Material flow planning for the construction of new office space

(see VDI 1978, p. 2). We will integrate strategic enterprise planning, BIS and material flow planning.

4.2.2 Procedure

Supplementing the BPO concept with material flow information consists of **three steps**:

❑ Determining the significance of material flow for the particular business process
❑ Defining guidelines for material flow planning and
❑ Defining guidelines for the implementation of standard software.

Initially, it must be determined whether examining **material flow** is **relevant** for a particular business process. This is the case in all processes directly or indirectly influencing the area of **logistics**. Logistics include:

❑ Procurement logistics,
❑ Manufacturing logistics,
❑ Distribution logistics and
❑ Waste management logistics

(see BECKER, ROSEMANN 1993, pp. 2-4). In these areas, material flow is the focal point of the process.
The new standard software focuses on illustrating and controlling the material flow (see SCHEER 1990a, p. 2-3). This encompasses

❑ Production planning and control, including order management, material and capacity management, manufacturing control and shipping management,
❑ Research and Development, where the "objects" of material flow are defined and the
❑ Execution of manufacturing functions, such as warehouse, transportation or assembly management,

(see BECKER, ROSEMANN 1993, p. 37).
If a business process is included in these functional areas, the scope of reconciling material and information flow must be defined. This should be carried out by means of examining the information flow from the perspective of material flow and vice versa (see BECKER, ROSEMANN 1993, pp. 36-37). The following are typical requirements of material flow regarding corresponding information systems, such as

❑ Including suppliers in the information cycle (for example, just-in time concepts) to reduce the depth of manufacturing,
❑ Integrating suppliers to reduce the depth of development,
❑ Replacing pure inventory management by flexible information and movement management,
❑ Supporting material turnover by means of indicators, the creation of logistical units and modeling the data and relationships in these units,
❑ Consistent support of warehouse management,
❑ Giving information as great a "head start" as possible vs. material flow, increasing planning leeway within distribution logistics,
❑ Implementing communication technology in the entire logistical chain between the supplier and the customer (for example, by implementing a status tracking system),
❑ Actively taking into account all waste management aspects during the entire manufacturing process of the product, especially regarding by-products resulting from manufacturing or consumption of the products,
❑ An IS link between waste management logistics and the remaining logistics sub-systems

(see BECKER, ROSEMANN 1993, pp. 53-160).

The following are examples of material flow relevant aspects of information systems:

❑ Supplementing logistical attributes (such as the weight of parts) of existing data and creating master data for logistical resources,
❑ Deploying a classification system for parts,

❏ Synchronizing material flow and information flow by deploying identification systems (such as bar codes),
❏ Using effective planning models for production planning and control (simultaneous planning models, MRPII concepts, retrograde scheduling, load oriented plant control systems OPT, electronic production scheduling systems, Kanban, cumulative quantity concepts),
❏ Implementing PPC methods for individual vertical markets (for example, in the furniture industry, route planning, followed by production planning),
❏ Taking logistical aspects into account, synchronous with product design,
❏ Integrating logistical processes in the development of routings and other manufacturing preparation activities, creating an appropriate data foundation for planning and controlling logistics (such as splitting up or overlapping manufacturing processes),
❏ Deploying CAM functions (manufacturing, assembly, warehouse and transportation control systems) and
❏ Implementing special organization forms, such as manufacturing islands

(see BECKER, ROSEMANN 1993, pp. 159-259).
The significance of these aspects regarding the reconciling of material and information flow can be determined by

❏ Material flow analysis or planning, respectively, or by the
❏ Strategy based BPO concept.

Based on this, one can determine whether and where material and information flows should be reconciled. If more information is required, representative products and parts will have to be physically traced along the entire logistical chain (see SCHULTE 1991, pp. 123-149).

If it becomes necessary to reconcile material and information flow, the necessary **guidelines** for **material flow planning** must be planned. Thus, material flow planning must make use of the possibilities offered by future deployment of standard software with the goal of optimizing material flow.

Strategically significant guidelines are adapted from the information models of the strategy based BPO concept. Indicators regarding additional guidelines for material flow planning derive from the reference model of the standard software or appropriate standard software product descriptions. Guidelines can be specified when the business processes are detailed according to the standard software at a later point in time. However, it is necessary to obtain indicators regarding material flow related changes as soon as possible, in order to take appropriate physical measures. For example, these can be the implementation of transportation systems, changes in the plant layout or negotiations with business partners (customers or suppliers), to be implemented before going live with the standard software. Detailed information models are generally not necessary.

Material flow **guidelines** for **implementing the standard software** must also be defined. To this end, the material flow requirements regarding the appropriate information systems must be defined. They are determined by current material flow analysis or planning, respectively, or by studying the flow of representative parts or products.

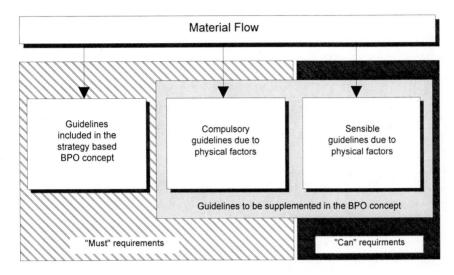

Fig. 4.7: Requirements of material flow when implementing standard software

Guidelines are drafted as **information models**, such as process, organizational, function or data models. This supplements the detail models designed in the strategy based BPO concept, providing they are not strategically important issues already included in the BPO concept.

When supplementing the BPO concept, there are

❑ Compulsory guidelines ("must" requirements) due to physical factors, or
❑ Desirable, but not necessarily compulsory requirements ("can" requirements).

"Must" and "can" requirements for implementing standard software are supplemented in the BPO concept. For example, lack of storage space for bulky metal parts can lead to a definite need for just-in-time delivery. Storing small parts that are continually needed for the final assembly stage of production, near the assembly line, can be sensible, but are not necessarily compulsory. Fig. 4.7 depicts what is necessary for material flow when implementing standard software. The procedure of supplementing the BPO concept according to material flow is depicted in Fig. 4.8.

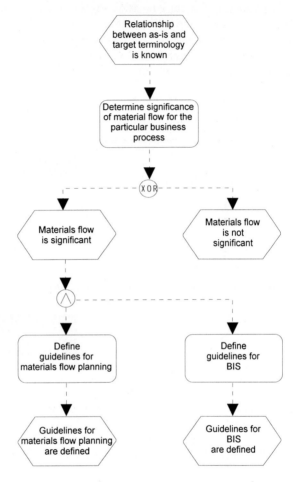

Fig 4.8: Procedure for supplementing the BPO concept according to material flow

4.2.3 Supporting Methods and IT Tools

There are many different ways to illustrate material flow. They can be classified in

❑ Two-dimensional models (process plans, flow charts or actual illustrations, as in blueprints),
❑ Three-dimensional illustrations (analogous, multi-layered, moving or scale models) and

❑ Mathematical illustrations (equations, matrices or mathematical models)
(see VDI 1975). These methods are used in material flow analysis and planning.
Although they contain significant information regarding the implementation of
standard software, they will not be described here in great detail because they are
not actively used in BIS.

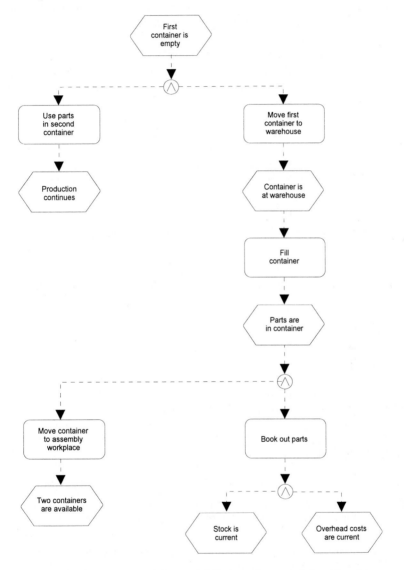

Fig. 4.9: Example of a process model, material flow requirements being taken into account

Information models describing guidelines for information systems to be designed in BIS can be illustrated by the methods used to establish the strategy based BPO concept for process, organization, function and data modeling. The models are designed with the ARIS Toolset, ensuring efficient reusability.

Requirements for material flow planning (such as necessary negotiations with suppliers or construction) can sometimes be phrased verbally. Guidelines are transformed into appropriate models during material flow planning.

Fig. 4.9 depicts an excerpt of the "Supplying continually used parts for assembly" process model of a company in the mechanical engineering industry. In the assembly area, there are two containers for all the frequently used parts. As soon as one of them is empty, it is refilled in the warehouse. The use of these parts is booked as consumption. This method makes it easier to provide the necessary parts because it is not necessary to remove, book and move every single part to the workplace in a certain sequence. However, during product costing analysis, this method does result in imprecise figures. This is due to the fact that it is not possible to allocate individual parts to certain orders. For further processing, the process model is included in the software based BPO model.

4.3 Detailing the BPO Concept on the Transactional Level

The next step in establishing a standard software based BPO concept is to detail the existing BPO concept on the transactional level of the software.

4.3.1 Goal

The goal of this BIS step is to **detail** the information models of the **business processes**, based on the requirements definition (business concept) of the **standard software**. The degree of detailing is a result of the structure of the standard software **transactions**. A transaction is a continuous sequence of individual user dialog steps within the software, necessary to supplement a task. Transactions classify the business administration contents of standard software (see SCHEER 1994a, p. 61).

The **strategic focus** of detailing must be ensured by taking significant detail models of the strategy based BPO concept into account. The resulting detail information models are designed to be transformed in the new **standard software**. Alternatively, one must define where supporting IT or organizational measures (such as developing additional modules or carrying out procedures manually) are necessary. These information models are the cornerstone for defining specific execution measures.

The organizational structure, i.e., **hierarchical and process organizations,** derives from the information models. The particular requirements of the function level concept must be taken into account.

4.3.2 Procedure

The BPO concept is detailed in four **steps**:

❑ Modeling process relevant objects according to the standard software,
❑ Modeling other data structures according to the standard software,
❑ Standard software based detailing of process models,
❑ Hierarchical organizational positioning of the processes.

The cornerstone of detailing the strategy based BPO concept is the **standard software reference model**. The standard software process model plays a major role, although data, function and organizational models are also necessary. Due to the fact that these reference models describe the business administration contents of the standard software, they must conform to the detailing predetermined by the software transactions. The degree of detailing must at least be on the transactional level, ensuring documentation of standard work processes. More detailed models can be aggregated on the transactional level.

Obtaining reference models is not regarded as a step within BIS because the models are viewed as part of the software product (i.e., documentation). If reference models are not available, the required models must be established within the BIS. This is done by means of software documentation and by examining the software itself.

Detailing according to software reference models, such as recommended by SAP AG (see KELLER, MEINHARDT 1994a, BANCROF 1996, pp. 36-39), ensures simultaneous detailing and specification of the information models of the strategy based BPO concept. The resulting models describe the future business processes in detail. Yet they can also be implemented by the standard software in question. Linking the specification and detailing processes ensures an efficient and effective procedure.

Step One in detailing the BPO concept is to define the **model** of process relevant **objects** in the **standard software**. They were previously defined in the strategy based BPO concept and partially documented in data models. If the processes or sub-processes to be detailed refer to end products, they are specified by a product model.

The way significant objects are modeled greatly influences the detail processes to be established later. For example, if the end products are modeled in open, variant BOMs, a specific product must be configured with every customer order. This determines the process flow documented in many detail process models.

If the significant **objects** are only named, but not modeled in detail, the model structure is strategically less significant. It is **not a differentiating factor**. For this reason, data structures required by the standard software, such as BOMs or customer order structures, are the cornerstone for modeling the objects. One should examine how to describe the particular objects within the standard data structure of the software. The data models should include as few elements and relations (i.e., we should take the simplest solution to describe the objects (e.g., products) within the standard software as possible. If this is not sufficient, alternatives must be examined. The data model for modeling objects corresponds with the reference data model of the standard software.

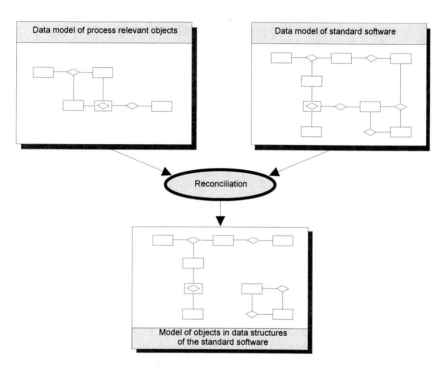

Fig. 4.10: Modeling process relevant objects in the standard software product

By creating a model in the standard software as precisely as possible, **competitive advantages** can be obtained or related material flow can be implemented efficiently - provided a data model of the strategy based BPO concept or the material flow related supplement exists for these **objects**. The model starts with the existing standard software independent data model. Then the functionality of the standard software for modeling the objects is examined, determining the most appropriate one. Thus, excerpts should be selected from the reference data model that describes the objects best, ideally without losing any information value.

End products or assemblies are modeled by using BOM structures of the standard software product. At times, standard BOMs or enhancements, such as non-variable part BOMs, plus-minus BOMs or multiple BOMs (see SCHEER 1994a, pp. 99-125), can be used. For example, additional attributes for describing the objects to be modeled should be included in a classifications system's feature lists. The objects are generally described by multiple or extensive excerpts in the reference data model of the standard software. A model of process relevant objects in the standard software is depicted in Fig. 4.10.

If process relevant objects can not be modeled in the standard software, the product is not suitable for supporting the processes in question. Thus, IT alternatives (such as individual software) or organizational alternatives should be considered.

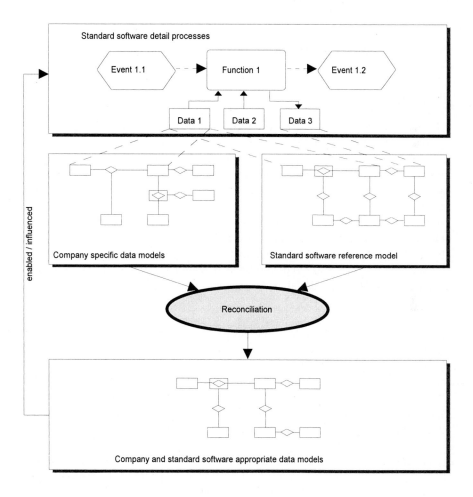

Fig. 4.11: Process related reconciling of data models

Step Two in detailing the BPO concept on the transactional level is to define the **model** of other standard software independent **data structures** in the standard software. Significant excerpts of the standard software reference data model are selected according to the semantic content of the existing data models. As opposed to models for process relevant objects, the data models to be examined can include multiple objects with corresponding relationships (customer and/or manufacturing orders, suppliers, orders, etc.). Standard software independent data models should be reconciled by comparing the semantic contents of the two data models. One should determine whether and how the contents of the company specific model can be modeled by means of the standard software model (see ENDL, FRITZ 1992, pp. 42-43). These **reconciling tasks** are facilitated by the fact that **process related excerpts** of the standard software data model, not entire company data models, are processed. This task is illustrated in Fig. 4.11.

Company specific enhancements of the standard software data model are usually linked to substantial maintenance efforts that are hard to quantify and frequently reoccurring. This is due to the fact that data structures need to be adjusted with every new software release. For this reason, developing standard software appropriate solutions is especially important. If certain aspects of company specific data models can not be modeled, organizational changes are usually preferable to manipulating the standard software. This can lead to appropriate adaptation of the process models in question. For example, if the relationship "manufacturing order to customer order" is not available in the software when standard products are ordered, an appropriate link can be made by interactively specifying the manufacturing orders (such as in comment lines) with the corresponding customer order number.

The next step is **standard software oriented detailing** of the processes defined in the strategy based BPO concept. We should differentiate between processes that are

❑ Not specified in further detail, and those described by
❑ Detail process or function models of the strategy based BPO concept or the material flow related supplement.

In the first case, the processes are **detailed** according to the standard software reference model. In the second case, the reference model and detail information model must be **reconciled**. This situation is illustrated in Fig. 4.12.

In order to **detail** the existing processes, the significant processes or process excerpts in the standard software reference model are determined by means of the appropriate description and functions included within. The **detail processes** of the reference model are **allocated** to the appropriate functions of the general process (coming out of the strategy based BPO concept). Triggering events and final events of the detail processes must correspond to the triggering events of the parent functions. Events and functions of the detail processes no longer necessary are removed, missing elements necessary for the processes, as required by the task to be fulfilled, are supplemented (see JOST, MEINHARDT 1994, pp. 547-548; KIRCHMER 1993, pp. 140-141).

Ideally, it should be possible to allocate exactly one **transaction** of the software to the **function** included in the detail processes. However, if the business administration contents of the standard software are only generally classified by the transactions, this degree of detailing is insufficient to describe the process organizational structure of the processes. In this case, one transaction should be allocated to two or more detail functions.

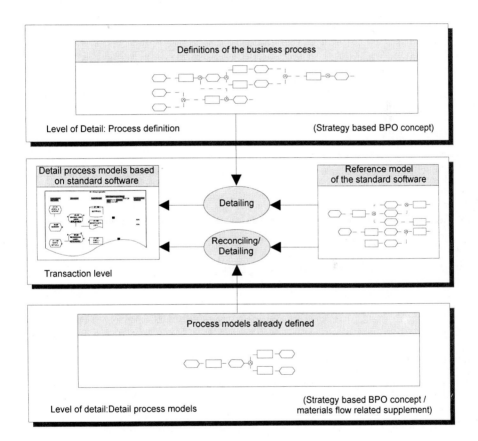

Fig. 4.12: Standard software detailing of the processes

If necessary, the reference model of the standard software should be supplemented. Drawing on practical experience of the author in implementing SAP R/2 and SAP R/3 standard software, one function of the business process definition of the strategy based BPO concept corresponds to approx. 20 - 30 detail functions on the transactional level. Fig. 4.13 depicts the allocation of general and detail processes.

Supplements in the standard software reference model are potential starting points for developing individual **enhancements** (add-ons) **for standard software**. These add-ons lead to additional development and maintenance efforts. One should therefore examine carefully whether these

❏ Model enhancements might already be implemented in the standard software -
  - or whether they might be available soon and only the corresponding documentation might be missing in the reference model -- or whether
❏ IT support might not be necessary for the supplemented functions, or whether the
❏ Functionality of the software might really need to be enhanced.

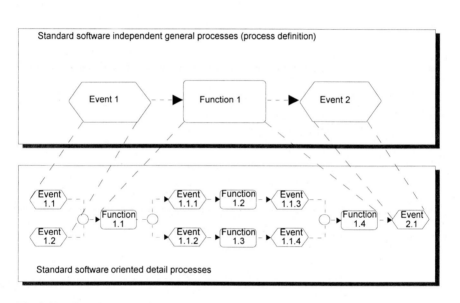

Fig. 4.13: Allocating general processes to detail processes

If possible, one should avoid defining software add-ons due to the additional effort resulting from it.

If **detail process** or **function models** for functions of the business process definitions are defined independently of the particular software application, they must be **reconciled** with the standard software reference model. To this end, individual functions and corresponding events of the independent models must be compared with corresponding elements in the reference model. This generally requires more detailed descriptions of the elements to be compared, due to the fact that different short names can be allocated to the same contents -- or vice versa. The use of business term models is useful here.

Software add-ons will probably have to be defined when detail processes with "must" requirements of the strategy based BPO concept or of material flow related supplements of the BPO concept are reconciled. This is due to the fact that corresponding functions -- or the process logic linked with them -- are compulsory.

These detail process models describe functions and their process logic. In order to simplify implementing these processes, additional information is supplemented. For every function, central **input** and **output data** are listed in aggregated form (data clusters). The degree of aggregation results from the degree to which the functions are detailed. Including these data further specifies the contents of the functions. The details can be taken from the reference model (see KELLER, MEINHARDT 1994a, p. 31), but can also be supplemented according to company specifics. Elements of the business term model are commonly used to name or describe the information objects.

Data objects are further characterized by central attributes. In BIS, at a minimum, the **archiving times** and the management of **historical data** should be defined. This defines topics, such as how long transactional data should be stored after being completely processed (for example, a closed customer order), or whether frequent change states of basic data or transactional data should be documented in a history (such as different change states of BOMs).

Including the names of **standard software transactions** (for example, system commands in live operations) as an attribute of the corresponding functions also simplifies implementation of the processes. These function attributes link the process model and subsequent deployment of the software. In participative implementations, transaction details support early system tests. This is also useful when deploying models in training classes. For standard software functions, transaction names should also derive from the reference model (see KELLER, MEINHARDT 1994a, p. 7). In functions to be supplemented in the software reference model, transactions should be defined according to company specifics, or be omitted totally (such as when functions are executed manually).

Supplementing the **type of processing** (interactive, automatic, manual) in the individual functions simplifies the characterization of the work processes and thus simplifies implementing the processes (designing work places, human resources,...).

Process type and transactions are IT attributes of business administration functions. The resulting process models must still be allocated to the requirements definition (business concept) level of the ARIS Architecture because the business administration design of the business processes is the driving factor, not the IT structure of the standard software.

Step Four of detailing the BPO concept on the transactional level entails **hierarchy organizational positioning** of standard software processes. According to the relationship between detail processes and the general processes of the strategy based BPO concept, this is followed by positioning the detailed processes in the **function level model**. This results in allocation of the processes to one or more organizational levels. The processes are positioned within the planned structure of the enterprise.

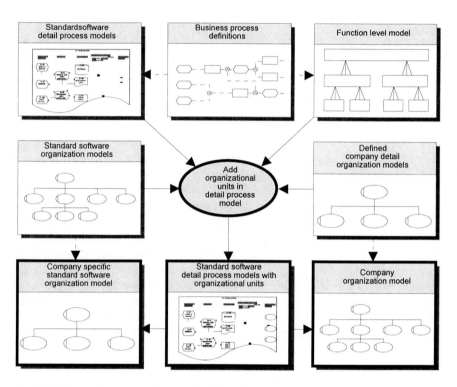

Fig. 4.14: Hierarchy organizational embedding of processes

Positioning detail processes in the function level model indicates whether a process is carried out more than once (such as in various regionals sales offices). If this is the case, a standard software based process model can be designed for one particular situation, such as a company site, and then deployed in other applications as a **company specific reference model**. Thus, special requirements of various company sites, such as country specifics, are supplemented and enterprise-wide process steps remain valid. This increases the efficiency of the procedure.

If **detail organization models** exist for the function levels in question, organizational units should be allocated to the standard software processes. Otherwise, appropriate organizational units are defined according to the processes and are supplemented in the detail process model. From case to case, existing organizational units describe in the as-is organizational model, can be

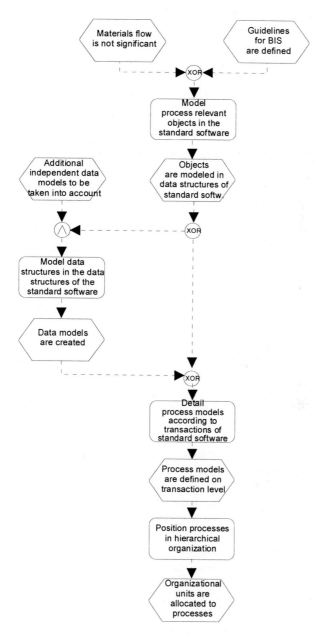

Fig. 4.15: Procedure for detailing the BPO concept on the transactional level

used. This is possible if the tasks of the units conform to the processes in question or can be modified accordingly.

The resulting process models include all the information system views: organization, functions and data, as well as their links with one another. This is the maximum scope of the models in the control view of the ARIS Architecture (see SCHEER 1990b, pp. 129-134). The organizational units in this process can be summarized in a **process oriented enterprise organizational model**. Thus, the hierarchical organization derives from the process structure, resulting in business process oriented organizational structures.

The necessary **user authorization** for employees of these organizational units is created by allocating the organizational units to the functions of the detail processes, to input / output data and to the corresponding transactions of the standard software. Access methods (create, display, update) are supplemented as attributes of these authorizations. One should examine whether it is possible to model authorizations by using the software documentation. If access to certain data objects must be defined in more detail, this is done while detailing the BPO concept on the screen level.

Hierarchy organizational embedding of the detail processes is depicted in Fig. 4.14.

The procedure for detailing the BPO concept on the transactional level is illustrated in Fig. 4.15.

Appropriate **standard software organizational units** should be determined for the functions of the detail process model resulting from the standard software reference model. These organizational units enable modeling of the enterprise hierarchical organization and the allocated work processes in the standard software. The various types of software organizational units (such as plan, company code or divisions in the SAP R/3 software), as well as functions and data to be allocated, result from the standard software reference model (see KELLER, MEINHARDT 1994a, p. 31). The relationship between the standard software based process model (with the company specific organizational units) and the standard software organizational model shows how to model organizational decentralization and centralization measures in standard software (and with that configure the software accordingly). The standard software organizational units should be designed to support the centralization or decentralization processes of the company as well as possible: At a minimum, they must not impede them. This results in a company specific standard software organization model containing the specific characteristics of the types of organizational units in the software.

The standard software organizational structure can support the planned enterprise hierarchical organization more or less. For example, if organizational units are to independently carry out release orders to suppliers, modeling separate standard software organizational units could avoid the risk of orders potentially influencing one another (such as grouping orders of different organizational units). Employees would neither be able to display nor change orders not pertaining to them. If it is not possible to model this situation in the standard software, then the desired effect would have to be achieved by organizational means, without the support of the standard software. **Errors in defining the standard software organizational units** have potentially **far-reaching** consequences because they influence multiple functions and data elements.

The BPO concept on the transactional level can be established by having the respective employees participate. It is also possible to utilize this concept to effectively keep users informed after the design is done. Thus, it supports the participative and the gate keeping approaches of implementing standard software. The gate keeping approach can be utilized whenever early involvement of the employees is not expected to result in increased efficiency or effectivity, such as when designing a prototype or when skill levels of potential employees are very low.

4.3.3 Supporting Methods and IT Tools

In order to illustrate the detail information models on the transactional level, the methods shown in the BPO concept for the organizational and data views can be used.

The process models of the control view on the transactional level differ from the models of the strategy based BPO concept by a higher degree of complexity. This is due to the fact that all the information system views and their relationships are taken into account. This can be illustrated in the **process chain diagram (PCD)** (see BERKAU 1991; BROMBACHER 1991, pp. 128-130; SCHEER 1990b, pp. 129-130; SCHEER 1994a, pp. 59-60). Its tabular form (see Fig. 4.16) makes it easier to read than free form techniques. The first two columns describe events and functions according to the EPCs already illustrated. They depict the chronological and logical order of the processes. The third column contains the necessary input and output data. These are shown in the form of data clusters, i.e., in an aggregated illustration. Thus, a data cluster (such as a customer order) can correspond to multiple entities and their relations in an ERM diagram. The next column denotes the medium that keeps the data. This information simplifies the definition of procedures for implementing the processes. For reasons of manageability, in efficient applications, the data and media columns are often grouped together (see KIRCHMER 1993, pp. 139-141). The data cluster name is annotated in the symbol of the medium, resulting in fewer diagram columns and corresponding symbols. However, it also makes methodically correct linking of data models –detailing the data clusters but not the corresponding media -- more difficult. The processing type, next in the process chain diagram, provides information regarding the degree of IT support (interactive, automatic or manual). In the next column, transaction names are listed. Normally in PCDs, the name of the application is listed (see KIRSCH 1994, p. 3.2-3.3). This would not be sufficient for the degree of detail (transactional level) required in this phase of BIS.

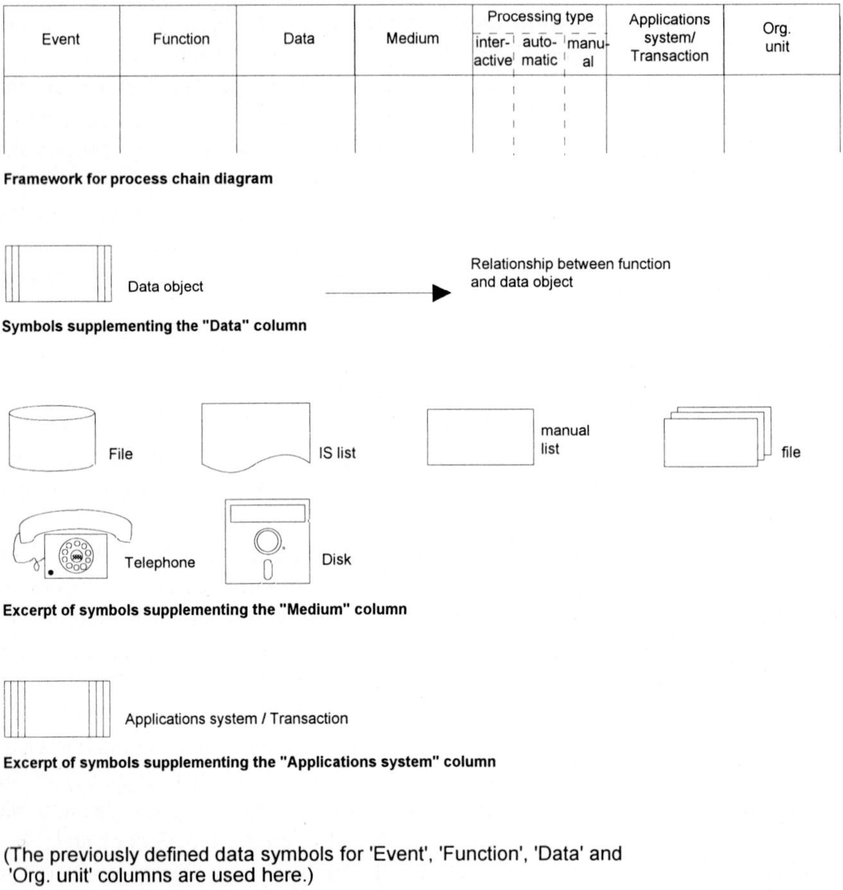

Event	Function	Data	Medium	Processing type			Applications system/ Transaction	Org. unit
				inter-active	auto-matic	manu-al		

Framework for process chain diagram

Data object   Relationship between function and data object

Symbols supplementing the "Data" column

File   IS list   manual list   file

Telephone   Disk

Excerpt of symbols supplementing the "Medium" column

Applications system / Transaction

Excerpt of symbols supplementing the "Applications system" column

(The previously defined data symbols for 'Event', 'Function', 'Data' and 'Org. unit' columns are used here.)

Fig. 4.16: Symbols illustrating process chain diagrams (PCDs)

This is why the PCD illustration is modified. Transaction names and type of description are also attributes of the IS concept level of the ARIS Architecture, simplifying the implementation of modeled work processes. The organizational units executing the functions are listed in the last column. Fig. 4.16 depicts the symbols for illustrating the PCDs.

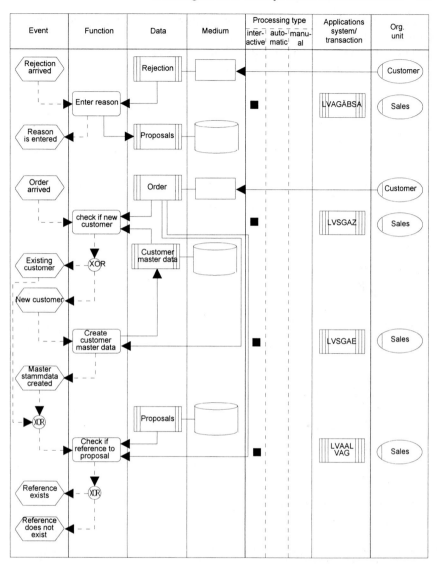

Fig. 4.17: Example of a process model on the transactional level

Fig. 4.17 depicts an excerpt of the "Customer order processing for standard products" detail process of a company in mechanical engineering using the PCD format. The process is based on the reference model of SAP R/3 standard software. Menu paths are listed in the "Transactions" column. Selecting these paths calls up the corresponding standard software transactions. This illustrates the link between the requirements definition (business concept) level and subsequent productive deployment of the software. For every function supported by the standard software there is a definition describing which system command should be selected as a starting point of the procedure.

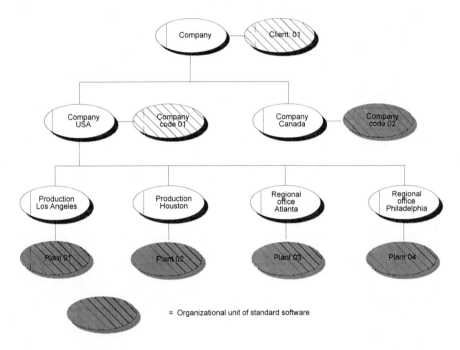

Fig. 4.18:Example of allocating company organizational units to standard software organizational units

Fig. 4.18 depicts an example of the allocation of **companies to standard software organizational units**. This, too, is based on a SAP R/3 project in the mechanical engineering industry. Standard software organizational units and their specifications are listed for every organizational unit in the company. An example of this specification would be whether an organizational unit is modeled as a plant or a warehouse in the SAP system and how to specifically name this unit, such as "Plant 01", the definition being applied according to the appropriate processes. Regional sales offices are modeled as stock locations because the standard software permits separate planning processes without impeding enterprise-wide customer order processing. Orders can be entered locally and then processed further at corporate headquarters. The required information results from the allocation of standard software functions to corresponding organizational units in the SAP R/3 reference model (see KELLER, MEINHARDT 1994a, p. 31), as well as from the allocation of organizational units to the appropriate functions on the function level model.

The PCD illustration can be modeled in the **ARIS Toolset** (see KIRSCH 1994, p. 3.-2 - 3.-3, 4.4.-20 - 4.4.-22). Detailed data models can be allocated to PCD data objects (see IDS 1994c, p. 4.-21 - 4.-22), establishing the relationship between process structures and detailed data structures. The PCD should be linked to parent processes of the strategy based BPO concept. All the models pertaining to a process or sub-process should be grouped by means of the ARIS Toolset, increasing manageability (see IDS 1994c, p. 5.-9 - 5.-13). An example would be "Customer order processing for standard products". Models are differentiated automatically by the ARIS Toolset, according to information system views, i.e., organization, functions, data and processes, and are positioned in the ARIS Architecture.

A key issue in deploying an IT tool in this phase of BIS is the availability of standard software reference models in the same tool environment. If an IT tool is not deployed, the effort of processing models is substantially increased because the information needs to be migrated into the modeling tool. To give a specific product example, ARIS Toolset's "ARIS Analyzer for R/3 (former "R/3 Analyzer")" provides SAP R/3 reference models (see KELLER, MEINHARDT 1994a, p. 5).

Due to the scope of the models, deploying an **IT tool** to design and maintain information models on the transactional level is key. Based on personal experience of the author in three SAP R/3 implementation projects in companies in machine and plant engineering, just to illustrate process models on the transactional level, between 3,000 and 5,000 individual information elements (functions, events, data objects, media, transactions and organizational units) had to be managed. If this had to be managed and maintained manually, this would result in an immense amount of additional effort.

4.4 Detailing the BPO Concept on the Screen Level

We will now detail the BPO concept further. The degree of detailing is defined by the sequences of screens in the standard software.

4.4.1 Goal

The goal of detailing the BPO concept on the screen level is to **increase** the **degree of detailing** in the conceptual design, augmenting the **efficiency** and **effectivity** of the subsequent **implementation**. The degree of detailing is a result of the **dialog steps** within a transaction which walk the user through the business administration task. They are reflected in individual screens representing business administration issues, leading to the term "detailing on the screen level".

Processing a screen, i.e. its display, entering data and executing it, can require several system steps, such as transforming and then storing data (see SCHEER

1994a, p. 61). Since modeling is still carried out on the requirements definition (business concept) level of the AIRS architecture, the system steps in this phase of BIS are not significant.

Detailing on the screen level is the last step in the conceptual design of BIS. After this step, implementation of BIS and thus, of the strategic goals by means of the measures yet to be taken, must be ensured. The **degrees of freedom** in the standard software based BPO concept still available must **decrease** to ensure an implementation according to the strategic goals.

In order to ensure an **efficient** procedure, as few excerpts of the BPO concept as possible should be detailed on the screen level. Every detailing step should be judged as to how useful it is for the implementation of the target system. If the scope of the BPO conceptual design on the screen level is unnecessarily wide, this can lead to substantially increased effort in design and maintenance of the models.

4.4.2 Procedure

The BPO concept on the screen level is detailed in **five steps**:

❑ Defining the model excerpts to be detailed,
❑ Defining the information system views to be detailed,
❑ Detailing the process models on the screen level,
❑ Detailing the data models on the screen level and
❑ Specifying access authorization, archiving times and historical data.

The first step is to **define** the still to be detailed **model excerpts** of the BPO concept on the transactional level. To this end, one should determine for which process steps the

❑ Contents should become more transparent, ensuring their implementation, or the
❑ Degrees of freedom should be limited, ensuring the implementation of the goals.

Both steps are dependent upon the business content of the dialog steps belonging to a transaction. Thus, they should be assessed according to the standard software documentation or by actually deploying the standard software.

Ideally, standard software reference models are used. The scope of these models, which is obviously large, and the substantial amount of effort required for changes (of the entire content of the screens or their process logic) make it unlikely that software vendors will ever provide reference models on this level of detail because this could slow down the development of new standard software products considerably. The author is not aware of any standard software reference models of this level of detail or similar development activities to this effect. For this reason, we will not focus on reference models in detail in the remainder of the activities on screen level.

It is generally necessary to **increase transparency** when dialog steps belonging to a transaction can -- due to their quantity, contents or process logic -- not be implemented by potential users. Each particular process step must be made less complex by further detailing. Whether it needs to be detailed depends on the design of the new standard software and the skill level of the future users. Thus, a decision regarding detailing should be made based on **standard software and company specifics.**

Degrees of freedom (i.e., in detail defined aspects) in models on the transactional level should be **reduced**, if this prevents a system configuration that would be contrary to the target system or impede the actual implementation. The potential content and the process logic of the dialog steps should be examined regarding such issues. It is also important to assess whether access authorization, as defined on the transactional level, is sufficient. It must be clear which users are allowed to create, update, delete and display data. The decision regarding reducing the degrees of freedom is generally **company specific**.

Regarding these aspects, in order to avoid any additional effort, one should carefully examine whether and where processes should be detailed further. If in doubt, detailing should be avoided. Should it become necessary to create detail models on the transactional level in the BPO implementation (such as for training classes), the standard software BPO concept on screen level can be supplemented at this time.

Once the process steps to be detailed on the screen level are determined, the **significant information system views** must be defined. This can require designing

❑ Detail process models or
❑ Detail data models.

If this affects functions or process logic of the dialog steps, more detailed **process models** must be designed. Function models generally can not be used on the screen level because increased transparency of the screen sequences or reduced degrees of freedom require an assessment of both functions **and** process logic. If the main focus is on transaction data, more detailed **data models** are necessary. Organizational models can not be designed on the screen level because the functions are already executed by users, i.e., the smallest organizational units, on the transaction level. Thus, maximum detailing is already carried out on the transactional level (step before).

The next step, if necessary, is to detail **process models** on the **screen level**. Dialog steps, according to the software documentation or standard software, lead to a sequence of individual business administration functions. The desired process logic sorts these functions by listing appropriate events. Process logic is either predetermined by the software or can, in some cases, be freely defined.

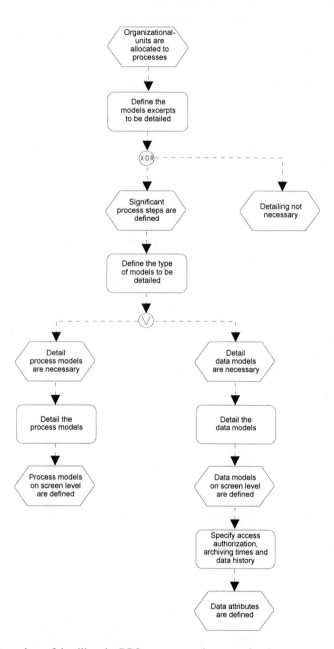

Fig. 4.19: Procedure of detailing the BPO concept on the screen level

Process logic should be defined in such a way to ensure an optimal work process, as required by the designed business processes. For example, it could aim for especially fast processes or processes with as few errors as possible. The dialog steps reflected in the individual screens can be structured very differently, according to the various standard software products or modules. This is a result of IT or ergonomic aspects, such as the number of characters that fit on the screen. The structure of the processes to be modeled is not geared to IT issues, but rather takes business administration aspects into account. In this case, the process structure must at times differ from the degree of detail required by the dialog steps. It can make business sense to process the information required by a screen -- in several functions of the process model – or vice versa. The appropriate screen name should be assigned to every function of the process models on the screen level.

This simplifies implementation at a later date, such as for training classes. Company specific supplements of the standard software, apparent in the dialog steps, should also be taken into account. The next step in detailing the BPO concept on the screen level can be to design **detail data models**. The difference between models on the transactional level is that they attribute entities and their relationships. This is carried out according to screen contents and by assessing control information (such as tables) which determines screen process logic. If necessary, attributes can be supplemented to the guidelines of the software – or omitted, too -, in turn resulting in additional -- or missing fields -- in screens during implementation.

The resulting data models can be used to specify different kinds of **access authorization**. Data models or excerpts are allocated to organizational units or specific persons, respectively. The software documentation establishes whether the desired authorizations can be modeled.

Archiving times and **historical data** can be specified according to the detail data models. This is always necessary when the input and output objects listed in the transactional level do not sufficiently describe the data contents to define all the eventualities regarding archiving and required histories. However, this is generally not the case.

The procedure for detailing the BPO concept on screen levels is depicted in Fig. 4.19.

4.4.3 Supporting Methods and IT Tools

In order to illustrate the models on the screen level, the methods previously described can be used. The processes should be modeled by means of EPCs. Details such as input data, output data or organizational units are not necessary to illustrate process logic and the functions of the dialog steps. However, for every function on the screen level, the appropriate screens should be supplemented (see KIRSCH 1994, p. 4.1.-14 - 4.1.-15), leading to enhancement of the EPC. The EPC illustrations are supplemented by listing attributes (see KIRSCH 1994, p. 4.2-10 - 4.2-11).

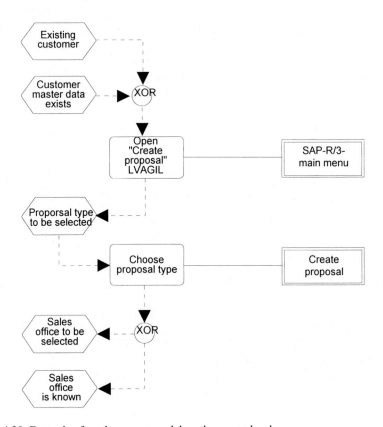

Fig. 4.20: Example of a sub-process model on the screen level

Fig. 4.20 depicts an excerpt of the "Create proposal for standard products" sub-process on the screen level. Once again, the process is based on the SAP R/3 system and was designed for a company in the mechanical engineering industry. The sequence of the first two functions is predetermined by the standard software. Users are not entitled to an option. Subsequently, the process branches out, depending on the entry in " Sales organization".

Modeling can be done using the ARIS Toolset (see KIRSCH 1994, p. 4.1.-14 - 4.1.-15, 4.2-10 - 4.2-11). Models are allocated to the transactional level, similar to information models on the transactional level being allocated to the strategy based BPO concept. Using an IT tool is a central prerequisite for efficient maintenance of models on the screen level. Changes are common, for example due to modification of screen sequences or screen contents during the implementation or during production phases of the standard software (or new releases or modifications in the software configuration).

4.5 Defining a Migration Plan

The last step in establishing a standard software based BPO concept is to define a migration plan.

4.5.1 Goal

The goal of defining the migration plan is to sufficiently detail and specify the implementation steps in the implementation strategy, creating a **framework** for the **BPO implementation phase** of BIS. This is to ensure execution of the implementation measures with appropriate contents and **timing**. These measures should be coordinated, in order to observe existing restrictions and to minimize any risk in the implementation.

❑ IT measures and
❑ Organizational measures

should be defined in this context. IT measures pertain to providing and implementing appropriate hardware, software and data, as well as to carrying out required tests. Organizational measures entail providing appropriate guidelines for personnel, processes, hierarchy organizational measures and office space (see HEINRICH, BURGHOLZER 1990, pp. 332-336). Timing and contents of these measures should be coordinated.

In the implementation strategy, we have discussed general guidelines regarding the execution of continuous, step-by-step and ad hoc migration of business processes. This results from the simultaneous and sequential order of implementation schedules for individual sub-processes. The migration plan should further specify the type of migration. Here we must define whether

❑ Migration is to be carried out on a key date or simultaneously -- or whether
❑ Migration to the target status should be immediate or whether the implementation should take place step-by-step

(see HEINRICH, BURGHOLZER 1990, pp. 326-330).

For every business process, the migration plan is the interface between business conceptual design and operational implementation. This is why company and standard software specific aspects are both equally important. Detailed definition of the necessary implementation measures in the migration plan is only possible for a particular company and a particular standard software product. The procedure for defining a migration plan can just provide a general outline.

The migration plan, similar to the implementation strategy, is a link to project management, defining the project structure and time-frame in the short-term.

4.5.2 Procedure

The migration plan is defined in **three steps**:

❑ Defining and scheduling IT measures,
❑ Defining and scheduling organizational measures and
❑ Defining and scheduling the begin of the live phase.

Contents and timing of the individual measures are coordinated. Therefore, it is irrelevant whether IT measures or organizational measures are first.

While engineering the entire enterprise was the focal point of the implementation strategy, the driving force is now to implement processes or sub-processes by means of the standard software. The finish date defined in the implementation strategy is the final date of activities of the migration plan. The earliest starting date is defined by the current date. This date is generally later than the starting date defined in the implementation strategy, because it entails processing of the standard software based BPO concept in the interim. Every measure defined in the migration plan involves appropriate preparation and execution (HEINRICH, BURGHOLZER 1990, p. 321). The duration to be allocated should be selected accordingly.

If, during BPO implementation, it becomes apparent from the preparation or execution of the measure that it is necessary to move the defined finish date back, the migration plan and implementation strategy must be adjusted accordingly. This is frequently due to external causes, such as lack of availability of standard software modules or hardware components. It is necessary to continuously monitor the time table. Any modifications from bottom-up feedback then flow into top down planning of implementation strategy and migration. This process continuously ensures high quality planning.

The general relationship between implementation strategy and migration plan is depicted in Fig. 4.21.

A **migration plan** should be made **simultaneously** with the information model of the standard software based BPO concept. In the BPO implementation, this permits measures to be implemented early.

This can be necessary for a number of reasons. It can be necessary to

❏ Coordinate timing and content with other activities in the company.
❏ Implement measures, in order to continue conceptual design. For example, detail processes on the screen level can only be verified by means of standard software, once the latter has been installed and is at least partially configured.
❏ The timing targets predetermined in the implementation strategy require simultaneous conceptual design and implementation.
❏ Available resource capacity (such as human resources) compels measures to be spread out over time

(see HEINRICH, BURGHOLZER 1990, p. 321).

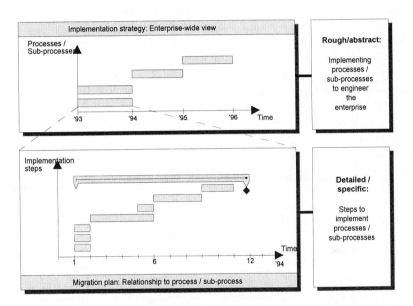

Fig. 4.21: Correlation between implementation strategy and migration plan

When defining measures to implement business processes, the implementation of other processes, as planned in the implementation strategy, should also be considered to achieve synergy effects. Examples: The purchase of hardware and execution of performance tests would be done for several processes. This is especially the case when implementing the same processes at various locations.

The first step in defining the migration plan is to define and schedule **IT measures**. These can be split up into

❑ Software,
❑ Data,
❑ Hardware and
❑ System tests

(see HEINRICH, BURGHOLZER 1990, pp. 335-336; SAP 1993).

Software measures include installation, business process specific configuration, development of necessary standard software add-ons and, if necessary, modification of the software. The scope of these measures results from standard software specific process models. **Data** measures include delivering IS-supported data, creating interfaces to third-party systems and, if necessary, manually maintaining and entering data. The scope of these measures results from process and data models of the standard software based BPO concept on the screen and transactional levels -- and from the volume and quality of existing company specific data. Providing CPUs, peripherals (such as printers or hard disks), networks and necessary system software (operating systems, networking software etc.) are various examples of **hardware** measures. They can derive from software and data measures. Furthermore, standard software specific process models are indicators of necessary hardware (such as necessary PC work places or printers).

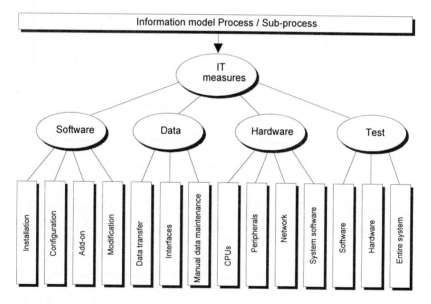

Fig. 4.22: Structure of IT measures

Finally, software, hardware and the entire software / hardware system must be **tested**. The scope of the tests results from software, hardware and data measures. Standard software tests are generally less substantial than individual software tests because software functionality is already ensured. Thus, only the specific configuration needs to be assessed.

The structure of the IT measures is illustrated in Fig. 4.22. The structure of the measures generally defines the degree of detail of the measures to be defined by the company. These general measures only apply to a specific company. For example, "Deliver data" would be specifically replaced by "Deliver material master data".

IT measures are **scheduled** according to specific standard software products and the specific user company. As in defining the implementation strategy, one should rely on the experience of the respective software vendor, hardware vendor and any external sources, such as specialized consulting companies. Logical interrelationships should be considered, such as the fact that software can only be tested after it has been installed, as well as the availability of necessary resources. The logical interrelationships between the IT measures result from their definition. The fact that IT measures are sometimes dependent on organizational measures can lead to changes in the original schedule. The next step is to define and schedule **organizational measures**. These pertain to
❏ Human resources
❏ Hierarchical and process organizations and
❏ Office space

(see HEINRICH, BURGHOLZER 1990, pp. 333-335; SAP 1993).
   Personnel measures include training classes for users and system administrators and, potentially, hiring personnel externally. The scope depends on existing process models (regarding users) and IT measures (for example, system administrators for certain networking systems). Changes in **hierarchical** and **process organizations** require creating organizational units (allocating certain persons) and providing job descriptions and necessary organizational resources, such as forms. The measures derive from standard software based information models. **Office space** for IS and business personnel must be provided for. This results from the IS and organizational measures.
   Fig. 4.23 illustrates the structure of the organizational measures.
   Organizational measures are also **scheduled** according to standard software and company specifics. Company specific aspects, such as the skill level of the future users, the current organizational structure or current office space are key. Defining the duration of implementation is based on company estimates, supplemented by external know-how.
   IS and organizational measures can be interdependent. For example, company specific user training classes are only possible after the configuration of the

standard software has been completed. Thus, reconciling the schedules of IS and organizational measures is necessary. In this context, every organizational measure needs to be assessed as to whether any results of IT measures are a prerequisite. Then, the IT measures should be assessed. If any necessary predecessor-successor relationships are infringed upon, the organizational or IT measures should be rescheduled.

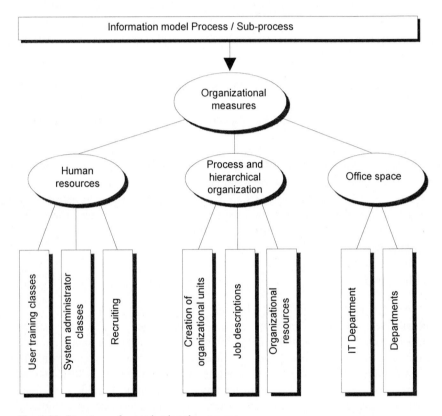

Fig. 4.23: Structure of organizational measures

The last step is to **define and schedule the begin of "going online"**, i.e. transition from the as-is to the target situation. This is defined by the start-up of the standard software. Various IS or organizational measures can be prepared, but not carried out until the actual begin of the production phase. For example, handwritten forms can only be replaced by IS supported ones after going live. The begin of the production phase ensures the flawless start of the standard software supported business processes.

Migration can be carried out by

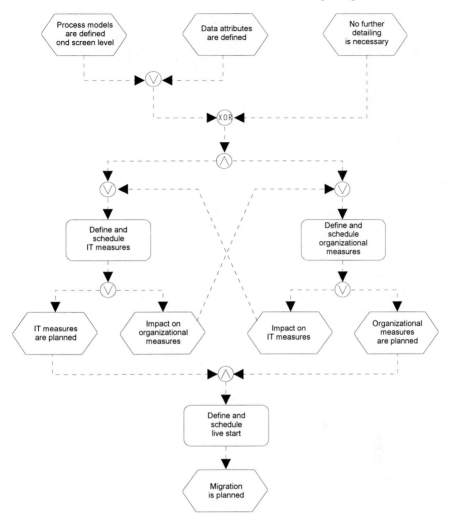

Fig.. 4.24: Procedure for defining the migration plan

❑ Key date migration, i.e., when the new standard software is started and the old system and related processes are shut down, or by

❑ Parallel migration, in which day to day tasks are carried out using both the new standard software, as well as the old systems

(see HEINRICH, BURGHOLZER 1990, pp. 328-329). **Key date migration** avoids redundant work which would be necessary in a parallel migration. There is, however, a potential risk that errors, such as in configuring the software, can impede the productive work process. Generally, the redundant work processes in parallel migrations impede work to such an extent that key date migration is necessary (see HEINRICH, BURGHOLZER 1990, p. 329). Exceptions, i.e., carrying out key data migration anyway, should only be made for processes or sub-processes, when potential errors caused by the new standard software would have unacceptable consequences.

One should also define whether to

❑ Immediately migrate to the target status or to migrate
❑ Step by step, i.e., implementing interim solutions

(HEINRICH, BURGHOLZER 1990, pp. 329-330). **Step by step migration** can be necessary due to external reasons, for example, if certain standard software features have been announced but are not yet available, or for internal reasons, such as if the skill level of employees is not sufficient. Step by step migration is necessary if immediate migration were to heavily strain company resources or would create a risk for the company. If this is the case, interim solutions should be used as information models on the transactional or screen levels, if they do not already derive from existing models. Generally, **migration** should be **immediate**, in order to utilize the predicted advantages of the target system as quickly as possible.

The begin of the live phase requires that IT and organizational measures or respective preparations have already been concluded (assuming the execution of the migration is only possible after the begin of the live phase). Its duration depends on these migration efforts and the measures to be carried out. Start-up of the standard software should also be supported (see HEINRICH, BURGHOLZER 1990, pp. 340-341). The begin of the live phase is **scheduled** in the same manner.

The procedure of defining the migration plan is illustrated in Fig. 4.24.

4.5.3 Supporting Methods and IT Tools

The migration plan details and specifies the implementation strategy. It should be fine-tuned in the **Gantt chart** drawn up in the implementation strategy.

Detailing refers to the BPO implementation. The implementation illustrated as a work process is then transformed into a collective process, grouping the individual implementation measures.

Based on the experience of the author, dependencies between individual implementation measures can be taken into account without using any special methods. If there are too many individual measures to permit this, network methods can be used (see HEINRICH 1994, pp. 205-214). Networks are usually illustrated in focused diagrams, depicting individual events by arrows or nodes (see HEINRICH 1994, pp. 209-212).

Based on the experience of the author, detailing the Gantt chart already designed in the implementation strategy requires a **project management system** (see MICROSOFT 1992, pp. 63-91). Without one, maintenance would be too time-consuming to ensure up-to-date migration, once organizational or IT changes are made.

5 BPO Implementation

In the BPO implementation, measures are undertaken to **execute** the standard software based, and thus strategy based, **BPO concept**. The result is a system describing the various human, task and technology factors in their entirety (see HEINRICH, BURGHOLZER 1990, p. 320). The measures are sufficiently pre-determined by these BPO concepts to ensure the implementation of **strategic goals**.

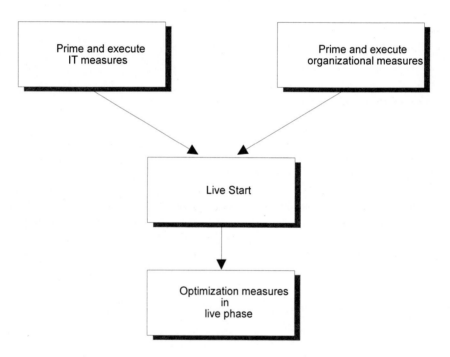

Fig. 5.1: Structure of Chapter Five

The measures should be primed and carried out on the **IS concept** or **implementation levels** of the ARIS Architecture. The main focus is on the IS concept level because the software product has actually already been implemented by the software manufacturer. Moreover, measures should be included that are not connected to technology in any way. The degree of detailing can be defined in accordance with the ARIS Architecture. Priming of the measures, i.e., basic definition of the implementation procedure and required tools, corresponds with the IS concept level. Execution, i.e., actual use of the tools, corresponds with the implementation level. **IT and organizational tools,** as well as physical **framework guidelines,** define the detailing of the measures. For example, standard software can be customized more or less automatically by means of the information models -- or multiple individual measures can be undertaken to set the respective parameters.

In BPO implementation, there are certain aspects in common with the installation phase of HEINRICH and BURGHOLZER's approach (see HEINRICH, BURGHOLZER 1990, pp. 319-324) and with the SAP customizing procedure model (see SAP 1993). However, the BPO implementation phase in BIS is less significant because, in order to achieve the strategic objective, the BPO concepts determine the measures of the BPO implementation. Efficient implementation of the concept is key now.

BPO implementation is carried out in **four steps**:

- ❑ IT measures
- ❑ Organizational measures, at the
- ❑ Live start
- ❑ Optimization measures in live phase.

BPO implementation should be carried out for each business process or sub-process of the standard software based BPO concept. As explained when defining the migration plan, some measures need to be started and executed simultaneously with the conceptual design of the BPO concept (see HEINRICH, BURGHOLZER 1990, p. 321). The structure of Chapter Five is depicted in Fig. 5.1.

The goal, procedure and possible method and IT tool support are illustrated for each step of BPO implementation. This discussion is limited to aspects linked directly with the deployment of the standard software and is independent of any particular standard software products.

5.1 Prime and Execute IT Measures

Firstly, we will discuss priming and executing the IT measures in the BPO implementation. The timetable results from the migration plan.

5.1.1 Goal

The goal of IT measures is to create an **IT infrastructure** enabling the **execution** of the **business processes** modeled in the standard software based BPO concept. The result is a configuration consisting of the necessary standard software, hardware and data for implementing strategic goals.

The following measures, defined in the migration plan, should be defined and executed:

❑ Software,
❑ Data,
❑ Hardware and
❑ System tests.

The results of the measures should then be included in the corporate IT infrastructure (see HEINRICH, BURGHOLZER 1990, p. 320).

Any latitude in the BPO implementation, i.e., issues not uniquely defined by the standard software based BPO concept, should be utilized to implement the strategic goals. One can assume that these latitudes will occur because to rule them out totally would require disproportionately complex modeling from the outset.

5.1.2 Procedure

IT measures are classified in **four groups**:

❑ Software measures,
❑ Data measures,
❑ Hardware measures and
❑ Testing.

The sequence of each measure results from the migration plan. In order to prime and carry out the measures, the individual activities are structured in accordance with the information system views of the ARIS Architecture. This makes the process less complex -- and more transparent.

Software measures commence with the **installation** of the standard software. Frequently, a direct line to the software vendor is installed, enabling technical support should technical problems arise (see SAP 1993, pp. 5-6). Appropriate hardware is obviously a prerequisite for the installation. Until the production phase, it can be purchased in increments. Therefore, the new software can be installed on existing hardware because increased processing power will not be necessary until several software modules are in the live phase.

The software measures focus on all the various activities necessary to adapt the standard software to the individual features of the enterprise -- in other words, **customizing.** The individual issues, i.e., the way the standard software is supposed to be used in each specific case, are described in the BPO concept, primarily in the standard software based BPO concept. The following tasks should be carried out during customizing:

❑ Organizational,
❑ Data,
❑ Function and
❑ Control tasks.

Business processes were originally the focus of the BPO concept. Now, this concept will be executed by using the standard software. Because the standard software design is usually function oriented, customizing results in a transition from the business process oriented BPO concept to function oriented standard software. Once the live phase has begun, this leads to process oriented deployment of the originally function oriented standard software. This is illustrated in Fig. 5.2.

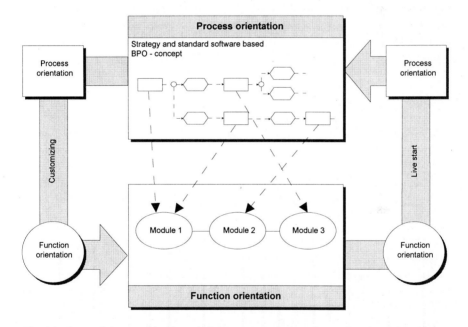

Fig. 5.2: Customizing resulting in a shift from process orientation to function orientation

In the course of **organization** tasks in customizing, the standard software organization model designed in the BPO concept on the transactional level should be implemented in the standard software (see SAP 1993, pp. 11-12). Generally, this task should be one of the first customizing tasks because successive parameters should only be valid for certain organizational units. Defining authorization types in the software program is another one of the organizational tasks. This can include general user profiles (for example, users that principally are only allowed to view data) that are then allocated to specific users (see SAP 1993, pp. 17-18). Further organizational customizing tasks can result from the specific standard software product.

Among other things, **data activities** can include

❑ Defining framework guidelines for master data (such as for number ranges),
❑ Defining forms (e.g., invoices for printing),
❑ Defining reports (e.g., evaluations) and
❑ Defining parameters for reorganization and archiving

(see SAP 1993, pp. 12-13, 16-17, 22). This involves structural parametrization, for the whole standard software. The parameters result from the information models on the transaction and screen levels of the standard software based BPO concept. Data models, on which forms and screens are based, are especially significant (see SCHEER 1993d, pp. 16-17). Technical aspects, such as the layout of forms or the definition of field lengths or number ranges, should be defined as required by the objectives. For example, the layout of proposals for customers could be more important than the layout of purchase orders.

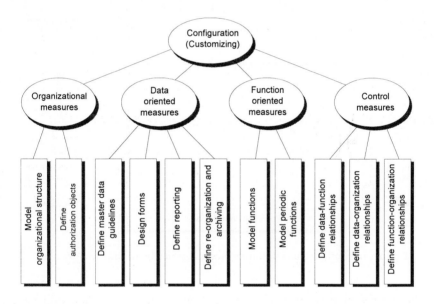

Fig.. 5.3: Structure of the measures for configuring standard software (customizing)

In **function activities**, the focus is on executing functions by means of the standard software. One should define which business administration functions in the standard software should be used and which should be deactivated --- thus, not needing to be configured in detail. Generally, detail parameters should be listed for active functions, for example providing an option between online and batch operations. Note the difference between functions (triggered by users) and periodical functions, such as month-end closing in financial accounting (see SAP 1993, pp. 13-15). Customizing activities result from the functions defined in the process models of the standard based BPO concept.

Finally, **control** activities define the relationship between

❑ Data and functions, for example, a function may only process data of a certain number range (see SAP 1993, p. 13),

❑ Data and organizations, i.e., which users (or general user profiles) are allowed to create, update, delete and display data (see SAP 1993, p. 17) and between

❑ Functions and organizations, by defining which users may execute certain functions (see SAP 1993, p. 179).

The necessary details can be taken from the process models of the standard software based BPO concept. This is where the links between the various information system views were modeled. Based on the experience of the author however, typically, there are still many degrees of freedom here, such as when defining display authorizations. They should be utilized to maximize the quality of implementing business processes.

The structure of the customizing activities is displayed in Fig. 5.3.

If standard software **add-ons** or **modifications** are necessary, they should be modeled in accordance with procedure models for developing software, as described in various publications (see BALZERT 1982 or MEYER 1990). In order to ensure integration, the rules for developing standard software should be observed.

After the presentation of the software measures, now the data measures are discussed. **Data measures** comprise the second group of IT measures. This affects the data view of the ARIS Architecture. The measures to be carried out refer to specific data instances, i.e., data contents. The following tasks should be carried out:

❑ Transfer the data already existing in other software systems (requiring a " one-time interface"),

❑ Develop interfaces for software systems still in use (permanent interfaces) and

❑ Manually transfer data, for example because existing data are only present as folders

(see HEINRICH, BURGHOLZER 1990, p. 336; SAP 1993, pp. 8-9, 15-16, 24-25).

When transferring data, in general only the data necessary for implementing the business process or sub-process should be transferred. In order to avoid redundant maintenance after the beginning of the production phase and possible data inconsistencies, it could become necessary to transfer more data than necessary for the process in question. For example, if only material masters of certain end products are necessary for complete customer order processing of standard products, it would be a good idea to maintain *all* the material masters in one new system.

The more data structures of the existing and new software overlap, the easier it is to automatically transfer data. Transferring records from multiple application software files to the standard software program can lead a considerable amount of individual programming. Therefore, one should consider case by case whether it might be more economical to interactively enter or to automatically transfer data.

Before designing **one-time interfaces**, the following core activities are necessary:

❑ Roughly compare the existing system with the new standard software,
❑ Maintain the data in the existing system, in order to ensure appropriate quality of the data,
❑ Define manual transfer activities (such as executing online commands),
❑ Define the transfer programs (provided by the software vendor) and
❑ Develop any additional transfer programs which are necessary

(see SAP 1993, pp. 8-9). The data should not be transferred until just before the beginning of the production phase of the standard software. This avoids redundant maintenance activities (in both existing and new systems).

The following should be done before defining **permanent interfaces**:

❑ During the production phase, define points in time and triggers that determine when data should be transferred,
❑ Define a control system, i.e. define which software system is supposed to trigger the data exchange,
❑ Define manual tasks (if necessary),
❑ Define which modifications of the existing system might be necessary and
❑ Develop interface programs for existing systems

(see SAP 1993, p. 9). Start-up is not possible until the beginning of the standard software production phase. For permanent interfaces, one should consider using standard interfaces (see SCHEER 1990a, pp. 57-67) because this avoids or at least reduces the effort of developing and maintaining individual interfaces.

If any interface programs are developed individually, this should be done in accordance with established procedure models for software development. You should inquire whether your standard software vendor provides program modules for these interfaces. This is quite probable because, during the course of the implementation, one-time interfaces are frequently used. Permanent interfaces are usually necessary to fill unavoidable gaps in the standard software -- for example, when linking technical and commercial systems. If program modules, that have been developed by the standard software vendor a partner, are reusable, this can facilitate the development effort considerably (see HESS 1993, pp. 8-10).

Hardware measures include providing the technical equipment necessary to deploy standard software in accordance with the BPO concept. The necessary hardware and system software also should be provided (see HEINRICH, BURGHOLZER 1990, p. 335). The ensuing activities should be included in the

❑ Organization view and
❑ Control view

of the ARIS Architecture. The distribution of functions and data, such as in client/server architectures, is defined in the control view (see SCHEER 1994a, pp. 70-76). Network topologies are defined in the organizational view (see SCHEER 1994a, p. 63).
This leads to requirements for

❑ User equipment, such as necessary PCs and printers,
❑ CPUs and related equipment (such as processors, RAM, hard drives), based on a rough estimate of the required amount (for example, the number of BOMs, routings or number of stock withdrawals per day),
❑ Precise network planning,
❑ Hardware configuration for testing and the production phase and
❑ Additional purchases that might become necessary

(see SAP 1993, p. 9). The measures result from the process and organization models of the standard software based BPO concept as well as from software and data specific guidelines, (see NEU 1991, pp. 179-188).

In order to prevent or at least reduce potential problems during the production phase of the standard software, the success of these measures should be evaluated in **tests** (see HEINRICH, BURGHOLZER 1990, p. 340). In addition to individual tests, the following measures should be carried out. An

❑ Integration test encompassing the entire system, including integrated existing systems. Furthermore,
❑ System load should be reviewed to ensure sufficient performance in the production phase

(see SAP 1993, pp. 23-24). If the test results are negative, the measures that were carried out should be corrected. Or it might be advisable to deploy more powerful hardware. Major deviations between the desired and actual test results can result in a delay of the migration plan timetable.

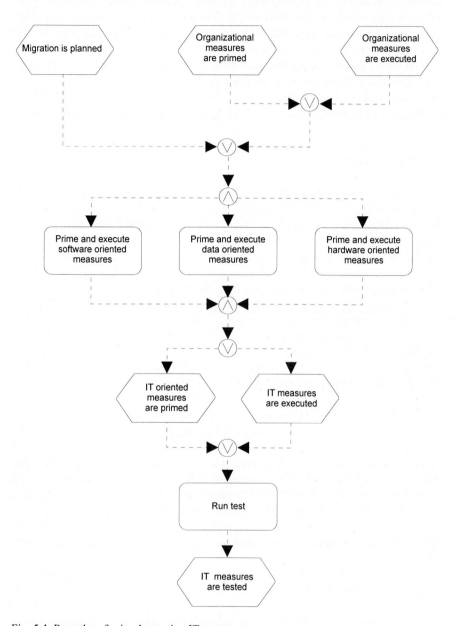

Fig. 5.4: Procedure for implementing IT measures

Integration tests are especially important. They are done in accordance with the processes defined in the standard software based BPO concept. Efficiency and effectivity of the concept are verified -- and optimized if necessary. Being bottom-up guidelines, the results can lead to a refitting of the BPO concept which was established top-down. This can make the BPO concept and standard software more acceptable to future users (see SCHEER 1990a, p. 69). In integration tests, IT test elements and organizational tests overlap because work processes are examined in addition to software processes.

The procedure for implementing IT measures is illustrated in Fig. 5.4.

5.1.3 Supporting Methods and IT Tools

IT measures are closely linked with the planned information technology, i.e. with programs (provided by the standard software vendor) and hardware. Methods and tools are therefore dependent upon this technology, i.e., specific products. Some examples are: Tools for augmenting installation of the software, transferring data and integrating third-party systems. Other examples are development environments for creating individual programs to supplement the standard software or for hardware testing (see SAP 1994, pp. 6-8 - 6-9, 8-1 - 8-32). Due to the fact that these technologies all refer to specific products, we will not discuss them in detail. Support issues should be discussed case by case with the software or hardware vendors, respectively, or with consultancies specializing in these particular products. The same is true when deriving a hardware concept from the standard software based BPO concept. Various professional publications discuss supporting procedures and IT tools for individually developing standard software add-ons (see BALZERT 1982; MEYER 1990; HEINRICH 1994, pp. 68-79; SCHEER 1990c, pp. 124-139).

Customizing, the main activity in IT measures, is also closely linked to the standard software application. However, parameters are generally selected according to the standard software based BPO concept created in accordance with the business administration reference model of the standard software. Various products are now commercially available to **automate** the transfer of conceptual guidelines to the standard software, such as by linking standard software with the ARIS Toolset. This functionality is available in the FI-2 Intelligent Production Scheduling System (Intelligenter Leitstand FI-2) by IDS Prof. Scheer GmbH, Germany (see SCHEER et al. 1994, p. 96) . In addition, a link to SAP R/3 standard software (see KELLER, MEINHARDT 1994b, pp. 87-88; SCHEER 1994, p. 732) is available.
Deploying a tool presupposes appropriate system design of the standard software (see SCHEER et al. 1994, pp. 94-96). **Model based customizing** using the ARIS Toolset offers the following **advantages**:

❑ Standard software specific aspects, such as special macro languages, must not
  be learned,
❑ Errors are avoided / reduced, such as by incorrect data entry,
❑ Saves time when customizing,
❑ Ensures precise representation of the actual standard software configuration by
  means of standard software based BPO concept models. This makes is easier to
  assess processes and software regarding previously defined goals,
❑ Ensures correct configuration, such as regarding the sequence of the individual
  functions

(see SCHEER et al. 1994, p. 100). Furthermore, IT tool support controls the shift
from process to function orientation during customizing. System administrators do
not require any specific training courses regarding the function oriented structure
of the standard software. The close link between standard software and ARIS
Toolset is illustrated in Fig. 5.5.

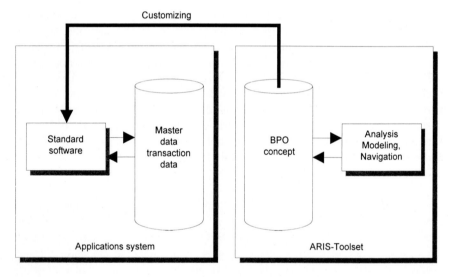

Fig. 5.5: Automating the customizing process by linking standard software and ARIS
Toolset

Nonetheless, when using this IT tool for customizing, specific parameters must
still be entered interactively. Deploying **knowledge based systems to configure
software** can support the customizing process (see LUDWIG 1992, pp. 4-12).
Various prototypes for the RM-Mat and RM-PPS modules of SAP R/2 standard
software are available (see LUDWIG 1992, pp. 57-66; PIETSCH 1993). The
execution of process oriented integration tests requires appropriate **test data**. They

should be defined to process the business cases in question. This simulates future daily operations.

For all the measures, the responsible persons as well as step-by-step and final deadlines (in accordance with the migration plan) should be defined. The contents of the measure should also be specified, for making reviews at a later point in time possible. This can require creating a migration plan and deploying a project management system (see MICROSOFT 1992, pp. 205-215).

5.2 Prime and Execute Organizational Measures

The next step is to prime and execute organizational measures of the BPO implementation. Once again, the timing of these measures should be coordinated with the guidelines of the migration plan.

5.2.1 Goal

The goal of organizational measures is to create **organizational conditions** ensuring the **implementation** of the **business processes** modeled in the standard software based BPO concept. This enables deployment of the standard software in accordance with the strategic goals.

The measures defined in the migration plan regarding

❑ Personnel,
❑ Hierarchical and process organizations and
❑ Office space

should be set up and carried out as completely as possible. Measures presupposing coordination with the standard software (see KLOTZ 1993, pp. 137-142) can not be implemented until the beginning of the live phase. For example, manual processing of documents should be continued until this information can be processed by means of the information system.

Any latitude in the BPO implementation should be utilized to implement the strategic goals.

5.2.2 Procedure

Organizational measures are classified in **three groups**:

❑ Personnel measures,
❑ Hierarchical and process measures and
❑ Office space measures.

In actual deployment, measures should be adapted to the specific company. The following procedure should only be regarded as a guideline.

Organizational measures are not explicitly classified within ARIS information system views because measures basically aim at implementing the organizational view. Therefore, structuring is not possible in this manner.

Personnel measures are of key importance because these future users and system administrators will be responsible for ensuring the implementation of the business processes (see BARTELS 1993, pp. 13-15; WILDEMANN 1990, p. 198). Personnel measures result from the contrariety between the as-is and the target situations because

❑ Some tasks are omitted,
❑ Existing tasks are modified and
❑ Other tasks are added.

BIS affects every area of human resources, including determining human resource requirements, hiring, training, deploying, retaining and also discharging staff (see JUNKER 1988, pp. 7-9). Thus, human resources should be adapted to the implementation.

When implementing standard software, we can distinguish between

❑ User training courses,
❑ System administrator courses and
❑ Personnel recruitment.

These are key measures in BPO implementation (see HEINRICH, BURGHOLZER 1990, pp. 333-334).

User training classes play a key role among personnel measures because it will be the users who will need to implement the processes, defined in the strategy based BPO concept making sure to meet the defined goals, in their day-to-day work. This should be done through appropriate qualification measures (see WILDEMANN 1990, pp. 198-201). Future standard software users need to get to know the standard software product as a "tool" and learn to use it in accordance with the BPO concept. This is ensured by a four-phase training course, based on the future business processes:

❑ Introductory training regarding business administration issues of the business processes,
❑ Introductory training regarding the standard software "tool",
❑ Process training regarding future processes,
❑ Start-up training, ensuring migration from the as-is to the target situation.

Business administration introductory training spans the entire context of the various business processes as well as ensuing specific business tasks that are key to the enterprise. This course mainly covers the contents of the strategy based BPO concept. Future users learn about their tasks in context with the entire process and are taught the contents of their day-to-day work in accordance with strategic goals and processes. In this phase, standard software does not play a major role.

Structure and technical handling of the standard software are the topic of the **standard software introductory training course**. The scope of this course includes the functionality necessary to use the standard for the processes defined in the BPO concept. The standard software should be available in a working production version. This is necessary for teaching the functionality and doing subsequent exercises. However, in this phase of training, it is not necessary to have the application system configured according to the BPO concept. This is because the objective here is to master the technical aspects, not teach business contents. By the end of the course, the standard software "tool" will be familiar.

The main focus of the user training course is on **process training**, covering the implementation of the business processes by means of the standard software. The topics are business administration contents and handling of the standard software for processing business tasks. The skills taught in the two previous courses are a prerequisite for this course. The process training course covers the link between the business processes of the enterprise and the new standard software. The foundation of this course is the standard software based BPO concept. Subsequently, users will be able to implement business processes with the standard software. The prerequisite for the process training course is the configuration of the software in accordance with the standard software based BPO concept. For the most part, customizing should be concluded by this stage.

The last step of the user training course is **start-up training**. Its goal is to lay the groundwork for the beginning of the live phase, i.e., the specific transition from the as-is to the target situation. The topics are the important changes after implementing the standard software based BPO concept and the correct procedure for dealing with any problems that might occur at the beginning of the live phase. This could entail consulting appropriate contacts or studying detailed documentation. This course is based on the standard software based BPO concept and the measures planned for BPO implementation.

The procedure of these process oriented user training courses is depicted in Fig. 5.6.

Depending on the situation, **training courses** can be held before or simultaneously with the implementation measures. As a matter of fact, they should be carried out as soon as possible, in order to maximize preparatory measures (see WILDEMANN 1990, p. 223). This rules out any resistance toward the BPO implementation which could result from misconceptions, uncertainty and, therefore, apprehension of the users (see MAYDL 1987, pp. 35-36). These courses are the basis for subsequent "learning by doing".

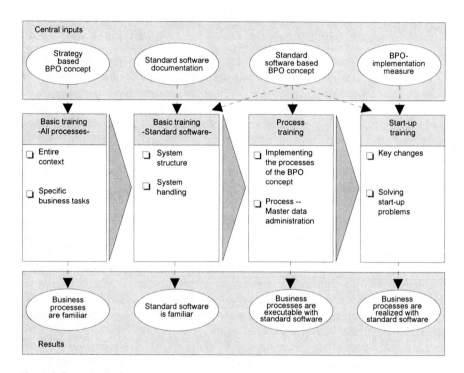

Fig. 5.6: Procedure of process oriented user training courses

They include the concept of

❑ Presentation,
❑ Explanation
❑ Emulation and
❑ Practice

(see WILDEMANN 1990, p. 226). While training courses may generally be held away from the specific workplace (off-the-job training), i.e., in classrooms, process and start-up training courses should be held on-the-job, in order to ensure optimal preparatory measures. The result of the courses, specifically of the exercises, can also be included in the standard software based BPO concept, in accordance with a bottom-up procedure.

System administrator courses aim to ensure IT support of the standard software.

These are some typical topics:

❑ System architecture of the standard software,
❑ Standard software administration
❑ Software specific programming languages that might be in use,
❑ Skills pertaining to the system software (operating system, database etc.)

(see SAP 1993, p. 7). To a large extent, these courses are determined by the technology of the specific standard software product. Therefore, their structure is predetermined by the software vendor. The basic parameters for user training courses already mentioned apply here as well.

In system administrator training courses, **technical system administration** during the production phase should be defined. Among other topics, the following issues should be addressed:

❑ High availability of the dialog system),
❑ Correct procedure for system starts or stops,
❑ Backups, recovery and restarts,
❑ Starting batch jobs or
❑ Spool and monitoring processing

(see SAP 1993, pp. 21-22). The responsible persons should be clarified for every aspect, and the necessary skills of the respective should be ensured.

If any missing skills can not be corrected by training the respective employees, external personnel should be hired. Measures regarding **personnel recruitment** should be initiated. This is valid for application departments (in executing the business processes) and for IT administration (see HEINRICH, BURGHOLZER 1990, pp. 333-334).

Process and **hierarchical / organizational** measures derive from the strategy and standard software based BPO concept. Process-organizational activities are usually addressed by means of customizing, training courses or personnel recruitment (see HEINRICH, BURGHOLZER 1990, p. 334). However, positions—being the most elementary organizational units—provide a close link between the process and hierarchical organization. Thus, measures such as

❑ Creating organizational units,
❑ Creating job descriptions and
❑ Providing organizational resources,

affect both views of the organizational structure.

Organizational units are **created** from organizational and process models of the BPO concept on the transactional level. Qualitative and quantitative personnel requirements derive from the allocation of organizational units to functions. Organizational units are based on this structure (see KLOTZ 1993, pp. 13-14). This determines the attendees of the user training courses. The tasks of the these new positions should be listed in **job descriptions** (see KLOTZ 1993, pp. 13-15; 219-222). Key tasks result from the standard software based BPO concept on the transactional and screen levels.

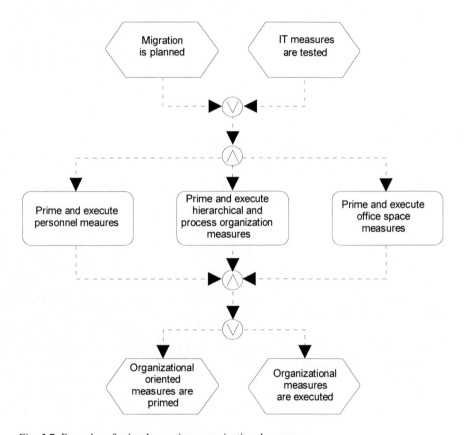

Fig. 5.7: Procedure for implementing organizational measures

Providing organizational resources entails all the organizational resources not provided by the standard software. For example, this would include printing forms and providing archives for receipts still filed manually, such as customer orders (see HEINRICH, BURGHOLZER 1990, p. 334). The requirement for these organizational resources results from the process models of the standard software based BPO concept. Content oriented structure, such as of forms, results from the appropriate data models (see SCHEER 1993d, pp. 16-17).

Office space measures describe office space required for implementing the BPO concept. We can distinguish between office space for

❑ IS equipment and
❑ Business departments

(see HEINRICH, BURGHOLZER 1990, pp. 334-335). **IT equipment** should be installed in an area that has appropriate features and is adequately large. For example, floor space and aspects such as air conditioning and proper floor support should meet the hardware requirements, based on the hardware measures. Appropriate office space is necessary for **business departments**, also. One should also allow for sufficient space for hardware, i.e., printers or PCs. Furthermore, one could consider creating new organizational measures within the context of hierarchical measures.

The procedure for implementing organizational measures is illustrated in Fig. 5.7.

5.2.3 Supporting Methods and IT Tools

For the most part, **user training courses** are supported by the **information models** created in the standard software based BPO concept. Thus, company specific user documentation is an integral part of the BPO concept. Specific deployment of models can be facilitated by **ARIS Toolset's navigation component**, enabling easy access to the model excerpts (see IDS 1994e). Models can also be printed, in order to provide every user with the necessary information. This is necessary if ARIS Toolset is not accessible to all the users or if printing the model contents were to make the models substantially more acceptable to the users.

A qualification profile can be extracted from the information models, if personnel need to be recruited. This results from the allocation of organizational units to functions.

User and system administrator training courses for standard software are supplemented by the appropriate **software documentation** (handbook). Today, more and more frequently, documentation is being provided online as an integral part of the standard software (see FREMMER 1992, pp. 117-125).

The advantages of online documentation vs. printed documentation are as follows:

❑ Documentation is available at every workstation deploying the standard software,
❑ Access to information is easy, for example by the integration of hypertext,

❑ There is a positive psychological effect because users are not confronted with -- potentially intimidating -- mountains of paper -,
❑ Exploratory learning (learning by doing) becomes easier,
❑ The workplace is consistent when documentation is integrated with the standard software product,
❑ Releases stay up to date,
❑ Company specific add-ons of the documentation are possible and easy to do,
❑ Distribution is easier,
❑ Online documentation requires less storage space

(see FREMMER 1992, pp. 126-128; SAP 1994, pp. 2-9). Therefore, training courses can sometimes be trimmed to only focus on handling online documentation and software help functions.

Ideally, there are direct IT links between the information models in ARIS Toolset and the online documentation (which is for example the case with SAP R/3). It is possible to directly access the appropriate software documentation from the standard software based BPO concept, in order to clarify any questions regarding the implementation. Information models, standard software and standard software user documentation form a unit, designed to train future users in an integrated environment.

Standard software introductory training courses and company independent topics within system administrator training courses can be held externally at the vendor site, although they can also be held in-house, at the customer site. External courses

❑ Prevent any interruptions caused by daily operations,
❑ Convey an overall impression of the software vendor and
❑ Provide the necessary infrastructure.

In in-house courses,

❑ Travel time is reduced,
❑ It is usually easier to address company specific issues, for example because any information which might be necessary can be obtained during the course,
❑ Results of the training course (entries in the standard software) can be utilized more efficiently, for example in individual exercises after the course.

In order to make an appropriate decision, these issues should be weighted from case to case. Company specific issues, such as are covered in the process and start-up training courses, are usually executed in-house.

Hierarchical and **organizational** measures of the BPO concept information models can be determined by evaluating the process models by means of **ARIS Toolset's navigation component**. This is how all the functions allocated to an organizational unit can be determined (see IDS 1994e, p. 3.-10 - 3.-11).

In order to support organizational measures, the **compensation system** can also be designed accordingly. Result based compensation systems play an important role, leading to appropriate salaries and, in addition, offering incentives for good results (see WILDEMANN 1990, pp. 230-231).

Responsible persons, completion and interim deadlines (according to the migration plan) should be defined for organizational measures, too. The contents of the measures should be listed, in order to ensure proper execution and monitoring at a later point in time. This can be carried out by means of the project management system.

5.3 Live Start of the Standard Software

IT and organizational measures are designed to prime the beginning of the live phase of the standard software program. This will be our next topic. The chronological sequence of the beginning of the live phase is also defined in the migration plan.

5.3.1 Goal

The goal of the live start is to **trigger** the **operational implementation** of the business processes modeled in the strategy and standard software based BPO concept. It represents the specific transition between as-is and the target situations, i.e., the shift between the build-time phase and the run-time phase of information system planning (see SCHEER 1990b, p. 16).

One should take care to avoid or at least reduce the potential for any **interruptions** of the processing of currently existing business issues, such as currently processed open customer orders. During transition to the target situation, migration should be triggered appropriately and users should be supported accordingly.

When designing work processes, any latitude still existing after the beginning of the live phase should be used in accordance with the goals defined in the target system.

5.3.2 Procedure

The beginning of the live phase of the standard software consists of **three steps**:

❑ Starting-up the standard software,
❑ Activating IS and organizational measures,
❑ Start-up support.

The procedure of the live start results from its role between the build-time and run-time phases of the business processes. The implementation of the goals is started operationally.

Measures that sometimes can only be activated once the software is up and running can be extracted from the strategy and standard software based BPO concept. They are activated during the beginning of the live phase. In order to ensure the implementation of the business processes, support of the live phase of the standard software is initiated. Activities of the beginning of the live phase thus range from build-time phase to run-time phase. Fig. 5.8 depicts the role of the lie start of the live phase as an interface between build-time and run-time.

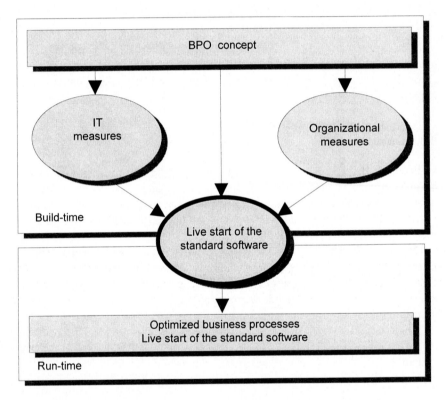

Fig. 5.8: Beginning of the live phase – interface between build-time and run-time

The first step of the live start is to get the **standard software up and running**. The time schedule defined in the migration plan is generally not sufficient to precisely define the starting date of the live phase. **Events** should be defined, determining the **beginning** of the work process in accordance with the standard software based BPO concept, such as processing a certain customer order in a company in the mechanical engineering industry (see HEINRICH, BURGHOLZER 1990, p. 340). Event types are defined in the process models of the standard software based BPO concept. Specific instances can be defined according to existing business issues. This leads to a uniquely defined starting date for every work step of the business processes. Thus, start-up does not occur at a uniquely defined point in time for the entire business process, but is rather a function of the process logic of the process. This "natural" spacing of the start-up activities enables corrections and supplements of BPO implementation measures and specific support of the start-up of the live phase (see HEINRICH, BURGHOLZER 1990, p. 341).

If **key date migration** is planned, the starting event for processing the business processes in accordance with the new standard software is identical with the final event for work processes, in accordance with the old software systems or other tools that need to be replaced. In **parallel migration**, the final events for terminating as-is processes should be defined separately (see HEINRICH, BURGHOLZER 1990, pp. 340-341).

In **step-by-step migration**, ranging from the as-is status to the target status defined in the BPO concept, appropriate interim steps should be established in the transactional and screen levels. This is carried out in accordance with the approach illustrated in the standard software based BPO concept. Individual interim steps are started up as described above.

In **an immediate migration** to the target status, it is frequently a good idea to define short-term interim solutions according to the IS structure of the standard software, i.e. its modules. Each module is **started up** individually, **according to its functions**. This makes it easier to localize any technical problems that might arise. Interim solutions are only in production as long as necessary for IT monitoring. They are then migrated to the target status defined in the BPO concept. This ensures business process orientation of the implementation.

Step Two of the live start is to **activate IT and organizational measures** that could not be executed until start-up of the standard software. This mainly affects process-organizational issues in business and IT departments, respectively. However, IT measures, such as transferring historical data, may not be initiated until the beginning of the live phase, if redundant maintenance or not up to date data are to be avoided. The implementation status of each IT and organizational measure should be reviewed and activated, if necessary.

The last step of the live start is to initiate measures to **support start-up**. This includes all activities that specifically support users in implementing the BPO concept, once the standard software is up and running. The duration and extent of this support depends on the skill level of the users and the complexity of the business processes in question. The following activities should be carried out:

❑ Monitor correct processing and assist accordingly, if any problems arise,
❑ Diagnose and correct any processing errors,
❑ Diagnose and correct any IT errors, such as in the interface programs or in customizing,
❑ Collect information regarding a realistic assessment of the BPO implementation

(see HEINRICH, BURGHOLZER 1990, p. 341). During this phase, users learn to use the BO concept, the standard software documentation, and other tools. These skills can be used to further optimize work processes in accordance with the goals.

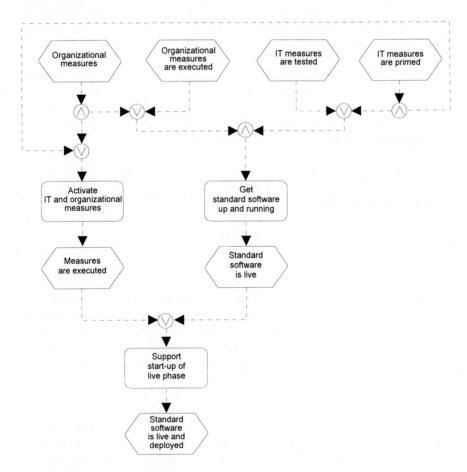

Fig. 5.9: Procedure for going live

The procedure regarding the live start phase is depicted in Fig. 5.9.

5.3.3 Supporting Methods and IT Tools

Event types for defining start-up are taken from the process models of the standard software based BPO concept. The **navigation component** of ARIS Toolset is useful because it can be used to locate various events. Module oriented interim solutions can be defined by means of the **standard software documentation**.

One way of activating IS and organizational measures is to use the documentation in a **project management system**. If necessary, specific work orders can be defined, ensuring implementation of the measures.

Both the BPO concept and standard software documentation can be used to support start-up. Fortunately, they are both included in the **Online Help** function in the **ARIS Toolset**. It might be necessary to print them, if this is more acceptable to users accustomed to conventional documentation. The ARIS Toolset provides user-friendly printing functionality to this end (IDS 1994c, p. 1.-92 - 1.-95).

5.4 Optimizing Business Processes in the Live Phase

The last step of the BPO implementation in BIS is to initiate optimization measures in the live phase of the standard software. These "post implementation" activities are especially important to trigger off a Continuous Process Improvement (CPI).

5.4.1 Goal

The goal of optimizing business processes during the live phase (i.e., after the beginning of the live phase) is to adapt BIS results and integrate theme with a **continuous improvement process**. The results of the implementation should not be viewed as static events, but rather as the first steps in a dynamic evolution – management, superiors and employees all working and thinking in a consistent, process oriented manner. BIS thus triggers enterprise-wide implementation of the KAIZEN concept (see IMAI 1993, p. 15).

In this context, optimization activities should aim at

❑ Measures carried out in the BPO implementation and at
❑ Enhancing or refitting the strategy and standard software based BPO concept and subsequent BPO implementation.

The cornerstone for optimization activities is to examine the business processes implemented according to the BPO concept.

5.4.2 Procedure

Business processes in the live phase are optimized in **four steps**:

❑ Reviewing the BIS frame conditions,
❑ Reviewing whether the strategic goals have been reached,
❑ Refitting the BPO implementation and
❑ Refitting the BPO concepts.

Optimization steps should be carried out continuously throughout the production phase of the standard software (Continuous Process Improvement CPI)

During the **review of the BIS framework conditions,** one should determine whether and how the business environment (that existed when the strategy and standard software based BPO concept were implemented) has changed. BIS conditions include all the issues that were initial input for the strategy based and the standard software based BPO concept. Changes in the business environment can be

❑ Determined within the company, such as by a reduction in the depth of manufacturing or
❑ Outside the company, such as by different market requirements or by enhancement of the standard software.

If **conditions are unchanged**, one should review whether the goals defined in the strategy based BPO concept have been reached. If necessary, the goal should be reached by refitting the BPO implementation already underway. If it becomes clear that **conditions have changed**, the strategy and / or standard software based BPO concepts should be refitted. BIS should then be partially (or totally) repeated.

When **reviewing whether the goal has been reached**, one should assess whether the target system defined in the strategy based BPO concept was actually implemented by means of the business processes designed. One should take into account that at the beginning of the live phase of the standard software, it is usually not possible to reach the goal completely. Goals such as reducing stock by 30% can not be reached at the beginning of the production phase, but rather take several months (see HEINRICH, BURGHOLZER 1990, p. 342).

If the **target system** still has **not** been **reached**, one should determine whether the implemented business processes actually correspond with the standard software based BPO concept. If deviations are determined between reality and the standard software based BPO concept, they should be analyzed. Adequate refitting of the BPO implementation should then be ensured.

There could be a number of reasons for these variations, such as:

❑ The tests were not carried out thoroughly or comprehensively enough,
❑ The IS or organizational measures were not complete or the
❑ IS or organizational measures were completed too late -- or with unsatisfactory results

(see HEINRICH, BURGHOLZER 1990, p. 341).

Refitting the **BPO implementation** eliminates deviations between real work processes and the standard software based BPO concept. To this end, company specific measures should be defined, primed and executed. If the unsatisfactory implementation of the BPO concept is caused by the fact that the degrees of freedom in the standard software based BPO concept are too expansive (for example because access authorization is defined too generally), the information models in question in the BPO concept should be detailed and/or supplemented. This avoids future deviations of the implementation. Refitting the BPO implementation is depicted in Fig. 5.10.

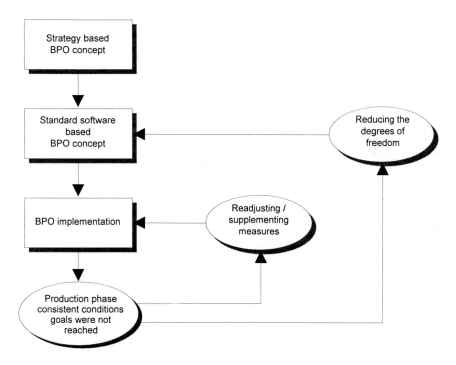

Fig. 5.10: Refitting the BPO implementation

If the goals are not reached, even though the conditions and the BPO implementation have not changed, the strategy and standard software based BPO concept should be reviewed. It would seem that various issues have not been considered sufficiently.

If framework conditions have changed, the standard software or strategy based **BPO concept** should be **refitted** -- or at least verified. The consequence of refitting a concept is to execute consecutive BIS phases.

Refitting the BPO concepts is illustrated in Fig. 5.11.

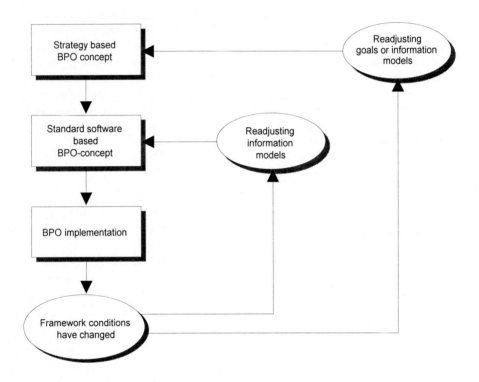

Fig. 5.11: Refitting the BPO concepts

Typical changes leading to refitting of the **standard software based BPO concept** are

❑ Deployment of new standard software releases or
❑ Enhancement of business partners' (customers or suppliers) IT equipment, permitting optimized integration (such as by means of EDI).

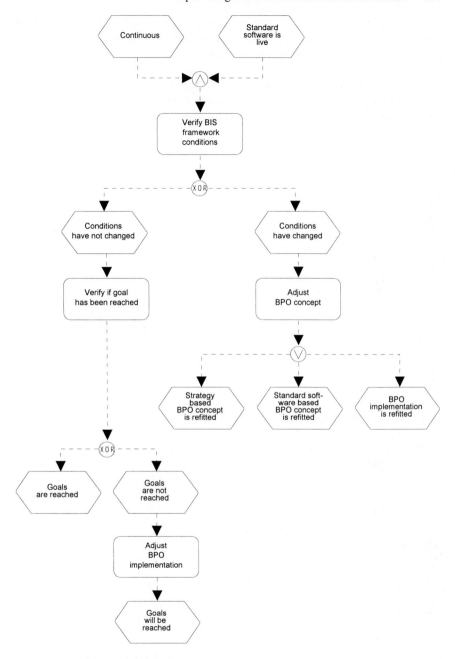

Fig. 5.12: Procedure for optimizing business processes in the live phase

Software vendors usually require deployment of new standard software releases, in order to continue maintenance. Before refitting the standard software based BPO concept, one should review to which extent business administration enhancements of the standard software can actually be utilized. Deployment of the new release is only advisable if it improves processes. If a standard software reference model is available, it can be used to determine the effects of deploying software enhancements. This is done by comparing it with the information models of the existing standard software based BPO concept.

Refitting the **strategy based BPO concept** can be triggered by the following framework conditions, such as:

❑ Enhancement of the product suite,
❑ New companies being bought up,
❑ New competitive products,
❑ A change in a company's position regarding customers or suppliers,
❑ New competitors or
❑ Changes affecting existing competitors

(see PORTER 1990, pp. 25-27). If it is necessary to refit the target system within the BPO concept. This can lead up to a complete BIS, possibly with another standard software product.

Fig. 5.12 depicts the procedure for optimizing business processes in the production phase.

5.4.3 Supporting Methods and IT tools

Methods and tool support for the optimization of business processes in the live phase includes **documentation** and **analysis** of the **as-is situation** at the beginning of the live phase. This optimization can be carried out in the various phases of BIS.

Here are some typical methods of getting information about the as-is situation:

❑ Interviews,
❑ Observation,
❑ Questionnaires,
❑ Personal notes and
❑ Document evaluation

(see HEINRICH 1994, pp. 366-373).
The results can be supplemented by special means of measuring time:

❑ Personal notes based on an activity log and the BPO concept,
❑ Estimates,

❑ Counting,
❑ Operational resources with built-in time recording devices,
❑ Evaluation based on technological data,
❑ Time recording or
❑ Interviewing co-workers

(see HEINRICH 1994, pp. 374-379).
For as-is analyses, various analysis methods are available, such as

❑ Checklists,
❑ Check matrices,
❑ ABC analyses and
❑ Interactivity analyses

(see HEINRICH 1994, pp. 380-386).
Communication analyses can be carried out by the use of

❑ Communication tables,
❑ Communication diagrams,
❑ Communication matrices
❑ Communication networks

(see HEINRICH 1994, pp. 387-394).
No specialized tools are required to apply these analysis methods. However, this requires manual effort, impeding continuous information gathering, analysis and with that any resulting improvement.

Therefore, in order to enhance performance, it is necessary to **deploy IT technology**. In BIS, the results of as-is information gathering should be transferred to ARIS Toolset, enabling IS supported **analysis**. Business processes documented in the process models of the standard software based BPO concept are evaluated interactively and evaluated as to how their process logic compares with the as-is situation. Time, cost attributes and the probability of certain events occurring can be defined in the functions or connection lines of the models. The toolset can then do index analysis (see IDS 1994b, p. 2.-70 - 2.-115). This leads to an increase in the efficiency of the analysis procedure.

Gathering information concerning current time, cost attributes and probabilities is often time-consuming. **This** can be made less complex by utilizing information that is automatically generated during operation of the software. Data that was specifically entered (such as feedback) can be used. On the other hand, all the activities of an information system can be protocolled by the operating system, tele-processing monitor, database management system or application software, and then used by analysts (see ÖSTERLE et al. 1994, p. 466).

Parameters and coordination of hardware, system software and application software can be optimized in accordance with **monitoring evaluations**.

Monitoring can be defined as the transaction of measuring performance and observing time-related processes in computer systems (see KLAR 1985, p. 37). The classic goal of deploying monitoring tools is to run application systems at the lowest hardware costs possible. For this reason, figures such as response time, system load and paging rates are measured (see XEPHON 1991).

However, monitoring data can also be used to analyze organizational links, i.e., to optimize business processes. This is also known as **organizational monitoring** (see ÖSTERLE et al. 1994, p. 466). There are two kinds of monitoring data:

❑ Monitoring data provided by the standard software itself, such as a change in certain master and transaction data, and
❑ Data provided by system software, such as a TP monitor listing the amount of calls in a given software transaction

(see ÖSTERLE et al. 1994, pp. 467-468).
Data can be determined regarding an

❑ Hierarchical organization, such as which organizational unit uses which system transactions; a
❑ Process organization, i.e., the time span between opening and completing a manufacturing order and
❑ Handling of a system, such as resource requirements, in order to process a certain activity, such as to book an invoice

(see ÖSTERLE et al. 1994, pp. 468-475).

In as-is information gathering and analysis, other benefits result from **automatically transferring monitoring data** and contents of the IT supported **master** and **transaction data** to **ARIS Toolset**, simplifying detail visualizing of the business processes and their analysis (see KRUPPKE 1994, pp. 466-467). The result is a direct link between information system planning (build-time) and subsequent information system management (run-time). This connection between ARIS Toolset (or the information models therein) and standard software or system software is possible because the process models of the standard software based BPO concept were created on transactional or screen levels. This is a standard software based degree of detail where also monitoring data can be provided. Thus, actual processing time (i.e., time span between start and completion of a manufacturing order) could derive from the transaction data of the standard software. Conversely, the time span between the IT technical release of a manufacturing order (with a corresponding transaction) and its completion (once again, with a corresponding transaction) derives from the monitoring data. If both of them are allocated to "parts processing" as an attribute, one can determine whether the data collection is up to date. By assessing the ratio of the yield planned in manufacturing vs. the amount of parts actually reported in the feedback, one can determine the probability of scrap material. This can be allocated to the models of the standard software based BPO concept. Likewise, monitoring data of hierarchical / organizational and system elements are transferred to information models of the standard software based BPO concept. The resulting monitoring and software data should be aggregated before being transferred to ARIS Toolset, for example by calculating averages of various processing times. Thus, business processes can be reviewed efficiently and resulting improvement measures can be initiated continuously. Thus, the "ARIS Toolset" planning tool turns into an operational information system. The link between standard software and ARIS Toolset for the purpose of analyzing as-is processes is depicted in Fig. 5.13.

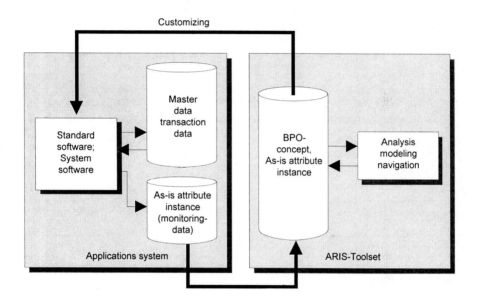

Fig. 5.13: Linking standard software to the ARIS Toolset for the purpose of analyzing as-is-processes

Changes in framework conditions are triggered by external events, such as by a new software release or by internal measures. Data entry and evaluation of these events are corporate activities, for which specific method support does not exist. Any decisions regarding new processing of BIS phases should be made case by case, in accordance with company specific issues.

If any potential changes have been documented, they are evaluated to determine whether the standard software or strategy based BPO concept might have been "strained". An example would be a new release of standard software reference models that need to be reconciled with the standard software based BPO concept. The **analysis component** of ARIS Toolset **automatically compares model versions** (see IDS 1994b, p. 2.-116 - 2.-150), if the following conditions are fulfilled:

❑ The models to be compared are of the same type, such as EPCs,
❑ The objects to be compared are of the same object type, such as functions, and
❑ The objects to be compared are linked with one another

(see IDS 1994b, p. 2.-119). If specifically the last condition is not fulfilled, preparing an automatic comparison can be so complex that a tool-supported, but interactive comparison, could be more efficient. However, when releasing software reference models, one can assume that the vendor will provide a link between the releases.

6 Comprehensive Model of Business Process Oriented Implementation

In Chapters One through Five, we described each individual BIS step, using sub-process models. Interdependencies of these implementation steps are shown in the fact that the same events are used in different sub-models. Next, the ensuing detailed BIS process model is aggregated in two steps. The result is a sub-process model for every implementation phase and a cross-phase comprehensive model. Thus, the BIS procedure model is described on three detail levels. By using this description type, we are able to transparently illustrate the interrelationship of the implementation steps.

In **project management,** using the BIS processes on three levels of detail makes it easier to derive the project structure. Furthermore, when planning **training courses** on the BIS process for persons implementing the standard software, this permits an efficient and effective top-down procedure.

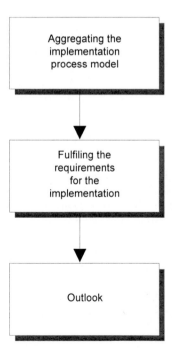

Fig. 6.1: Structure of Chapter Six

After aggregating the BIS process model, we will summarize how this procedure fulfills the requirements defined in Chapter Two. Finally, we will take a look at what we think will be in store for BIS in the future.

The structure of Chapter Six is illustrated in Fig. 6.1

6.1 Aggregating the Implementation Process Model

The BIS detail process model illustrated in Chapters Three through Five was developed top-down by detailing and specifying the ARIS Architecture procedure model. The process logic of the individual functions to be carried out in BIS are described by means of event-driven process chains. In order to emphasize the structure of the BIS phases and the interrelationship of these implementation phases, the existing **process models** are **aggregated** bottom-up. This is carried out in **two steps**.

❑ First, a sub-process model is developed for every BIS phase. The interdependencies between the phases result from using the same events in several sub-processes.
❑ The sub-process models are then grouped within a model, transparently describing the interrelationship between the BIS phases.

The result is an illustration of the BIS **procedure model** in **three detailing levels:**

❑ Implementation level
❑ Phase structure level
❑ Function level

The models of the implementation and phase structure levels will be derived subsequently, the models of the individual function level are discussed in Chapters Three through Five. Fig. 6.2 depicts the detailing levels for describing the BIS procedure model.

Sub-process models for every BIS phase result from grouping the models of the individual implementation steps within a BIS phase into one function each, along with the respective start and finish events. In a function of a general process model, start events are characterized by detail model events that are not created by a function of the same detail sub-process. In a function of a general process model, finish events are characterized by detail model events that do not trigger a function within the described sub-process. Thus, aggregated process models of the **phase structure model** result from the process model of the individual function level. Focusing on the essential steps of the implementation phase emphasizes the structure of the implementation process of every BIS phase.

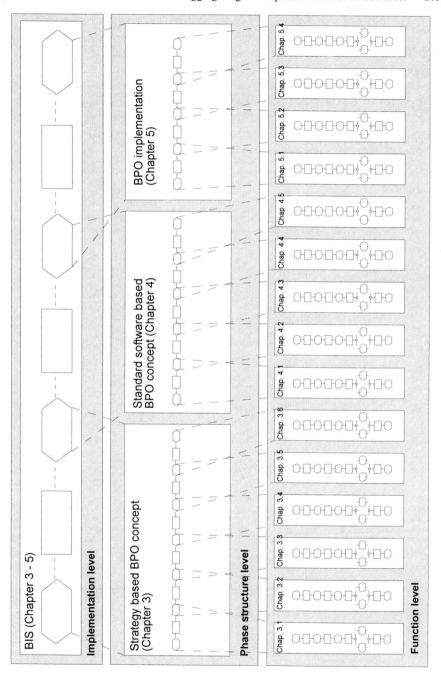

Fig. 6.2: Detailing levels for describing the BIS procedure model

The procedure for designing the strategy based BPO concept is depicted in Fig. 6.3. This phase of BIS can commence once the as-is analysis has been concluded and BIS has begun, resulting in defined sub-processes of the enterprise to be supported by the standard software program. Successive BIS phases are scheduled for every sub-process. The design of the standard software based BPO concept commences as soon as the strategy based BPO concept is concluded and BIS must be continued for a sub-process. Fig. 6.4 illustrates the procedure of designing the standard software based BPO concept. Migration for processed business processes or sub-processes is scheduled at the end of this BIS phase. This triggers BPO implementation.

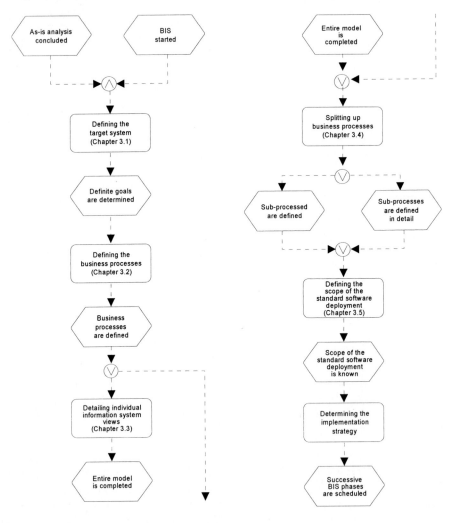

Fig.. 6.3: Procedure for designing the strategy based BPO concept

The corresponding process model is depicted in Fig. 6.5. Consequently, the goals defined in the strategy based BPO concept will be reached. Alternatively, the BPO concept or BPO implementation, respectively, will have to be refitted in accordance with the altered conditions.

Fig. 6.4: Procedure for establishing the standard software based BPO concept

The process model of the phase structure level is aggregated as described above, leading to the **BIS model** in the **implementation phase level**. This describes the interrelationship of the BIS phases. The ensuing process model is illustrated in Fig. 6.6. BIS is triggered by completion of as-is analysis and the beginning of the standard software implementation. Once implementation is concluded, implementation of the strategic goals is ensured. Alternatively, the results of individual phases of implementation should be refitted in accordance with the altered conditions, thus ensuring reaching the goal.

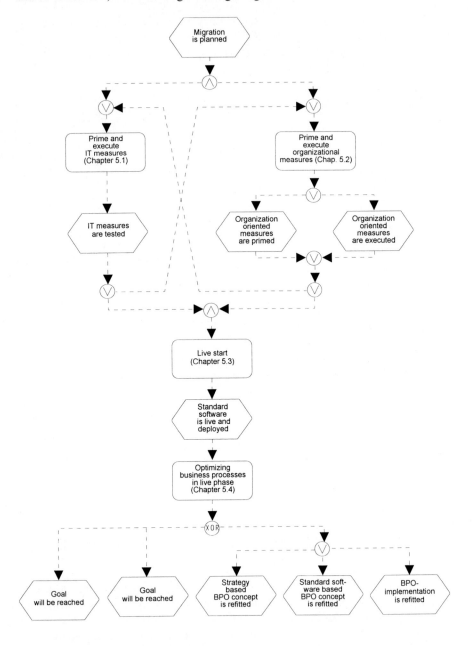

Fig. 6.5: Procedure of the BPO implementation

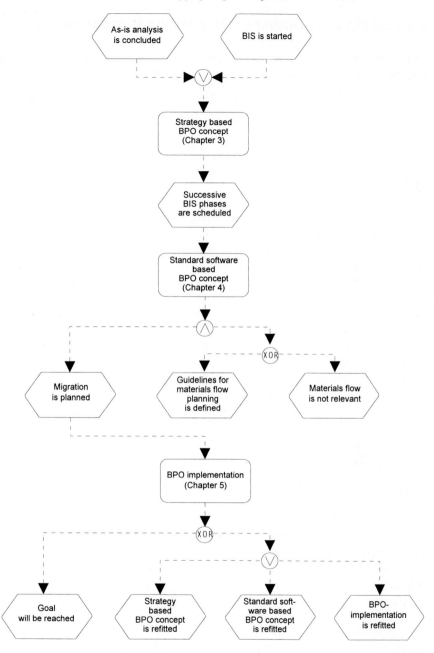

Fig 6.6: Procedure for BIS

6.2 Fulfilling the Requirements for the Implementation

The **BIS** procedure model takes into account the **requirements** defined in Chapter Two, regarding the **implementation** of business process oriented **standard software**:

❑ Reconciling object and function orientation,
❑ Enabling integration,
❑ Specifically decentralizing business processes,
❑ Taking dynamic aspects into account and
❑ Specifically involving employees.

The key requirements for **reconciling object oriented** organizational structures and **function oriented** standard software structures are fulfilled, as shown here. In accordance with business processes defined independently of any particular standard software and by means of the strategy based BPO concept, strategic corporate goals are initiated by defining the processes and then implemented by defining the target system in subsequent phases. This takes into account the strategic significance of the results of implementing the standard software. The implementation strategy developed in accordance with the strategy based BPO concept defines the "direction of diffusion" of the standard software. Simultaneous detailing and specification of the BPO concept are ensured by using standard software reference models when designing the standard software BPO concept. In this context, any necessary software add-ons and/or modifications for implementing the business processes are defined. If necessary, the results of reconciling material and information flow should be included in the design of the BPO concept. The implementation becomes less complex since consistent methodology is used, in accordance with the Architecture of Integrated Information Systems (ARIS). Various modeling methods and IT tool support optimize the implementation of the standard software product.

Integration requirements for implementation are taken into account by the following BIS tasks. By defining (cross-module, if necessary) software support of the business processes early on in the implementation strategy, consistent use of the standard software's integration functionality is initiated. Business process orientation of the following detailing and specification steps systematically includes this integration functionality in implementation tasks. Any effects of the implementation on indirectly affected departments of the enterprise are taken into account by an enterprise-wide definition of the processes. This is also achieved by structurally splitting up the processes in the strategy based BPO concept. Any replacement or integration of existing application software is designed in the implementation strategy and migration plan, and executed during the BPO implementation.

In BIS, **work processes** are specifically **decentralized or centralized**. In the strategy based BPO concept, business processes and/or the functions therein are allocated to individual organizational levels. In the standard software based BPO concept, they are allocated to specific organizational units. According to corporate strategic goals, decentralized units and overlying coordination functions are thus defined. During BPO implementation, step-by-step specification in the standard software based BPO concept leads to execution by organizational measures. Specifics of vertical markets are included in BIS by means of vertical market reference models. The size of a particular company is recorded in the definition of the organizational levels and also when defining the implementation strategy. Any restrictions brought about by the size of a company are included in designing the migration plan and the subsequent BPO implementation. IT infrastructure derives from the strategy and standard software based BPO concept.

Dynamic aspects of implementation are consistently taken into account. The implementation strategy lays the groundwork for either continuous, step-by-step or ad hoc migration of business processes. These migration strategies can also be combined. Continuous optimization of business processes starts at the beginning of the live phase of the standard software. Deployment of either key date or parallel migration is defined in the migration plan and executed in the BPO implementation. During BPO implementation, preparatory measures for both organizational and software measures are carried out as simultaneously as possible and then executed in the BPO implementation. The key element in ensuring efficient implementation is consistent use of reference models. After deploying vertical market reference models in the strategy based BPO concept, the next step is modeling in accordance with standard software reference models of the standard software based BPO concept. The information models to be designed are only detailed as far as is necessary to implement the goals. The new standard software determines the degree of detailing in the standard software based BPO concept and should be adequate for the implementation. This reduces the total effort necessary for carrying out conceptual design tasks during the implementation. Efficiency can be increased even further by consistently deploying an IT tool. Efficient and effective processing of the standard software implementation is supported by designing the implementation process in accordance with the BIS process model. This indicates that the implementation task itself is of a strategic nature.

BIS enables **employees** to be **specifically included** in the implementation process. Information models for individual sub-processes can be designed either with the respective employees in workgroups or can be established as a guideline. This enables either participative or gate-keeping implementation types. These approaches can also be combined, especially when detailing the models on transactional or screen levels. In the course of implementation, BIS ensures business administration and standard software - related skills of the employees.

This becomes especially clear when process oriented user training courses are designed during BPO implementation.

6.3 Outlook

The **BIS** procedure model for implementing strategic goals developed in this work is responsible for transforming the implementation of standard software into a **strategy driven implementation of information systems**. It implements business administration concepts by means of information technology. Any differing organizational structure and standard software structure, such as process and function orientation, are overcome. At the same time, any identical design types in business oriented standard software are utilized systematically.

BIS shifts the focal point in standard software implementation from implementation and IS concept levels to the requirements definition (business concept) level of the ARIS Architecture. Processes or sub-processes are specifically supported by the standard software, independently of the standard software structure. Implementing strategic goals is key.

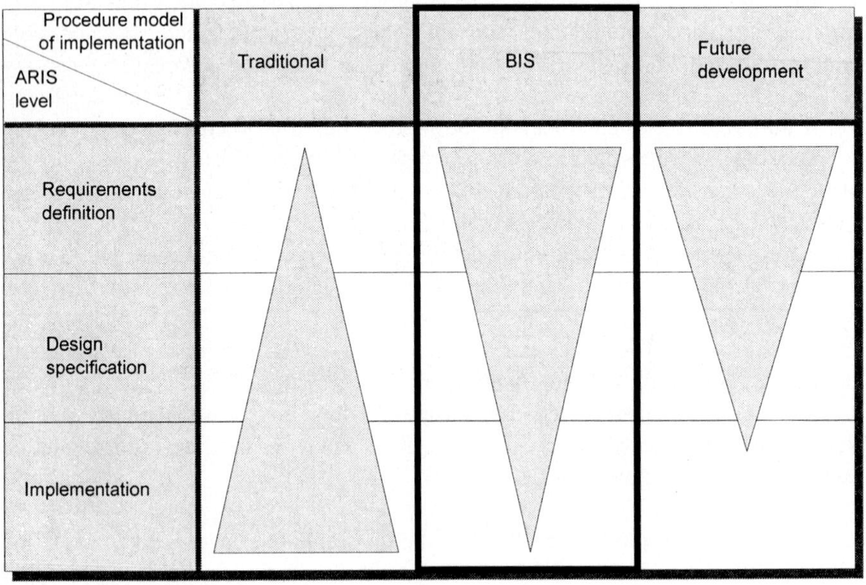

Procedure model of implementation / ARIS level	Traditional	BIS	Future development
Requirements definition			
Design specification			
Implementation			

Fig. 6.7: IT technology and the implementation of standard software

In standard software implementation in the future, tasks linked to implementing standard software on IS concept and implementation levels can be minimized further by

❑ Enhancing integration between the IT tool supporting the implementation (such as the ARIS Toolset) and the standard software product; and also by
❑ Optimizing standard software reference models. This makes it possible to model the information necessary for customizing as completely as possible.

Basic developments are already underway (see SCHEER 1991b, p. 7; SCHEER et al. 1994). Ideally, standard software measures will be omitted totally. The change in the significance of IT activities for implementing standard software is depicted in Fig. 6.7.

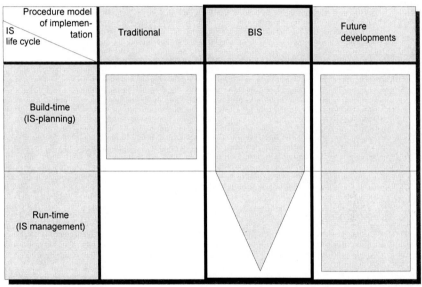

IS = Information system

Fig. 6.8: Implementation of standard software and the life cycle of information systems

Due to the dynamic evolution in creating enterprise-related markets and in developing standard software, increased **integration** of IS **build-time** and **run-time phases** is necessary. Implementation of standard software is not concluded, once the software is up and running. Moreover, implementation evolves into a **Continuous Process Improvement** (CPI). BIS addresses this issue by optimizing business processes in the live phase. Continuous deployment of the information models created in BIS (for the purpose of registering changes in the business environment and triggering the appropriate phases in BIS) can be simplified by

❑ Optimizing the continuous review of the as-is process of business processes and
❑ Making the analysis of target vs. as-is conditions easier.

It seems apparent that, eventually, information system planning and management will become integrated (see KRUPPKE 1994, p. 463-467). The implementation process described in BIS will gradually become part of the business processes of the enterprise. Fig. 6.8 illustrates the shift in classifying standard software implementation within the IS life cycle.

Implementing standard software is becoming a key issue in information management. Its key tasks are focused on business administration and helping design business processes, in order to implement strategic goals.

References

AMPONSEM, MARKHOFF 1994

Amponsem, H., Markhoff, H.: Marktorientierte Organisationslösungen: Prozesse und Strukturen. In: Booz, Allen & Hamilton Inc. Düsseldorf/München (Ed.): Gewinnen im Wettbewerb: erfolgreiche Unternehmensführung in Zeiten der Liberalisierung. Stuttgart 1994, pp. 128-153.

AMR 1998

AMR Research (Publ.): AMR Research predicts ERP market will reach $52 billion by 2002. Press Release, Boston, August 6, 1998.

APFEL 1994

Apfel, O.: Die SAP: Positionierung und Ziele. In: Institute for International Research (Ed.): SAP-R/3 - Wege, Chancen und Probleme bei Einführung, Koexistenz und Migration. Dokumentation zur Tagung am 25. und 26. Januar 1994 in Köln, Köln 1994.

AWK 1987

AWK Aachener Werkzeugmaschinen-Kolloquium (Ed.): Produktionstechnik - Auf dem Weg zu integrierten Systemen. Düsseldorf 1987.

BALANTZIAN 1992

Balantzian, G.: Les schémas directeurs stratégiques - démarche pratique. 4. Auflage, Paris et al. 1992.

BALZERT 1982

Balzert, H.: Die Entwicklung von Software-Systemen. Mannheim et al. 1982.

BANCROF 1996

Bancrof, N.: Implementing SAP R/3 – How to introduce a large system into a large organization. Greenwich 1996.

BANOS 1990

Banos, D., Malbosc, G.: Merise Pratique - 1. Les points-clé de la méthode. Paris 1990.

BARTELS 1993

Bartels, R.: Partizipative CIM-Einführung - Einsatz von Planungsgruppen zur Gestaltung einer CIM-Struktur. München et al. 1993.

BAUMANN, GERBER 1990

Baumann, W., Gerber, W.: Entscheidung gegen Standardsoftware am Beispiel FERAG. In: Österle, H. (Ed.): Integrierte Standardsoftware, Band I. Hallbergmoos 1990, pp. 55-66.

BECKER 1991

Becker, J.: Objektorientierung - eine einheitliche Sichtweise für die Ablauf- und Aufbauorganisation sowie die Gestaltung von Informationssystemen. In: SzU, Band 44. Wiesbaden 1991, pp. 135-152.

BECKER 1991

Becker, J.: CIM-Integrationsmodell - Die EDV-gestützte Verbindung betrieblicher Bereiche. Berlin, Heidelberg et al. 1991.

BECKER, SCHEER, WEIN 1991

216   References

Becker, J., Scheer, A.-W., Wein, R.: CIM-Teilstrategien. In: Scheer, A.-W. (Ed.): CIM-Strategie als Teil der Unternehmensstrategie. Köln 1991, pp. 139-159.

BECKER 1994

Becker, J.: Informationsmanagement und -controlling. Würzburg 1994.

BENJAMIN, BLUNT 1993

Benjamin, R. I., Blunt, J.: Informationstechnik im Jahr 2000 - ein Wegweiser für Manager. In: Harvard Business Manager 1/1993.

BERKAU 1991

Berkau, C.: VOKAL (System zur Vorgangskettendarstellung und -analyse) - Struktur der Modellierungsmethode. In: Scheer, A.-W. (Ed.): Veröffentlichungen des Instituts für Wirtschaftsinformatik. Saarbrücken 1991, Heft 82, pp. 73-85.

BODENSTAB 1970

Bodenstab, C. J.: 10 Tips for successful Implementation of Computer Systems. In: Financial Executive, Nr. 11, 1970, pp. 64-70.

BOLL 1993

Boll, M.: Prozeßorientierte Implementation des SAP Softwarepaketes. In: Wirtschaftsinformatik, 5/1993, pp. 418-423.

BOOZ, ALLEN & HAMILTON 1994

Booz, Allen & Hamilton Inc. Düsseldorf/München (Ed.): Gewinnen im Wettbewerb: erfolgreiche Unternehmensführung in Zeiten der Liberalisierung. Stuttgart 1994.

BRENNER 1990

Brenner, W.: Auswahl von Standardsoftware. In: Österle, H. (Ed.): Integrierte Standardsoftware, Band II. Hallbergmoos 1990, pp. 9-24.

BROMBACHER 1991

Brombacher, R.: Effizientes Informationsmanagement - die Herausforderung der Gegenwart und Zukunft. In: SzU, Band 44. Wiesbaden 1991, pp. 111-134.

BROMBACHER, HARS, SCHEER 1993

Brombacher, R., Hars, A., Scheer, A.-W.: Informationsmodellierung. In: Scheer, A.-W. (Ed.): Handbuch Informationsmanagement: Aufgaben - Konzepte - Praxislösungen. Wiesbaden 1993, pp. 173-188.

BULLINGER, NIEMEIER, SCHÄFER 1993

Bullinger, H.-J., Niemeier, J., Schäfer, M.: Wege zu schlanken Informations- und Kommunikationssystemen. In: Management & Computer, 2/1993, pp. 121-128.

BULLINGER, FÄHNRICH, ILG 1993

Bullinger, H.-J., Fähnrich, K.-P., Ilg, R.: Benutzungsoberflächen und Entwicklungswerkzeuge. In: Scheer, A.-W. (Ed.): Handbuch Informationsmanagement: Aufgaben - Konzepte - Praxislösungen. Wiesbaden 1993, pp. 939-964.

BÜNTE 1992

Bünte, P.: Geschäftsprozesse und Kommunikationssysteme. In: Peltzer, M. (Ed.): Unternehmenserfolg und Informationsmanagement. Bonn et al. 1992.

CALDWELL, STEIN 1998

Caldwell, B., Stein, T.: Beyond ERP. In: Information Week, Issue 711, Section: Top of the week, November 30, 1988.

CHEN 1976

Chen, P.P.: Entity-Relationship Model: Towards a Unified View of Data. In: ACM Transactions on Database Systems, 1/1976, pp. 9-36.

DAENZER 1989

Daenzer, W. F. (Ed.): Systems engineering: Leitfaden zur methodischen Durchführung umfangreicher Planungsvorhaben. 6. Auflage, Zürich 1989.

DAHLHEIM 1993

Dahlheim, P.-M.: Optimierung der Vertriebsabwicklung - Wettbewerbsvorteile mit Standardsoftware. In: Computerwoche Extra: Software-Trends '93, 1/1993, pp. 34.

DAVIDOW, MALONE 1993

Davidow, W. H., Malone, S. M.: Das virtuelle Unternehmen: der Kunde als Co-Produzent. Frankfurt/M., New York 1993.

ELGASS, KRCMAR 1993

Elgass, P., Krcmar, H.: Computergestützte Geschäftsprozeßplanung. In: Information Management, 1/1993, pp. 42-49.

ENDL, FRITZ 1992

Endl, R., Fritz, B.: Integration von Standardsoftware in das unternehmensweite Datenmodell. In: Information Management, 3/1992, pp. 38-44.

ERKES 1989

Erkes, F. E.: Planung flexibler CIM-Systeme mit Hilfe von Referenzmodellen (Teil 1). In: CIM Management 1/1989, pp. 62-68.

ESSER, KIRSCH 1979

Esser, W. M., Kirsch, W.: Die Einführung von Planungs- und Informationssystemen - Ein empirischer Vergleich. München 1979.

EVERSHEIM, KRUMM, HEUSER 1994

Eversheim, W., Krumm, S., Heuser, T.: Ablauf- und Kostentransparenz - Methoden und Hilfsmittel zur

Optimierung der Geschäftsprozesse. In: CIM Management, 1/1994, pp. 57-59.

FERDOWS 1989

Ferdows, K. (Ed.): Managing international Manufacturing. Amsterdam et al. 1989.

FRANK 1980

Frank, J.: Standard-Software: Kriterien und Methoden zur Beurteilung und Auswahl von Software-Produkten. 2. Auflage, Köln 1980.

FREMMER 1992

Fremmer, G.: Das Online-Handbuch: Die Unterstützung des Benutzers in der Mensch-Computer-Interaktion. Inaugural-Dissertation an der Ludwig-Maximilian-Universität zu München. München 1992.

FRESE 1993

Frese, E.: Grundlagen der Organisation: Konzepte - Prinzipien - Strukturen. 5. Auflage, Wiesbaden 1993.

FRESE 1994

Frese, E.: Aktuelle Informationskonzepte und Informationstechnologie. In: Management & Computer, 2/1994, pp. 129-134.

FREY 1990

Frey, M.: Der Markt für Standardsoftware - Daten, Fakten, Trends. In: Österle, H. (Ed.): Integrierte Standardsoftware, Band I. Hallbergmoos 1990, pp. 107-129.

FÜGLISTALER 1990

Füglistaler, U.: Technische Integration von Standardsoftware. In: Österle, H. (Ed.): Integrierte Standardsoftware, Band II. Hallbergmoos 1990, pp. 153-167.

FÜLLER 1990

Füller, E.: Entscheidung für Standardsoftware - am Beispiel der Firma Dr. Karl Thomae GmbH. In: Österle, H. (Ed.): Integrierte Standardsoftware, Band I. Hallbergmoos 1990, pp. 37-54.

GAITANIDES 1983

Gaitanides, M.: Prozeßorganisation: Entwicklung, Ansätze und Programme prozeßorientierter Organisationsgestaltung. München 1983.

GERBECKS 1994

Gerbecks, P.: SAP-R/3-Einführung bei der MD Papier GmbH. In: Institute for International Research (Ed.): SAP-R/3 - Wege, Chancen und Probleme bei Einführung, Koexistenz und Migration. Dokumentation zur Tagung am 25. und 26. Januar 1994 in Köln, Köln 1994.

GOLDHAR 1989

Goldhar, J. D.: Implications of CIM for International Manufacturing. In: Ferdows, K. (Ed.): Managing international Manufacturing. Amsterdam et al. 1989, pp. 259-265.

GOLDRATT 1990

Goldratt, E. M., Cox, J.: Das Ziel - Eine Methode ständiger Verbesserung. Maidenhead 1990.

GÖRGEL 1991

Görgel, U. B.: Computerintegrated Manufacturing und Wettbewerbsstrategie. Wiesbaden 1991.

GROCHLA 1980

Grochla, E. (Ed.): Handwörterbuch der Organisation. 2. Auflage, Stuttgart 1980

GRÖGER 1992

Gröger, M.: CIM und strategisches Management. Wiesbaden 1992.

GRÖNER 1991

Gröner, L.: Das Produkt im Mittelpunkt - Beispiel: Logistikstrukturen und -abläufe bei Pfaff. In: Beschaffung aktuell, 11/1991, pp. 39-42.

HAMACHER 1991

Hamacher, W., Papae, D.: Effiziente PPS-Einführung: Voraussetzung für zukunftssichere Mittelbetriebe. Köln, 1991.

HAMMER, CHAMPY 1994

Hammer, M., Champy, J.: Business reengineering: die Radikalkur für das Unternehmen. 2. Auflage, Frankfurt, New York, 1994.

HANSEN, AMSÜSS, FRÖMMER 1983

Hansen, H. R., Amsüss, W. L., Frömmer, N. S.: Standardsoftware: Beschaffungspolitik, organisatorische Einsatzbedingungen und Marketing. Berlin et al., 1983.

HANSEN 1986

Hansen, H. R.: Wirtschaftsinformatik I - Einführung in die betriebliche Datenverarbeitung. 5. Auflage, Stuttgart 1986.

HATTKE 1994

Hattke, W.: Von der sympathischen Software-Schmiede zum Software-Multi: SAP, Märkte und Anwenderleiden - eine Einführung. In: Institute for International Research (Ed.): SAP-R/3 - Wege, Chancen und Probleme bei Einführung, Koexistenz und Migration. Dokumentation zur Tagung am 25. und 26. Januar 1994 in Köln, Köln 1994.

HEINRICH 1994

Heinrich, J. : Systemplanung I - Planung und Realisierung von Informatik-Projekten. 6. Auflage. München, Wien 1994.

HEINRICH, BURGHOLZER 1990

Heinrich, J., Burgholzer, P.: Systemplanung II. 4. Auflage. München, Wien 1990.

HEß 1993

Heß, H.: Wiederverwendung von Software - Framework für betriebliche Informationssysteme. Wiesbaden, 1993.

HOFFMANN 1980

Hoffmann, F.: Organisation, Begriff der. In: Grochla, E. (Ed.): Handwörterbuch der Organisation. 2. Auflage, Stuttgart 1980.

HOPP 1990

Hopp, D.: Standardsoftware - CIM-Einstieg für den Mittelstand?. In: CIM Management 1/1990, pp. 30-31.

HORVÁTH, PETSCH, WEIHE 1986

Horváth, P, Petsch, M., Weihe, M.: Standard-Anwendungssoftware für das Rechnungswesen: Marktübersicht, Auswahlkriterien und Produkte für Finanzbuchhaltung und Kosten- und Leistungsrechnung. 2. Auflage, München 1986.

HOUY, SCHEER, ZIMMERMANN 1992

Houy, C., Scheer, A.-W., Zimmermann, V.: Anwendungsbereiche von Client/Server-Modellen. In: Information Management, 3/1992, pp. 14-23.

HUBER, GUMSHEIMER 1991

Huber, H., Gumsheimer, T.: Methodik zur strategischen Planung der Informationsverarbeitung - Ein Ansatz zur Überwindung des Planungsproblems. In: Office Management, 5/1991, pp. 29-35.

HÜTTENHEIM 1990

Hüttenheim, T.: Managementregeln zur Einführung von Standardsoftware. In: Österle, H. (Ed.): Integrierte Standardsoftware, Band II. Hallbergmoos 1990, pp. 131-146.

IDS PROF. SCHEER GMBH 1994

IDS Prof. Scheer GmbH (Ed.): Business Reengineering mit dem ARIS-Toolset. Saarbrücken 1994.

IDS PROF. SCHEER GMBH 1994

IDS Prof. Scheer GmbH (Ed.): ARIS-Handbuch Analyse. Buch 3, Version 2.0, Stand 05/94, Saarbrücken 1994.

IDS PROF. SCHEER GMBH 1994

IDS Prof. Scheer GmbH (Ed.): ARIS-Handbuch Modellierung. Buch 2, Version 2.0, Stand 05/94, Saarbrücken 1994.

IDS PROF. SCHEER GMBH 1994

IDS Prof. Scheer GmbH (Ed.): ARIS-Toolset Handbuch. Buch 1, Version 2.0, Stand 05/94, Saarbrücken 1994.

IDS PROF. SCHEER GMBH 1994

IDS Prof. Scheer GmbH (Ed.): ARIS-Handbuch Navigation. Buch 4, Version 2.0, Stand 05/94, Saarbrücken 1994.

IMAI, KAIZEN 1993

Imai, M.: Kaizen - Der Schlüssel zum Erfolg der Japaner im Wettbewerb. 8. Auflage, München 1993.

JÄGER

Jäger, E., Pietsch, M., Mertens, P.: Die Auswahl zwischen alternativen Implementierungen von Geschäftsprozessen in einem Standardsoftwarepaket am Beispiel eines Kfz-Zulieferers. In: Wirtschaftsinformatik, 5/1993, pp. 424-433.

JOST 1993

Jost, W.: Werkzeugunterstützung in der DV-Beratung. In: Informations Management, 1/1993, pp. 10-19.

JOST 1993

Jost, W.: EDV-gestützte CIM-Rahmenplanung. Wiesbaden, 1993.

JOST, MEINHARDT 1994

Jost, W., Meinhardt, S.: DV-gestützte SAP-Einführung mit dem R/3-Referenzmodell und dem ARIS-Toolset. In: Scheer, A.-W. (Ed.): Rechnungswesen und EDV, 15. Arbeitstagung. Saarbrücken 1994, pp. 521-551.

JUNKER 1988

Junker, R.: Einführung von Informations- und Kommunikationstechnologie. Berlin et al. 1988.

KALKS 1990

Kalks, U.: Strategieimplementierung: ein anwenderorientiertes Konzept. Wiesbaden 1990.

KAUMANN 1993

Kaufmann, F.: Erstellen von Modellen für Organisations- und DV-Lösungen: Entwurf und Spezifikation betrieblicher Objektsysteme mit der grafischen Entwurfssprache GRAPES. Berlin, München 1993.

KEEN 1991

Keen, P. G. W.: Shaping the future: Business Design through Information Technology. Harvard 1991.

KELLER, NÜTTGENS, SCHEER 1992

Keller, G., Nüttgens, M., Scheer, A.-W.: Semantische Prozeßmodellierung auf der Grundlage "Ereignisgesteuerter Prozeßketten (EPK)". In: Scheer, A.-W. (Ed.): Veröffentlichungen des Instituts für Wirtschaftsinformatik, Heft 89, Saarbrücken 1992.

KELLER 1993

Keller, G.: Informationsmanagement in objektorientierten Organisationsstrukturen. Wiesbaden 1993

KELLER, MEINHARDT 1994

Keller, G., Meinhardt, S.: SAP R/3-Analyzer - Optimierung von Geschäftsprozessen auf Basis des R/3-Referenzmodells. In: SAP AG (Ed.): SAP R/3-Analyzer. Walldorf 1994.

KELLER, MEINHARDT 1994

Keller, G., Meinhardt, S.: DV-gestützte Beratung bei der SAP-Softwareeinführung. In: Handbuch der modernen Datenverarbeitung - Theorie und Praxis der Wirtschaftsinformatik, 31/1994, pp. 74-88.

KENGELBACHER 1990

Kengelbacher, K.: Konzeptionelle Integration von Standardsoftware. In: Österle, H. (Ed.): Integrierte Standardsoftware, Band II. Hallbergmoos 1990, pp. 141-151.

KIESER, KUBICEK 1992

Kieser, A., Kubicek, H.: Organisation. 3. Auflage, Berlin, New York 1992.

KIRCHMER 1993

Kirchmer, M.: Prozeßorientierte Planung und Realisierung des Einsatzes von Standardsoftware - Vorgehensweise zur strategiegesteuerten Einführung integrierter Informationssysteme. In: Management & Computer, 2/1993, pp. 135-144.

KIRCHMER 1995

Kirchmer, M.: Markt- und produktgerechte Definition von Geschaeftsprozessen. In: Management & Computer, 4/1995, pp. 268-270

KIRCHMER 1998a

Kirchmer, M.: Vom Unternehmensziel zur Tabelleneinstellung: Geschaeftsprozess-orientierte Einfuehrung von SAP R/3. In: Pressmar, B., Scheer, A.-W. (Ed.): SAP R/3 in der Praxis. SZU, Band 62, Wiesbaden 1998.

KIRCHMER 1998b

Kirchmer, M.: Business Driven Implementation of ERP Systems. In: PlanetIT Online, planetit.com, 11/1998.

KIRCHMER, LAMETER 1994

Kirchmer, M., Lameter, F.: Geschäftsprozeßoptimierung - Kernaufgabe der SAP-Einführung. In: Scheer, A.-W. (Ed.): Rechnungswesen und EDV, 15. Arbeitstagung. Saarbrücken 1994, pp. 497-520.

KIRSCH 1994

Kirsch, J.: ARIS-Methodenhandbuch. Buch 5, Version 2.0, Stand 05/94, Saarbrücken 1994.

KIRSCH, BÖRSIG, ENGLERT 1979

Kirsch, W., Börsig, C., Englert, G.: Standardisierte Anwendungssoftware in der Praxis: empirische Grundlagen für Gestaltung und Vertrieb, Beschaffung und Einsatz. Berlin 1979.

KLAR 1985

Klar, R.: Hardware/Software Monitoring. In: Informatik Spektrum, 1/1985, pp. 37-40.

KLEIN 1990

Klein, J.: Vom Informationsmodell zum integrierten Informationssystem. In: Information Management, 2/1990, pp. 6-16.

KLOTZ 1991

Klotz, U.: Die zweite Ära der Informationstechnik. In: Harvard Manager, 2/1991, pp. 101-112.

KLOTZ 1993

Klotz, M.: Integrierte Anwendungssoftware und Unternehmensorganisation - Ein neues aufbauorganisatorisches Konzept zum Abbau von Hierarchieebenen. Berlin 1993.

KNETSCH 1987

Knetsch, W.: Organisations- und Qualifikationskonzepte bei CAD-CAM-Einführung: Voraussetzungen erfolgreicher Anwendung flexibler Automatisierungssysteme. Berlin 1987.

KÖLLE

Kölle, J.: Projektmanagement bei der Einführung von Standardsoftware dargestellt am Beispiel PPS. In: Österle, H. (Ed.): Integrierte Standardsoftware, Band II. Hallbergmoos 1990, pp. 45-54.

KRAUS, KRAEMER 1993

Kraus, M., Kraemer, W.: Zum Stand der papierlosen Beratung - Ein Schnappschuß der Unternehmensberatungspraxis in der Bundesrepublik Deutschland oder "trägt der Schuster selbst die schlechtesten Schuhe?". In: Information Management, 1/1993, pp. 6-9.

KRCMAR 1993

Krcmar, H.: CATeam - Computer Aided Team für die Verbesserung der Gruppenarbeit im Unternehmen. In: Management & Computer, 1/1993, pp. 5-10.

KRICKL 1994

Krickl, O. C. (Ed.): Geschäftsprozeßmanagement: Prozeßorientierte Organisationsgestaltung und Informationstechnologie. Heidelberg 1994.

KRICKL 1994

222   References

Krickl, O. C.: Business Redesign: Prozeßorientierte Organisationsgestaltung und Informationstechnologie. In: Krickl, O. C. (Ed.): Geschäftsprozeßmanagement: Prozeßorientierte Organisationsgestaltung und Informationstechnologie. Heidelberg 1994.

KRUPPKE 1994

Kruppke, H.: Leitstände zur Geschäftsprozeßoptimierung - Modellgestütztes Reengineering. In: Scheer, A.-W. (Ed.): Rechnungswesen und EDV, 15. Arbeitstagung. Saarbrücken 1994, pp. 455 - 469.

KÜTING 1983

Küting, K.: Grundsatzfragen von Kennzahlen als Instrument der Unternehmensführung. In: WiSt 5/1983, pp. 237-241.

KÜTING 1993

Küting, H.: Informatikplanung - Informatikmanagement: Strategien und Methoden zur Innovation im Unternehmen. Düsseldorf 1993.

LAIDIG 1993

Laidig, K.-D.: Standardisierungen: Offene Systeme. In: Scheer, A.-W. (Ed.): Handbuch Informationsmanagement: Aufgaben - Konzepte - Praxislösungen. Wiesbaden 1993, pp. 783-808.

LAMETER, KIRCHMER, KLINGSHIRN 1994

Lameter, F., Kirchmer, M., Klingshirn, C.: Schlanke Organisationsstrukturen auf Basis der SAP-R/3-Software. In: Management & Computer 1/1994, pp. 57-64.

LAMETER 1994

Lameter, F.: Einführung SAP-R/3 bei der Kaeser Kompressoren GmbH - ein Anwenderbericht. In: Institute for International Research (Ed.): SAP-R/3 - Wege, Chancen und Probleme bei Einführung, Koexistenz und Migration. Dokumentation zur Tagung am 25. und 26. Januar 1994 in Köln, Köln 1994.

LANG 1989

Lang, G.: Auswahl von Standard-Applikations-Software - Organisation und Instrumentarien. Berlin et al. 1989.

LAY 1990

Lay, G.: Entwicklungstendenzen, Problemfelder, Gestaltungspotentiale und FuE-Bedarf im Zusammenhang mit CIM-Strategien. In: Noack, M., Wegner, K., Gluch, D., Dienhart, U. (Ed.): CIM - Integration und Vernetzung: Chancen und Risiken einer Innovationsstrategie. Berlin et al. 1990, pp. 75-94.

LIEBETRAU, BECKER 1992

Liebetrau, G., Becker, M.: Die Auswahl von Standardsoftware. In: io Management Zeitschrift, 3/1992, pp. 59-61.

LOOS 1992

Loos, P.: Datenstrukturierung in der Fertigung - Ein methodischer Modellierungsansatz für die Gestaltung von Fertigungsinformationssystemen. München, Wien 1992.

LUDWIG 1992

Ludwig, L.: Beiträge zur wissensbasierten Parametereinstellung von Standardsoftwarepaketen - dargestellt am Bereich Materialbedarfsplanung des SAP-Systems RM. Inauguraldissertation an der Friedrich-Alexander-Universität Erlangen-Nürnberg, Erlangen-Nürnberg 1992.

MAIER-ROTHE 1985

Maier-Rothe, C.: Wettbewerbsvorteile durch höhere Produktivität - Strategien für CIM. Wiesbaden 1985.

MARKMILLER 1989

Markmiller, R.: Strukturiertes Auswahlverfahren verhindert Fehlinvestitionen. In: CIM Management, 3/1989, pp. 10-14.

MARTIN 1990

Martin, J.: Information Engeneering - Planing & Analysis. Book II, Englewood Cliffs 1990.

MARTINY, KLOTZ 1990

Martiny, L. Klotz, M.: Strategisches Informationsmanagement: Bedeutung und organisatorische Umsetzung. 2. Auflage, München, Wien 1990.

MASSBERG 1993

Massberg, W. (Ed.): Fertigungsinseln in CIM-Strukturen: Leitfaden zum Erfolg. Berlin et al. 1993.

MATTHEIS 1993

Mattheis, P.: Prozeßorientierte Informations- und Organisationsstrategie: Analyse, Konzeption, Realisierung. Wiesbaden 1993.

MAYDL 1987

Maydl, E.: Technologie-Akzeptanz im Unternehmen - Mitarbeiter gewinnen für neue Informationstechnologien. Wiesbaden 1987.

MERTENS, KÖNIG

Mertens, P. (HauptEd.), König, W. et al. (Ed.): Lexikon der Wirtschaftsinformatik. 2. Auflage, Berlin et al. 1990.

MEYER 1990

Meyer, B.: Objektorientierte Softwareentwicklung. München, Wien 1990.

MEYERSIEK, JUNG 1989

Meyersiek, D., Jung, M.: Kopplung von System- und Unternehmensstrategie als Voraussetzung für Wettbewerbsvorteile. In: Spremann, K., Zur, E. (Ed.): Informationstechnologie und strategische Führung. Wiesbaden 1989.

MICROSOFT CORPORATION 1992

Microsoft Corporation (Ed.): Microsoft Project zum Nachschlagen: Microsoft Project for Windows - Projektplanungssystem. Version 3.0, Irland 1992.

MORVAN 1988

Morvan, P.: Dictionaire de l'informatique - concepts, matériels, langages. Paris, 1988.

MÜLLER 1990

Müller, G.: Einflußfaktoren einer Software-Beschaffungsentscheidung - Empirische Untersuchung und Implikationen. In: Information Management, 3/1990, pp. 34-40.

NAGEL 1988

Nagel, K.: Nutzen der Informationsverarbeitung - Methoden zur Bewertung von strategischen Wettbewerbsvorteilen, Produktivitätsverbesserungen und Kosteneinsparungen. München, Wien 1988.

NEU 1991

Neu, P.: Strategische Informationssystemplanung - Konzepte und Instrumente. Berlin et al. 1991.

NOACK, WEGNER, GLUCH, DIENHART 1990

Noack, M., Wegner, K., Gluch, D., Dienhart, U. (Ed.): CIM - Integration und Vernetzung: Chancen und Risiken einer Innovationsstrategie. Berlin et al. 1990.

NOLAN, GOODSTEIN, PFEIFFER, 1993

Nolan, T., Goodstein, L., Pfeiffer, J. W.: Plan or die! - 10 keys to organizational success. San Diego 1993.

224   References

OCDE 1989
OCDE (Ed.): L'internationalisation du logiciel et des services informatiques. Paris 1989.
OLIFF, ARPAN, DUBOIS 1989
Oliff, M. D., Arpan, J. S., DuBois, F. L.: Global Manufacturing Rationalization: The Design and Management of International Factory Networks. In: Ferdows, K. (Ed.): Managing international Manufacturing. Amsterdam et al. 1989, pp. 41-65.
ÖSTERLE 1990
Österle, H.: Vorwort. In: Österle, H. (Ed.): Integrierte Standardsoftware, Band I. Hallbergmoos 1990, pp. 9-10.
ÖSTERLE 1990
Österle, H.: Unternehmensstrategie und Standardsoftware: Schlüsselentscheidungen für die 90er Jahre. In: Österle, H. (Ed.): Integrierte Standardsoftware, Band I. Hallbergmoos 1990, pp. 11-36.
ÖSTERLE 1990
Österle, H. (Ed.): Integrierte Standardsoftware, Band I. Hallbergmoos 1990.
ÖSTERLE 1990
Österle, H. (Ed.): Integrierte Standardsoftware, Band II. Hallbergmoos 1990.
ÖSTERLE, BRENNER, HILBERS 1991
Österle, H., Brenner, W., Hilbers, K.: Unternehmensführung und Informationssystem: Der Ansatz des St. Galler Informationssystem-Managements. Stuttgart 1991.
ÖSTERLE, SAXER, HÜTTENHAIN 1994
Österle, H., Saxer, R., Hüttenhain, T.: Organisatorisches Monitoring in der Gestaltung von Geschäftsprozessen. In: Wirtschaftsinformatik, 5/1994, pp. 465-477.
OETINGER 1989
Oetinger, R.: Die Benutzerschnittstelle in einer CIM-Umgebung. In: Information Management, 3/1989, pp. 28-36.
PAGE-JONES 1991
Page-Jones, M.: Praktisches DV-Projektmanagement: Grundlagen und Strategien; Regeln, Ratschläge und Praxisbeispiele. München, Wien 1991.
PETERS 1984
Peters, T. J., Waterman Jun. R. H.: Auf der Suche nach Spitzenleistungen - Was man von den bestgeführten US-Unternehmen lernen kann. 10. Auflage, Landsberg 1984.
PETRI 1990
Petri, C.: Externe Integration der Datenverarbeitung - Unternehmensübergreifende Konzepte für Handelsunternehmen. Berlin et al. 1990.
PIERCE 1987
Pierce, W.: Unterschiede in der Architektur von amerikanischen und europäischen Softwareprodukten. In: Internationaler Software-Congress Karlsruhe, Kongreßhandbuch. Walldorf 1987.
PIETSCH 1993
Pietsch, M.: PAREUS-RM - ein Tool zur Unterstützung der Konfiguration von PPS-Parametern im SAP-System R/2. In: Wirtschaftsinformatik, 5/1993, pp. 434-445.
PLATTNER 1993
Plattner, H.: Neue Trends in der Informationstechnologie. In: Scheer, A.-W. (Ed.): Rechnungswesen und EDV, 14. Arbeitstagung, Saarbrücken 1993, pp. 95-106.
PLATTNER 1993
Plattner, H.: Client/Server-Architekturen. In: Scheer, A.-W. (Ed.): Handbuch Informations-management: Aufgaben - Konzepte - Praxislösungen. Wiesbaden 1993, pp. 923-937.

POCSAY 1991

Pocsay, A.: Methoden- und Tooleinsatz bei der Erarbeitung von Konzeptionen für die integrierte Informationsverarbeitung. In: In: SzU, Band 44. Wiesbaden 1991, pp. 65-80.

PORTER 1989

Porter, M. E.: Wettbewerbsvorteile: Spitzenleistungen erreichen und behaupten. Sonderausgabe, Frankfurt, New York 1989.

PORTER 1989

Porter, M. E.: Der Wettbewerb auf globalen Märkten: Ein Rahmenkonzept. In: Porter, M.E. (Ed.): Globaler Wettbewerb. Wiesbaden 1989, pp. 17-68.

PORTER 1989

Porter, M. E. (Ed.): Globaler Wettbewerb. Wiesbaden 1989.

PORTER 1990

Porter, M. E.: Wettbewerbsstrategie: Methode zur Analyse von Branchen und Konkurrenten. 6. Auflage, Frankfurt, New York 1990.

PRESSMAR, SCHEER 1998

Pressmar, B., Scheer, A.-W (Ed.).: SAP R/3 in der Praxis. SZU, Band 62, Wiesbaden 1998.

PROBST 1992

Probst, G. J. B.: Organisation: Strukturen, Lenkungsinstrumente und Entwicklungsperspektiven. Landsberg 1992.

RAU 1991

Rau, K.-H.: Integrierte Bürokommunikation: Organisation und Technik. Wiesbaden 1991.

REICHL 1985

Reichl, M.: CAD erfolgreich einführen: Leitfaden für die Grobkonzeption des CAD-Einsatzes. Zürich, 1985.

RICHTER 1991

Richter, S., Pflieger, H.: Standortbestimmung mit VDMA-Kennzahlen - ein Schlüssel zur Zukunftssicherung für Maschinenbau-Unternehmen. Frankfurt 1991.

RIEDER 1988

Rieder, B.: Die Gestaltung des Implementierungsprozesses bei der Einführung von integrierter Standardsoftware, Dissertation an der wirtschaftswissenschaftlichen Fakultät der Universität Regensburg, Regensburg 1988.

ROCKART 1982

Rockart, J. F.: Current uses of the critical success factors process. In: Proceedings of the fourteenth annual conference of the Society for Information Management. o.O. 1982, pp. 17-23.

ROOS 1993

Roos, E.: Benutzerbeteiligung bei der PPS-Einführung - Konzept einer teamorientierten Vorgehensweise. In: CIM Management, 1/1993.

SAP AG 1992

SAP AG (Ed.): SAP-Implementation Ware. Release 5.0, Walldorf 01.10.1992.

SAP AG (Ed.): Customizing Vorgehensmodell. R/3, Walldorf, Juli 1993.

SAP AG 1994

SAP AG (Ed.): SAP-R/3-Software-Architektur. Walldorf, Juni 1994.

SAP AG 1997

SAP AG (Ed.): The Efficient R/3 Implementation Roadmap ... ASAP. Walldorf, 1997.

SCHÄFER

Schäfer, H.: CAD/CAM - Planung langfristiger Gesamtkonzeptionen. Düsseldorf 1990.

SCHEER 1990

Scheer, A.-W.: CIM - Der computergesteuerte Industriebetrieb. 4. Auflage, Berlin et al. 1990.

SCHEER 1990

Scheer, A.-W.: Architektur integrierter Informationssysteme - Grundlagen der Unternehmensmodellierung. Berlin et al. 1990.

SCHEER 1990

Scheer, A.-W.: EDV-orientierte Betriebswirtschaftslehre - Grundlagen für ein effizientes Informationsmanagement. 4. Auflage, Berlin et al. 1990.

SCHEER 1990

Scheer, A.-W., Berkau, C., Kraemer, W.: CIM: Eigenentwicklung oder Standardsoftware? In: Österle, H. (Ed.): Integrierte Standardsoftware, Band I. Hallbergmoos 1990, pp. 79-106.

SCHEER 1991

Scheer, A.-W. (Ed.): CIM-Strategie als Teil der Unternehmesstrategie. Köln 1991.

SCHEER 1991

Scheer, A.-W.: Papierlose Beratung - Werkzeugunterstützung bei der DV-Beratung. In: Information Management, 4/1991, pp. 6-16.

SCHEER 1992

Scheer, A.-W.: CIM und Lean Production. In: Scheer, A.-W. (Ed.): Rechnungswesen und EDV, 13. Arbeitstagung. Saarbrücken 1992, pp. 137-151.

SCHEER 1992

Scheer, A.-W. (Ed.): Rechnungswesen und EDV, 13. Arbeitstagung. Saarbrücken 1992.

SCHEER, OETINGER 1992

Scheer, A.-W., Oetinger, R.: Prozeßorientierte Einführung von funktionsintegrierter Standardsoftware - ein Widerspruch? In: Unabhängiges SAP-Anwender-Forum. München 1992.

SCHEER 1993

Scheer, A.-W. (Ed.): Handbuch Informationsmanagement: Aufgaben - Konzepte - Praxislösungen. Wiesbaden 1993.

SCHEER 1993

Scheer, A.-W.: ARIS - Architektur integrierter Informationssysteme. In: Scheer, A.-W. (Ed.): Handbuch Informationsmanagement: Aufgaben - Konzepte - Praxislösungen. Wiesbaden 1993, pp. 81-112.

SCHEER 1993

Scheer, A.-W. (Ed.): Rechnungswesen und EDV, 14. Arbeitstagung. Saarbrücken 1993.

SCHEER 1993

Scheer, A.-W.: Reorganisation von Unternehmensprozessen: vom Vorstandsbeschluß zum neuen Formular. In: Scheer, A.-W. (Ed.): Rechnungswesen und EDV, 14. Arbeitstagung. Saarbrücken 1993, pp. 3-18.

SCHEER 1994

Scheer, A.-W.: Wirtschaftsinformatik - Referenzmodelle für industrielle Geschäftsprozesse. 5. Auflage, Berlin et al. 1994.

SCHEER 1994

Scheer, A.-W. (Ed.): Rechnungswesen und EDV, 15. Arbeitstagung. Saarbrücken 1994.

SCHEER 1994

Scheer, A.-W.: Unternehmen 2000: Opfer von Reorganisationswellen oder Phönix aus der Asche. In: Scheer, A.-W. (Ed.): Rechnungswesen und EDV, 15. Arbeitstagung. Saarbrücken 1994, pp. 3-14).

SCHEER 1998a
Scheer, A.-W.: ARIS – Business Process Frameworks. 2nd edition, Berlin et al. 1998.
SCHEER 1998b
Scheer, A.-W.: ARIS – Business Process Modelling. 2nd edition, Berlin et al. 1998.
SCHEER, HOFFMANN, WEIN 1994
Scheer, A.-W., Hoffmann, W., Wein, R.: Customizing von Standardsoftware mit Referenzmodellen. In: HMD - Theorie und Praxis der Wirtschaftsinformatik, 31/1994, pp. 92-103.
SCHMIDT 1991
Schmidt, G.: Methode und Techniken der Organisation. 9. Auflage, Gießen 1991.
SCHOLZ 1987
Scholz, C.: Strategisches Management - Ein integrativer Ansatz. Berlin, New York 1987.
SCHOLZ-REITER 1991
Scholz-Reiter, B.: CIM-Schnittstellen - Konzepte, Standards und Probleme der Verknüpfung von Systemkomponenten in der rechnerintegrierten Produktion. 2. Auflage, Berlin 1991.
SCHRÖDER 1993
Schröder, J.: Standardsoftware bei der Sandoz AG - "Make and Buy" ist die bessere Lösung. In: Computerwoche Extra: Software-Trends '93, 1/1993, pp. 32-33.
SCHRÖDER
Schröder, J.: SAP als Basis wirtschaftlicher und innovativer Datenverarbeitung. In: Institute for International Research (Ed.): SAP-R/3 - Wege, Chancen und Probleme bei Einführung, Koexistenz und Migration. Dokumentation zur Tagung am 25. und 26. Januar 1994 in Köln, Köln 1994
SCHÜLE 1992
Schüle, H., Schumann, M.: DV-gestützte CIM-Planung. In: CIM Management, 2/1992, pp. 56-63.
SCHÜLE 1994
Schüle, H.: DV-Unterstützung beim Planen und Einführen von CIM-Lösungen. Heidelberg 1994.
SCHULTE 1991
Schulte, C.: Logistik: Wege zur Optimierung des Material- und Informationsflusses. München 1991.
SCHWARZER 1994
Schwarzer, B.: Prozeßorientiertes Informationsmanagement in multinationalen Unternehmen: eine empirische Untersuchung in der Pharmaindustrie. Wiesbaden 1994.
SIEPE 1991
Siepe, J.: Einführung eines PPS-Systems bei einem mittleren Unternehmen der Zulieferindustrie. In: Information Management, 3/1991, pp. 20-26.
SPANG 1991
Spang, S.: Modellierung internationaler Organisationen - Ein methodischer Ansatz für die Datensicht. In: Information Management, 4/1991, pp. 36-44.
SPANG 1993
Spang, S.: Informationsmodellierung im Investitionsgütermarketing. Wiesbaden 1993.
SPREMANN, ZUR 1989
Spremann, K., Zur, E. (Ed.): Informationstechnologie und strategische Führung. Wiesbaden 1989.
STAHLKNECHT 1983

228   References

Stahlknecht, P.: Customizen. In: Informatik-Spektrum, 3/1983.
STAHLKNECHT 1990
Stahlknecht, P.: Standardsoftware. In: Mertens, P. (HauptEd.), König, W. et al. (Ed.):
    Lexikon der Wirtschaftsinformatik. 2. Auflage, Berlin et al. 1990.
STAMPP 1994
Stampp, P.: SAP-Einsatz bei der Festo KG: Von der Projektorganisation bis zur
    Implementierung und Migration - ein Anwenderbericht. In: Institute for International
    Research (Ed.): SAP-R/3 - Wege, Chancen und Probleme bei Einführung, Koexistenz
    und Migration. Dokumentation zur Tagung am 25. und 26. Januar 1994 in Köln, Köln
    1994
STEIN, SWEAT 1998
Stein, T., Sweat, J.: Killer Supply Chains. In: Information Week Online, November 9,
    1988.
STEINBEIßER, DRÄGER 1989
Steinbeißer, K., Dräger, U.: Ein betriebstypologisches Verfahren zur Segmentierung des
    Anwendungssoftware-Marktes. In: Mertens, P. (Ed.): Arbeitspapiere Informatik-
    Forschungsgruppe VIII der Friedrich-Alexander-Universität Erlangen-Nürnberg,
    Forschungsprojekt DV-Unterstützung des Vertriebs. Erlangen, 1989.
STEINKE 1979
Steinke, D.: Standard-Anwender-Software: Darstellung und Beurteilung kommerzieller
    Datenverarbeitungsprogramme aus organisatorischer Sicht. Berlin, 1979.
STEINMETZ 1992
Steinmetz, O.: Information Processing for Integrated Product Engineering - How modern
    Software Technologies and Organizational Methods can Help Improve Time-to-Market,
    Quality and Costs. Dissertation an der Rechts- und Wirtschaftswissenschaftlichen
    Fakultät der Universität des Saarlandes. Saarbrücken 1992.
TAYLOR 1913
Taylor, F. W.: Die Grundsätze wissenschaftlicher Betriebsführung. München, Berlin 1913.
TSCHIRA, ZENCKE 1994
Tschira, K., Zencke, P.: Geschäftsprozeßoptimierung mit dem SAP-System R/3. In: SAP
    infor - Das Magazin der SAP-Gruppe, März 1994.
URBAN 1991
Urban, G.: Prozeßorganisatorische Grundlagen einer CIM-Fabrik. Dissertation an der
    Fakultät Geschichts-, Sozial- und Wirtschaftswissenschaften der Universität Stuttgart,
    Stuttgart 1991.
VDI-GESELLSCHAFT 1975
VDI-Gesellschaft Materialfluß und Fördertechnik (Ed.): VDI-Richtlinie 3596,
    Darstellungsmethoden für den Materialfluß. Düsseldorf 1975.
VDI-GESELLSCHAFT 1978
VDI-Gesellschaft Materialfluß und Fördertechnik (Ed.): VDI-Richtlinie 2498, Vorgehen
    bei einer Materialflußplanung. Düsseldorf 1978.
WARNECKE 1993
Warnecke, H.-J.: Revolution der Unternehmenskultur: Das Fraktale Unternehmen. 2.
    Auflage, Berlin et al. 1993.
WATTEROTT 1993
Watterott, R.: Ein Beitrag zur strategischen CIM-Planung unter besonderer
    Berücksichtigung der Bewertung von CIM-Technologien. In: Fortschritts-Berichte VDI,
    Reihe 20, Nr. 95. Düsseldorf 1993.

WILDEMANN 1987
Wildemann, H.: Strategische Investitionsplanung: Methoden zur Bewertung neuer Produktionstechnologien. Wiesbaden 1987.

WILDEMANN 1990
Wildemann, H.: Einführungsstrategien für die computerintegrierte Produktion (CIM). München 1990.

WILDEMANN 1992
Wildemann, H. (Ed.): Lean Management - Der Weg zur schlanken Fabrik. München, 1992.

WILDEMANN 1992
Wildemann, H.: Strategien zur Realisierung "schlanker Strukturen" in der Produktion. In: Wildemann, H. (Ed.): Lean Management - Der Weg zur schlanken Fabrik. München, 1992.

WOMACK, JONES, ROOS 1992
Womack, J. P., Jones, D. T., Roos, D.: Die zweite Revolution in der Autoindustrie. 6. Auflage, Frankfurt 1992.

ZEPHON PLC 1991
Xephon plc (Ed.): Xephon Consultancy Report: CICS Tuning and Performance. Berkshire, 1991.

ZANGL 1990
Zangl, H.: Wirtschaftlichkeitsnachweis beim Einsatz von Standardsoftware. In: Österle, H. (Ed.): Integrierte Standardsoftware, Band II. Hallbergmoos 1990, pp. 93-124.

ZENTES, ANDERER 1993
Zentes, J., Anderer, M.: Warenwirtschaftssysteme. In: Scheer, A.-W. (Ed.): Handbuch Informationsmanagement: Aufgaben - Konzepte - Praxislösungen. Wiesbaden 1993, pp. 343-368.

ZIMMERMANN 1994
Zimmermann, V.: Client-Server ist Prozeßorientierung! In: Management & Computer, 1/1994, pp. 68-69.

Table of Figures

Abbreviations

ARIS	Architecture of Integrated Information Systems
BIS	Business process oriented Implementation of Standard software
BPO	Business Process Optimization
CAD	Computer Aided Design
CAM	Computer Aided Manufacturing
CATeam	Computer Aided Team
CIM	Computer Integrated Manufacturing
CPI	Continuous Process Improvement
DP	Data Processing
EDI	Electronic Data Interchange
EPC	Event driven Process Chain
ERM	Entity Relationship Model
ERP	Enterprise Resource Planning
et al	and others
Fig.	Figure
i.e.	that is (id est)
IS	Information System
IT	Information Technology
MRPII	Management Requirements Planning
OPT	Optimized Production Technology
p.	page
PC	Personal Computer
PCD	Process Chain Diagram
pp.	pages
PPS	Production Planning System
SCM	Supply Chain Management
TQM	Total Quality Management

A.-W. Scheer

ARIS - Business Process Modeling

2nd completely rev. and enlarged
ed. 1999. XIX, 218 pp. 179 figs.
Hardcover DM 89,-*
ISBN 3-540-64438-5

ARIS (Architecture of Integrated
Information Systems) is a unique
and internationally renowned
method for optimizing business
processes and implementing
application systems.
This book describes in detail how
ARIS methods model and realize
business processes by means of
UML (Unified Modeling Language), leading to an information
model that is the keystone for a
systematic and intelligent method
of developing application
systems.
Multiple real-world examples -
including knowledge management, implementation of workflow systems and standard software solutions (SAP R/3 in particular) - address the deployment
of ARIS methods

*This price applies in Germany/Austria/Swit-
zerland and
is a recommended retail price.
Prices and other details are subject to change
without notice.

A.-W. Scheer

ARIS - Business Process Frameworks

2nd completely rev. and enlarged ed. 1998. XVII, 186 pp.
94 figs. Hardcover DM 79,-* ISBN 3-540-64439-3

A.-W. Scheer

CIM Computer Integrated Manufacturing

Towards the Factory of the Future

3rd rev. and enl. ed. 1994. XV, 303 pp. 155 figs. Hardcover
DM 94,-* ISBN 3-540-57964-8

A.-W. Scheer

Business Process Engineering

Reference Models for Industrial Enterprises

2nd, completely rev. and enlarged ed. 1994. XXIV, 770 pp.
580 figs., 26 in colour Hardcover DM 128,-*
ISBN 3-540-58234-7

A.-W. Scheer

Business Process Engineering Study Edition

Reference Models for Industrial Enterprises

1998. XXII, 757 pp. 554 figs. Softcover DM 75,-*
ISBN 3-540-63867-9

Springer-Verlag · Postfach 14 02 01 · D-14302 Berlin
Tel.: 0 30 / 82 787 - 2 32 · http://www.springer.de
Bücherservice: Fax 0 30 / 82 787 - 3 01
e-mail: orders@springer.de

Errors and omissions excepted. Prices subject to change without notice
d&p · 65575/1

Springer

Springer
and the
environment

At Springer we firmly believe that an international science publisher has a special obligation to the environment, and our corporate policies consistently reflect this conviction.

We also expect our business partners – paper mills, printers, packaging manufacturers, etc. – to commit themselves to using materials and production processes that do not harm the environment. The paper in this book is made from low- or no-chlorine pulp and is acid free, in conformance with international standards for paper permanency.

 Springer